Chocolate Legs

Sweet Mother—Savage Killer?

Her story begins as an Ursid Shirley Temple, a cute blond phenom amid the real-life Shangri-la of Glacier National Park's most scenic mountain valley. In time, however, the curtsying knockout zoomed to National Velvet-style celebrity, demanding more from fans than admiring glances and the flashing bulbs of paparazzi cameras. It was those Garbo-sized demands and an ever-growing haughtiness that attracted officialdom's attention.

Exile followed.

Life turned hard for the young bear in the peopleless mountains where the helicopter deposited her. And for her first year along this most isolated region of the Crown of the Continent, Chocolate Legs barely walked the knife-edge of survival.

But if nothing else, the young bear proved she was a survivor. She learned when to hold 'em and when to fold 'em—running without shame from bigger, older, meaner bears and avoiding the occasional humans wandering into her domain. Gradually she expanded her home range, always learning to access new foods in new terrain. She learned to swill fermenting grain along railroad derailments and to feast on cutworm moths on mountaintops. And eventually a decade passed and the blond bombshell found herself once more amid the haunts humans frequent.

By then, she was a mother several times over, with needs more than her own. By then she'd come to a fork in her life's trail. By then she'd reverted to old ways in old places, recalling her haughtiness at the same time as she recalled herself from exile.

It was then that her tale morphed into one that captured the imagination of reporters from as far away as the eastern seaboard and carried by international media around the globe. It was then that the *New York Times* headlined their story: "The Tale of Three Bad News Bears Who Became Killers." And it was then, after Chocolate Legs had been painted with a "Ma Barker" sobriquet, that the blond knockout with chocolate-colored legs most needed her own Johnny Cochrane in defense.

Chocolate Legs is an investigative journey into the life and death of one of the world's most fascinating creatures by a long-time journalist who has lived (and sometimes brushed near death) with the bears.

Other Books by Roland Cheek

Learning to Talk Bear

The Phantom Ghost of Harriet Lou

Dance on the Wild Side

My Best Work is Done at the Office

Montana's Bob Marshall Wilderness

Chocolate Legs

Sweet Mother Savage Killer?

Chocolate Legs

Sweet Mother
Savage Killer?

Roland Cheek

a Skyline Publishing Book

Cover design by Laura Donovan
Text design and formatting by Michael Dougherty
Copy editing by Jennifer Williams

Publisher's Cataloging in Publication
(Prepared by Quality Books, Inc.)

Cheek, Roland.
Chocolate Legs : sweet mother, savage killer? / Roland Cheek. — 1st ed.
p. cm.
LCCN: 00-092703
ISBN: 0-918981-07-7

1. Grizzly bear—Montana—Glacier National Park. 2. Bear attacks—Montana—Glacier National Park—prevention 3. Grizzly bear—Behavior 4. Glacier National Park (Mont.) I. Title.

QL795.B4C442001 599.784'0978652
QBI00-901966

Published by Skyline Publishing
P.O. Box 1118
Columbia Falls, Montana 59912

Printed in Canada

Table of Contents

Dedication

... to the proposition that wild, free-roaming grizzly bears will still exist at the turn of the next millennium.

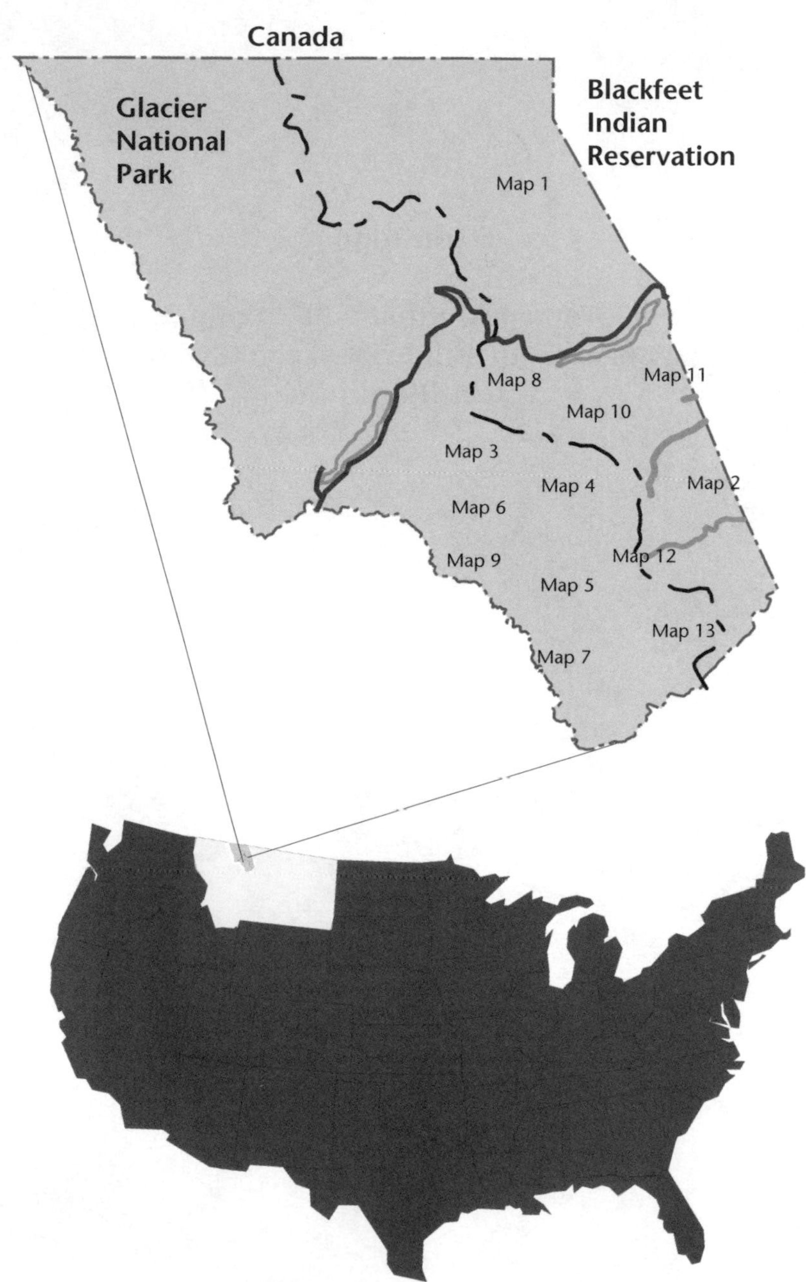
Canada
Glacier National Park
Blackfeet Indian Reservation
Map 1
Map 8
Map 11
Map 10
Map 3
Map 4
Map 2
Map 6
Map 9
Map 12
Map 5
Map 13
Map 7

Guide to Maps

Key to Illustrations

"What is man without the beasts? If all the beasts were gone, men would die from a great loneliness of spirit."

—Chief Seattle

Acknowledgment

I'm not sure how it is with others, but I need challenge for motivation. That a constant need to eat, stay warm and dry, to clothe oneself—all are of sufficient physical challenge to motivate. But what of the intellect?

My second great lifetime love is outdoors adventure. It's an avocation also packed with copious quantities of physical challenge. But there are even more intellectual ones: the connection between bee and flower, rainbow and raindrop, mountains and the movement of continental plates. As a consequence, my loftiest regards go to individuals who, perhaps by their very being, challenge me to understand God's natural wonders.

Dr. John Montagne is such a person. The former instructor, Professor Emeritus, now, of geology at Montana State University and a part-time landform interpreter during our wilderness trips, opened my eyes to the earth's geological processes, challenged me to search and think instead of merely look and listen and accept by rote.

By sending me off on a five-year search for a lost flower (Cypripedium passerinum), the late Danny On, much admired Flathead National Forest silviculturist, made my personal "cut list" of folks who challenge, by asking me, by example, to learn a little of botany in general and wildflowers in particular.

Then there are the biologists.

They're the ones who, when I began musing about bears, principally grizzly bears, nourished the interest, whetted the appetite, and challenged the learning curve.

They're the ones who've worked unflaggingly to keep me rooted, at least in some degree, in reality. They've listened patiently to my sometimes cockeyed analyses, shared their visions, and worked diligently to correct what they've perceived to be mistaken impressions.

There's Shawn Riley who got me started on bears; Rick Mace who shared reams of information and research; Dan Carney who gave me the benefit of much sensible experience; Steve Gniadek who went out of his way to counsel reining in creative instincts while rooting this story in as much scientific fact as possible.

Tim Manley, Carrie Hunt, Mike Madel, Terry Werner, John Waller, and Jim Williams all shared personal knowledge and gave personal time.

There's Mike Aderhold who provides management insight on Montanan's relationship with grizzly bears.

And there's Chuck Jonkel, perhaps foremost among all challengers to my sensibility toward grizzlies—not because he has insight denied others, but because he's one of the world authorities on the great beasts while still remaining accessible outside the lofty towers of academia.

It's because of them—and the lay people across America who care about grizzly bears—that I dared attempt this book. You can blame them for my imagination if you wish, they certainly whetted it and challenged it. But don't blame them for the errors—if they exist. Those are all mine.

Introduction

My first real introduction to the bear, Chocolate Legs, came during a reading, lecture, and autograph party a local Kalispell bank had been kind enough to organize for me in their community room. The occasion was during release of my second book, *The Phantom Ghost of Harriet Lou*, about elk. To effectively publicize the event, Three Rivers Bank had mailed flyers to customers on their mail list, as well as utilized lobby posters of both the new book, and the previous year's release, *Learning to Talk Bear*, about grizzlies.

Lots of folks turned out—many were Jane's and my friends, neighbors, and acquaintances established over decades. Quite a few, however, were strangers, there to learn, I suppose, about elk and my years as a wilderness guide. But surprisingly, some might have wished to find out how one talks bear. And, as it turned out, others wished to listen to a lecture from a guy they assumed was a bear expert.

As I recall, the reading went well. And there's little doubt I did okay during a question and answer session directed more to elk than grizzly bears. But after the lecture and after copies of our books dutifully signed to purchasers, two young ladies, probably in their early twenties, approached my table. One of them carried a dog-eared copy of *Learning to Talk Bear*. She asked if I would be kind enough to sign it.

It gave me much pleasure to do so, of course. But when I handed it back, the lady asked what I thought of the bear, "Chocolate Legs." It was obvious by her body language, and by the way she and her friend stood on edge at the table, that they held great sympathy for an animal who was, at the time, under a cloud of suspicion.

Frankly, I didn't handle their query well. Jane and I had

just returned from an autograph tour and I had not followed the news sufficiently. I was barely aware of the name Chocolate Legs and that her case—and that of her teenage cubs—were under investigation. The ladies, I could see, were disappointed with a reply from a pseudo bear expert admitting ignorance of the issue.

I wished many times later, as events unfolded, that I'd taken the ladies' names, but I didn't. However, I did save the letter from Lucille Guderski of Markesan, Wisconsin.

> *Hi,*
>
> *Just a few lines to tell you I have finished your book,* Learning to Talk Bear. *It was great, really enjoyed it. It is very well written, the vocabulary was easy to understand.*
>
> *I worry about the bear Chocolate Legs and her cubs. How unfortunate a life was lost. She made a mistake and it sounds like her penalty is death. We have been to Two Medicine Lake many times. I know exactly where the trail is.*
>
> *I plan to join Dr. Jonkel and his group to Churchill this year [to view polar bears]. I'm all excited about it. Sounds wonderful!*
>
> *Thanks again for sending me the book. I loved every page.*
>
> *Have a great week.*
>
> *Lucille Guderski*

Letters-to-the-editor about the case also tumbled in to local newspapers. Themes of most of those letters proved their writers were troubled in the same vein as Lucille and the two Kalispell ladies.

Taken as a whole, all the manifested concern started me thinking. And wondering.

The embryo for this book, then, was implanted in a Kalispell bank in late May, 1998. That the germination was so slow in fruiting was because I was tardy in investigation and dawdled in digesting the information as it came in. In addition, I agonized over the form I planned to use for doing the work about Chocolate Legs, then postponed its writing for a year while pursuing another project.

To make matters even more puzzling, the form the book finally took is not at all as I envisioned at its beginning and I'd apologize—except for what? Who can control the muse? I'm not the only writer to see their work take on a life of its own, nor am I the only one to comment on the phenomenon. Besides, the form you'll read is, in my view, better than the convoluted way I'd plotted the original before beginning its first draft.

As I've tried to make clear throughout this book, much creative latitude was exercised. My reason was not to skew its storyline to achieve a controlled response, but to strive for a more encompassing vision about what the span of years of a real-life bear in a real-life natural setting is like.

Each of the events transcribed within this book are real events occurring in the lives of other bears in other places, either as witnessed by the author, or by individuals in whom I place a great deal of trust. That all—or certainly most—also occurred in the life of Chocolate Legs is, I believe, a logical conclusion.

Instead, where the book is more likely to err is in other, unreported events that must have happened to the blond bombshell bruin during a fascinating and challenging life. And I regret those events aren't included because of the author's own lack of skill and imagination. Her's was a fascinating life—one that should be told in its entirety in order to strive for understanding. To attempt her story without trying to capture that entirety would, in my view, be deceptive.

Make no mistake, however. This is not a *textbook*, but a *test-book*. It's about my own fumbling efforts to understand a species of God's creatures I find more fascinating than any other.

1

Countdown to Destiny

With the snow squall sweeping Mexico-bound from Nunavut Land, the hiker paused to slip from his daypack, propping it atop a whitened, buckskin log. The log was remnant from an ages-old wildfire that savaged the flanks of this mountain; indeed, that had raged through much of the Swiss-look-alike valley below.

The hiker shrugged from his down jacket, folded and stuffed it into the knapsack. Straightening to his slender six-foot height, the man pulled a big blue handkerchief from his jeans' pocket and carefully wiped beads of moisture from a pair of bottle-lens eyeglasses.

With the glasses back in place and vision restored, the man snatched off his stocking cap and, while turning a full 360 degrees, swiped the handkerchief across his forehead and beneath the collar of his denim shirt, all the while gazing in rapture at the full sweep of surrounding snowcapped mountains. How glorious to be alive! Especially in such place.

He didn't yet know all their names, but he would. Martin and Deidre had told him the big one thrusting up from north of the lake—the lofty one with the exposed redrock shoulders—was Rising Wolf. And one of them mentioned Sinopah, too. He wondered why such a strange name should stick in his mind?

He watched a Park Service pickup tortoising along the macadam road far below, studied it for a moment, then turned to peer at the mountain to the west. Appistoki, Deidre had said. Still mostly snow-covered. He'd been told there would be mountain goats here. Hard to see white goats against white snow. The man dug into his daypack for a pair of battered binoculars, then swept the nearby open slopes for five minutes.

At last he grinned and shook his head. "Not yet. But if you're here, I'll spot you," he muttered. "And with luck, maybe I'll see a grizzly bear, too. Or," gazing down at a couple of beaver ponds near the lake, "maybe a moose."

The man dropped the binocs back into his daypack, slung it, and, skirting a weeping snowbank, trudged on up the trail. He chuckled aloud while thinking of his new friends—how they'd promised to join him on today's hike, but dropped out because of predictions of a spring storm. Because of them, he'd started late, not even leaving East Glacier until noon and not getting on the trail until an hour later.

Craig Dahl was twenty-six years old, in the prime of life and at the peak of his physical strength. With a degree in sports management, the young man was already a veteran outdoorsman, an accomplished hunter, angler, skier, canoeist, and backpacker. As such, he'd led canoe adventures in northern Minnesota and overnight hiking groups in Colorado's Rocky Mountains. Although new to Glacier National Park and the Northern Rockies, Dahl possessed a veteran outdoorsman's polished instinct for learning new landscapes, traveling new trails, riding new rivers, and spotting new wildlife.

He could read mountain weather, too. And, if he correctly read the dark clouds boiling over mountains to the west, the storm front wouldn't be long in arriving. A chill breeze began gusting around Craig Dahl.

The bears knew of the man's presence long before the man knew of the bears. There were three: a sow and her brace of two-year-old cubs.

They made a handsome family—Chocolate Legs and her two mirror-image offspring; each a classic blond shading to dark brown on their legs—as if they'd just waded from a muddy marsh—and with raccoon-like masks around beady, penetrating eyes.

The mother wore a fading yellow collar, nearly hidden by her still-thick winter coat. Though even more difficult to spot, she had aluminum tags clipped into each ear. The stocky young male cub sported a tag in only his left ear. The tags and collar were evidence the bears had at least some exposure to humans. Given the time (May 17, 1998) and their location (Two Medicine Valley/

Glacier National Park), that evidence suggested much more....

For several years, Glacier National Park has had a policy discouraging radio collaring of bears for research, holding that visitor experiences might be diminished by sighting animals wearing man-installed devices. Only in incidents involving risk to humans—or occasionally to the animals themselves—are bears trapped and relocated. In extremely rare occasions problem bears are fitted with radio collars and their movements monitored.

Though she and her offspring had become something of a nuisance around campgrounds and trails in the Two Medicine area, Chocolate Legs had not yet been deemed a sufficient problem for official action.

Not so outside the Park.

The boundary between Glacier National Park and the Blackfeet Reservation lies but three miles east of the Scenic Point Trail Craig Dahl hiked that day—and where the bear family busied themselves digging for marmots and ground squirrels and early tubers. What's more to the point, the Blackfeet hold a jaundiced view of—and a low tolerance for—grizzly bears who invade campgrounds, demonstrate little respect for humans, and who ransack garbage cans, camp coolers, and food boxes. Thus the previous year, when Chocolate Legs and her brood entered the Red Eagle Campground, two miles into the Blackfeet Reservation, then ignored attempts by campers and management to haze them from the vicinity, the tribal office was alerted.

Chocolate Legs paused in pursuit of a hoary marmot and lifted her snout to the wind. The breeze was fickle and she soon returned to excavating football-sized rocks and pea gravel, thrusting her nose into the deepening hole and snorting, then once again digging furiously, stone and dirt spewing between her wide-spraddled hind legs.

A hundred feet up the hill and to the left, the blocky male pursued his own marmot with more enthusiasm and even less finesse than the mother. His more refined sister perched near her mother, watching intently should one of the beagle-sized ground hogs try to flee. She, too, lifted nostrils to the wind and whined. But her mother needed no warning. Again the sow paused. Yes, there! A man-smell.

In some ursid circles the scent would have been sufficient to send bears beelining for distant ridges. But not this bear. Not these bears. Instead Chocolate Legs stared down the mountain for a moment, then resumed her excavation. Above, her male offspring paused to peer down the hill at his mother and sister. He, too, had the human's odor. But, following his mother's lead, he resumed furious digging.

Soon, they heard the human's approach; first the clink of a rock, then the scuff of a boot. Next was the "feel"—the faintest of vibrations from the man's footsteps. The sow discontinued her digging to drift into a thick patch of head-high limber pines, the female cub crowding hard against her. The male cub made one more furious pass at his excavation, then galloped down the hill to join the two females. Standing as they were, it was apparent each of the two-year-olds were only a few inches shorter and half the heft of their mother.

Dark clouds nearly covered the heavens, leaving only a line of intense turquoise-blue to the east. Craig Dahl hurried to climb as high as he could before the storm broke. His head-down direction took him around the copse of stunted trees, passing only a few scant feet from where three grizzly bears stood motionless against the mounting wind.

A few feet further and he came to another trail switchback and started to swing around it when something caught his eye. It looked as though a backhoe had been rooting around on the hillside directly before him. He kicked at the dirt pile, wondered what had caused it, then turned and hiked on up-trail. Now his path led him away from the bears, back toward the point where he could look out into the valley. And Craig desperately wanted to see as much of the surrounding terrain as he could before he must turn for the parking lot and his car.

As the man tramped away, the sow stepped from her hiding place and peered after. The male leaped behind to whine and stare fixedly around his mother at the retreating man. The female cub whimpered in hunger and her sibling whined again and shuffled his feet. But the sow only stared until the man disappeared around the brow of the hill, then returned to work furiously at her marmot dig.

Ten minutes later, the man popped out on a trail switchback

far above, where he shrugged off his backpack, and pulled out and slipped into his windbreaker. While doing so, his thoughts returned to the strange excavations he had seen far below. Leaning into the rising, howling gale, he resumed his climb.

A half-hour later, the storm broke about him—rain mixed with snow—and Craig Dahl knew he would not make Scenic Point. Nor, even if he did, would he enjoy what he was told was one of the most fabulous vistas in Glacier Park. Even from here his view into the valley below was gone. Shrugging at the fickleness of fate, the man turned to head back the way he'd come.

Traveling downhill was easier and with thoughts of the warm car and hot coffee driving him, his strides were mammoth, the passage swift.

Snow mixed with rain squalled all about him, fogging his glasses. Dahl laughed aloud at thought of how he needed windshield wipers and defrosters. Then his mind turned to the long drive back to his room and bed, and the new job he'd begun only a couple of days before.

Soon Craig Dahl reached the level of the strange excavations. He paused to stare curiously at the one nearest the trail. If anything, the wind was picking up intensity and an eerie keening swept through the thick and windswept waist-high trees—called krummholz he'd heard. He bowed his head into the biting, driving rain and snow and deliberately wiped a finger across the right lens of his eyeglasses. Then he took a step toward the mounds of dirt, and the krummholz beyond....

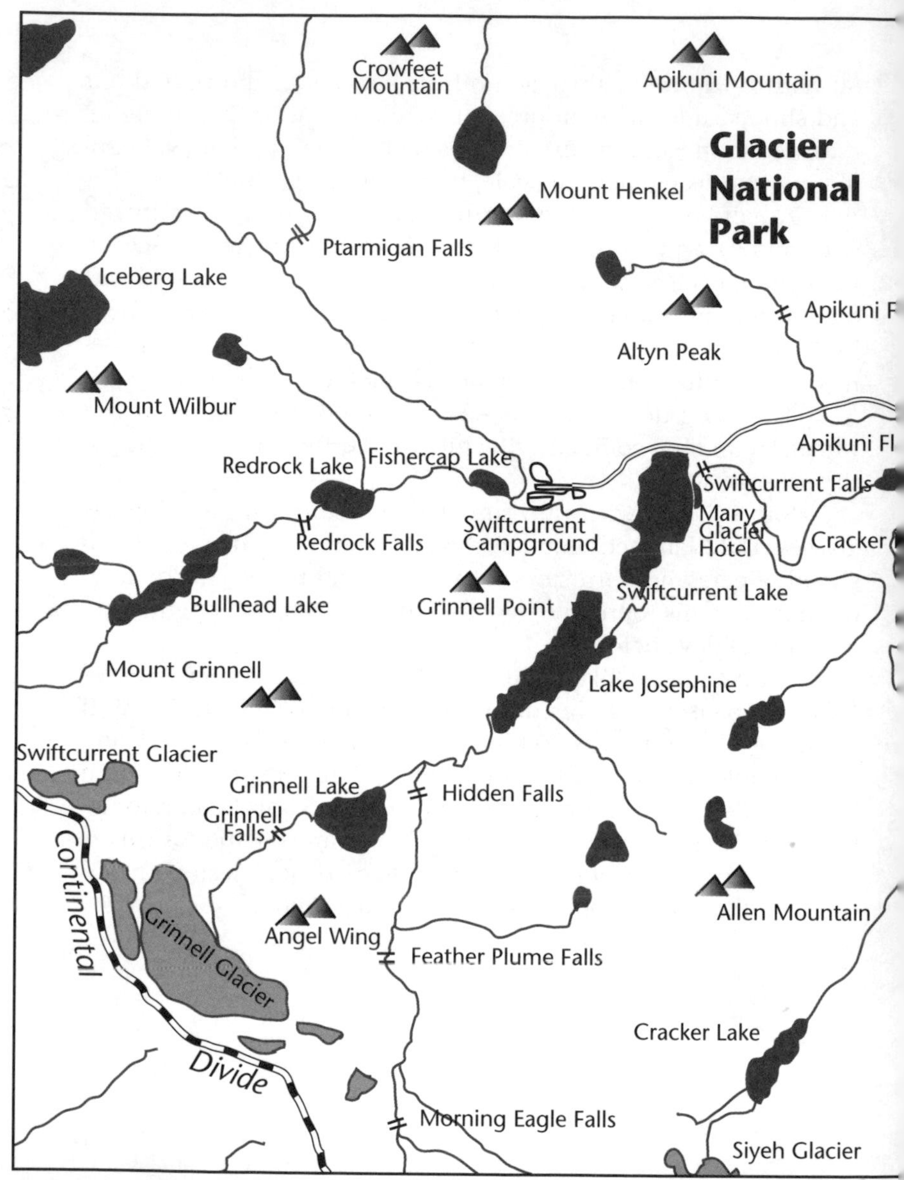

The Many Glacier Valley is most easily accessed by vehicle, via Glacier Rou Three, from U.S. 89 at Babb. U.S. 89, for much of its 300 Yellowstone-to-Glacie miles, curves leisurely through scenic mountain country. But it's in the final la before passing into Canada that God really had His act together.

**This map and others within these pages were produced in part through a DeLorme (Yarmouth, M system that, in turn, used U.S.G.S. quads as their base. Detail–1:50,000*

2

Show-Stopping Blond

The grizzly bear who would someday make national newswires as "Chocolate Legs" first attracted attention near Many Glacier, as a show-stopping roadside attraction. The year was 1983. She was but two-and-a-half years old.

From the first, Chocolate Legs demonstrated a disquieting "indifference" toward humans. Initially that indifference may have seemed charming, but it soon morphed into sobering, escalated to annoying, and, as later events show, perhaps even turned sinister.

The name Chocolate Legs, much like Topsy in Uncle Tom's Cabin, sort of "fetched up." The first mention of chocolate-colored legs was by a Glacier Park Naturalist leading a group of tourists on the Swiftcurrent Pass Trail. The observation report of this incident specifically referred to a blond grizzly (age unknown) with *chocolate colored legs*. This excerpt came from the same report:

> *Bear was 2-3 meters away. People shouted and bear ran away.*

There was a similar incident with another naturalist-led group occurring the same day in much the same area. Fortunately the second encounter provided enough space between grizzly and humans for a more comprehensive analysis of the bear in question. According to the second observation report, the bear, also termed "blond with chocolate legs," was a "yearling"—which meant, in this case, a two-year-old. Since the young bruin was alone, it's reasonable to assume she had just been cast out by a mother inclining toward nature's reproductive call. This encounter-report observed that the bear was "less than 200 lbs."

Again, the young bear demonstrated little fear of humans:

Bear feeding along trail. Emerged again 50 meters down trail. Naturalist relieved by rangers [assumedly responding to a radio distress call] who got folks out. They [rangers?] returned to area and encountered bear again.

What was considered coincidental at the time was that another young blond grizzly with dark-colored legs was reported in an adjoining valley on the same day. According to the report from yet another Park employee, this bear, too, exhibited a certain indifference toward humans:

Bear lounging below trail approx. 100 meters. After approx. 10 minutes, bear walked away, downhill.

It's probable this second young bear was in better condition:

Coat of bear looked like summer coat.

Life is not usually easy for a young bruin unceremoniously dumped from the nest by a mother whose thoughts are turning to Douglas Fairbanks of the ursid kind. Hence the young bear with dark legs was reported "chasing a deer" by a Park Service trail crew working the Iceberg-Ptarmigan Trail on the following day (June 29).

Assumedly the chocolate-legged juvenile bruin failed in her attempt to run down the deer, but her humiliation at being made the butt of jokes from other wild creatures was just beginning. Also reported near the Iceberg-Ptarmigan trailhead by a Park Service employee on July 1 was a bear with:

... chocolate legs, blond upper body. Approx. 1/2 mile up Wilbur Creek from Iceberg Trailhead. Had blond guard hairs with dark under fur. Dark ears. Bear first seen traveling in meadow ... from Iceberg Trail. Had lost sight of it, later coyotes were nearby. Lost sight of bear after 45 minutes. Seen with 3 coyotes harassing it from 3 different sides. Bear would chase.

If she was nothing else, however, Chocolate Legs proved to

be adaptable. And her chosen method for survival was by engaging in modest association with people. Lots of people. As reported on July 14:

Yearling grizzly. Blond with dark below knees. Mt. Altyn side between hotel and picnic area. Bear was seen from road side by many visitors. Bear was turning rocks and also feeding on vegetation. Bear was traveling slowly west when feeding. Actual number of observers was 150.

Some young bears learn that a sort of "buffer strip" exists between normal zones of human activity and that of larger, mature bears. It's possible this young bear learned that not only might close association with humans lead to a smorgasbord of exotic, good-tasting foods, but that the strange bipeds' very nearness provided security.

Still, Chocolate Legs *was* a young bear with young bear attitudes and aptitudes. A July 5 report by a boating concessioner on Josephine Lake reported:

Bear was playing and frolicking in water when aware of canoe. Bear left water. Witnessed at 8:00 p.m. by two hikers.

Near Redrock Falls on July 8, reported by Park visitor:

Blond grizzly. Beige back - dark legs. Coyote nearby barking. Bear rolling rocks and digging.

On July 12, came this report of a blond yearling grizzly near the old, abandoned Josephine Mine:

Blond - dark legs. Group of hikers having lunch. Observed bear walking uneasily on snow. Shy, non-aggressive! Some photos taken. Observers said they would send copies.

But, as shown earlier, by mid-July the young bear with brown legs was turning into a show-stopper. On the 15th, this report from a Park Service employee:

Blond yearling grizzly. Long blond guard hairs. Sheep curve - Many Glacier Road. Bear heading east from Mt. Altyn. Bear remained on lower slopes. Bear habituated to developed area and has hung around the last few days.

On July 16:

Blond yearling grizzly. On or along road. Lower slopes of Mt. Altyn. There were numerous observers.

Finally on July 18, the young bear formally received the name that was to follow her through the remainder of her life. It came via the simple substitution of a noun instead of an adjective:

Iceberg-Ptarmigan Trail. Blond yearling grizzly. "Chocolate Legs." Side of Mt. Henkel. Bear was foraging on side of Mt. Henkel, while people watched from parking lot.

It's not clear whether the decision to relocate the young bear, now routinely called Chocolate Legs, was as much a management decision for visitor safety as it was to benefit the animal. Certainly prevailing wisdom from that era was that humans and bears should not have too much togetherness.

By now, the young bruin was demonstrating little fear of humans, shouldering right up to an automobile and pausing to swing her head first up the road, then down, standing patiently, nose inches from window glass, mouth slightly open, drool leaking from her lips while windows were rolled down sufficiently to throw out half a candy bar or the remains of a sandwich while the obligatory photographs were snapped. She ambled through campgrounds while tremulous tourists sat at (or stood on) picnic tables and pointed. Garbage cans became the young bear's regular beat.

During those months of first known contact with people, the young blond bear with dark-colored legs was never known to contest humans *for* food. There was no record of hostility, no aggression. Neither was there any record of petty pilfery. It was almost as if there was a socially acceptable line beyond which the juvenile bruin felt she shouldn't pass—albeit a line drawn nearer humans than ones drawn by most other bears. If Chocolate Legs, by demeanor and action, respected humans, she also made it clear she had little fear of them. Nor did she love them. To her, it seemed people were of no more consequence than trees that provide shade, streams where fish swim, or rock ledges where mountain goats gambol. People were the possessors of a great assortment of treats, however. And if she waited patiently enough, some of those treats inevitably found their way to the young bear. There was no need for her to cross the line.

Hers was a shrewdness not usually present in such youthful bears. Probably she employed survival traits most often learned at a mother's knee. Unfortunately, there's nothing in the record about Chocolate Legs' mother, or why the young bear first turned up alone. True, the timing was right for the sow's next breeding season and the juvenile to be kicked from the nest. But still, there exists no record of an older sow who might have demonstrated a modicum of carelessness toward humans. There was no information about the gene pool from which the juvenile blond bear with brown legs emanated. Simply one day there appeared a traffic-jamming young blond ursid with brown legs who demonstrated a roadside proclivity for candy bars and half-eaten sandwiches. Somewhere down her backtrail, there'd been a fork. Somewhere down her backtrail, the young bear had chosen the one that took her among people.

Many Glacier Valley scores well in most folks' sweepstakes for highland grandeur. The valley is surrounded by sharp-topped mountains rising four and five thousand feet above the eastern plains; sculpted by yet-remaining glaciers and carved by avalanche and wind and water; forested by spruce and fir and lodgepole pine at the lower elevations, aspen and whitebark pine at mid-range, and by limber pine and alpine fir reaching to timberline; studded with high, wild mountain meadows and two-thousand-foot cliffs; sprinkled with jewel-like lakes, and hanging basins; criss-crossed with wide and walkable trails. Many Glacier panoramas have been subjects for thousands of camera angles held by untold numbers of open-mouthed tourists from all over America and the world.

There's a panoply of wildlife here, too: moose and bighorn sheep and mountain goats, grizzly and black bears, mountain lions, wolves, wolverine, elk and mule deer and an entire host of lesser creatures. Golden and bald eagles soar above, as do falcons and hawks. Waterfowl pass through—Canada geese and snow geese and assorted ducks. Some are summertime residents.

The valley earned the attention of early proponents for Glacier National Park—the likes of George Bird Grinnell, James Hill, Lyman Sperry—and its boundary was drawn to include the stunning valley. With enactment of the bill making Glacier Park a reality, Hill, the Great Northern Railway magnate, wasted no time in building a mammoth and magnificent hotel near the mouth of the valley. The hotel still broods on the shores of Swiftcurrent Lake, still attracts thousands of visitors every year. A campground was added a mile beyond, and a motel, and a store where souvenirs and groceries are sold. There are picnic grounds and roadside pull-outs where travelers driving the 13-mile dead-end road can pause to glass mountainsides for animals, snap pictures, or drink deeply from the visual cup God hath wrought.

Imagine, then, what a godsend a photogenic grizzly bear with little fear of humans and a proclivity for feeding along roadsides might add to Many Glacier's attractions.

Yet, amid all the glory and grandeur of God's best, there's a dark side to the Many Glacier country—people die here. They die through falls from cliffs or glaciers, they drown, they get into auto accidents. As one might expect where masses of people congregate, there's the occasional seizure, stroke, or coronary. And, because Many Glacier is a land that is popular for both bears and people, each have met their Maker by the hand of the other.

Three streams that would be called rivers in most other places all contribute to the character and structure of Many Glacier Valley: Swiftcurrent, Grinnell, and Canyon Creeks.

Josephine and Grinnell Lakes nestle in the Grinnell Creek Valley. Trails follow lakeshores and creeksides, ultimately forking to climb to Grinnell Glacier or Piegan Pass.

There are records of periodic human encounters with Grinnell area grizzlies. While the frequency of those encounters are not alarming to most trail travelers, they do occur often enough that experienced hikers are wary and are usually sufficiently prepared with warning devices and, since its development, defensive canisters of pepper spray.

Swiftcurrent Valley has fewer out-sized lakes, but its big-screen scenery arguably compares with any. Iceberg Lake is a pilgrimage gem for many hikers seeking a "just right" walk leading to spectacular silence and splendor. Should one choose to climb to the top of Swiftcurrent Pass, it's but a short jaunt down the western slope to Granite Park Chalet—among the most scenic overnight destination-chalets in all backcountry America. And finally, horseback riders or shanksmare hikers can take the Ptarmigan Trail through spectacular Ptarmigan Tunnel, into the remote Belly River drainage of Glacier, also a land of lakes and streams and forests and stunning mountains.

Fatal encounters with grizzlies have occurred in Swiftcurrent Valley and across Swiftcurrent Pass, at Granite Park Chalet. So, too, has death stalked the campground at Belly River's Elizabeth Lake, at the end of the Ptarmigan Trail.

Compared to the Grinnell or Swiftcurrent Valleys, Canyon Creek and its Cracker Lake source (a picturesque valley in its own right) is nevertheless considered the ugly stepchild of Many Glacier. There are old mining claims at Cracker Lake predating establishment of the Park. Though long since abandoned, those claims are complete with test holes and abandoned equipment.

Oddly, the six-mile-long, dead-end trail to Cracker Lake, leaving as it does from the hotel parking lot, attracts considerable hiker use. Equally odd, grizzly bears seem to proliferate in the Cracker Lake country. Analyzing past records of Glacier Park bear/human altercations, some experts suggest Cracker Lake bears might hold the record for acting more aggressively toward humans than bears elsewhere in Glacier. In short, though no Cracker Lake Trail grizzly attack has yet been carried through to a fatal conclusion, the suggestion is that Cracker Lake grizzlies might have a few extra-cranky genes.

All the foregoing was, of course, grist to the information mill for Park authorities who watched with growing alarm the subadult blond bear with chocolate-colored legs who appeared so suddenly on their 1983 scene. They watched with skepticism her fearlessness around humans, watched her growing sophistication at roadside begging, watched her apparently burgeoning interest in picnic grounds and campgrounds containing people and food. Finally a decision was made that the young bear was headed down a one-way road with a dead-end ticket leading to injury to

Park visitors and death for the bear. A decision was made to relocate her.

On July 20, a report came in that Chocolate Legs was at Iceberg Point. Rangers armed with a drug-loaded dart gun approached. From the report:

> *Bear ran when first seen. Later tried to dart. 2 shots. 1st dart low and 2nd missed. Irregular behavior. Bear remained in area. Bear 40 meters away most of the time. Moved away a couple of times and moved back.*

Aside from the report being noteworthy for what it didn't say, wouldn't you like to have been a pine siskin watching the day's activities from a tree limb? Still, a couple of things can be gleaned: a) that the rangers missed and b) that the young bear, though becoming agitated, never turned aggressive.

Yet Chocolate Legs had apparently became so acclimated to the Many Glacier area that she never left the valley and the next day was reported on the trail to Redrock Falls, "moving east." She remained in the same area through the 22nd and 23rd of July, but on the 24th a blond sow with a brown cub had moved into the same terrain, dislodging Chocolate Legs. She returned near people and on the 26th was again working the roadside at Sheep Curve on the Many Glacier Road:

> *... Closest was seen to road was approx. 10 yards. Bear was seen from trail between road and Swiftcurrent Falls to past the incinerator road. Bear was going across road. Some people tried to get close for pictures.*

The next day, a small blond grizzly was spotted from a boat on Josephine Lake. And another sighting was made of the bear at base of Grinnell Point. And finally, this noon report from Swiftcurrent Lake:

> *Seen from Swiftcurrent boat on west shore of lake. Hikers approaching bear. Hikers on north side of trail climbed tree. People in boat yelled. Bear sniffed, then went up slope. Hikers continued 10 minutes later. Bear was seen walking along shore.*

On July 28:

Blond yearling grizzly on or along road. Dark legs - blond back - dark hump. Heliport - Many Glacier Road. Bear first seen at Many Glacier heliport. Then near hotel intersection. A visitor was going uphill to photograph. Bear darted below water tank construction at 2:45 p.m.

The report ends with this simple sentence:

Transported by helicopter to upper Pinchot Creek.

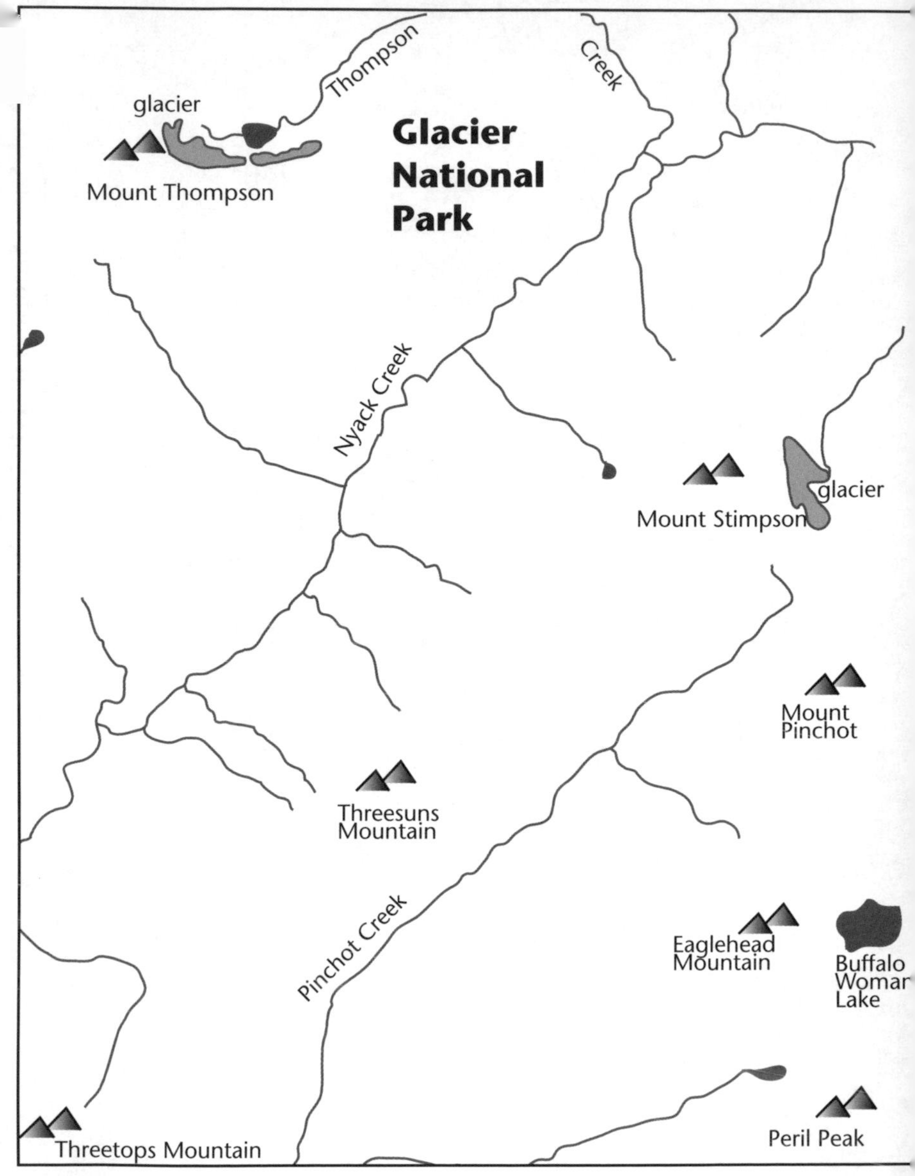

It was at the head of Pinchot Creek, on the ridge between the imposing twi mounts, Stimson and Pinchot, that Chocolate Legs was dropped on the evenin of July 28, 1983, and her world turned upside-down. She first feinted toward th glacier to the east of Stimson, then scurried back over the ridgetop to drop int Pinchot Creek. From there, she expanded outward.

**This map and others within these pages were produced in part through a DeLorme (Yarmouth, ME system that, in turn, used U.S.G.S. quads as their base. Detail–1:50,000*

3

Exiled Without Appeal

In all of million-acre Glacier National Park, there is but one sec-tion where overnight trail hikers are not required to stay in a designated campground. That heart-shaped fifty-thousand-acre region near the southern tip of Glacier is called the Nyack/Coal Creek Camping Zone. Backpackers hiking within the area are allowed to choose their own campsites based on judgment and whim, rather than regimented to particular locations, as they are throughout the rest of the Park. Though required to practice "no trace" camping while within the zone, the area provides opportunity for backpackers seeking wilderness freedom.

This particular zone was set aside as additional opportunity for freedom-loving hikers because the region is lightly utilized by most of the two million annual human visitors to Glacier.

Pinchot Creek slices at a diagonal through the center of the heart-shaped area, beginning near the Continental Divide on the upper quarter of the ventricles' left and continuing down until it empties into Coal Creek, just prior to that drainage joining the Wild & Scenic Middle Fork of the Flathead River, near the heart's point. There is no regularly maintained hiker's trail up Pinchot Creek. And it was at the creek's headwaters where biologists dropped the drugged Chocolate Legs on the afternoon of July 28, 1983.

The bear was fitted with a radio transmitter collar and an antidote serum was administered. According to the *Case/Incident Record*:

> *1743 - 65J [helicopter] touches down Pinchot Creek headwaters: UTM 308.00E; 5375.5N*
>
> *1750 - Bear removed from flight bag; seems in satisfactory condition.*

1750 - 1.77 cc-1.8cc M50/50 injected IM to right rump area.

1802 - Bear appears to respond to antidote (approx. 12 min. post injection.)

It is interesting to peruse the 1983 grizzly bear sighting record in the Many Glacier valley *after* the darting and removal of Chocolate Legs. For instance, at 1:40 p.m. on July 29—the day after Chocolate Legs' relocation, a visitor reported a blond grizzly with "tawny rump and legs" 500 feet upstream from Redrock Falls.

Just in case rangers were inclined to be dubious, another visitor reported a young blond grizzly with brown legs in the same area, this time at 3:10 p.m.

And on August 4, a Park Service employee spotted a "light blond grizzly with dark back legs" on the Iceberg-Ptarmigan trail, adding: "Subadult seen on trail twice. Bear feeding along trail. Not afraid of people, but did not approach anyone."

A blond yearling grizzly with dark legs was spotted on the Cracker Lake Trail on August 13, and on the same day, a second blond grizzly was reported on Grinnell Point.

There were a total of 18 reports of blond grizzlies in the Many Glacier Valley after the relocation of Chocolate Legs to Pinchot Creek. All in all throughout the 1983 season, reports of blond grizzlies in the Many Glacier area reached 71, leading some observers to suggest a beautiful blond bear with dark legs might not have been as distinctive as attractive.

Another avenue of analysis would be to take stock of how many blond grizzlies with cubs were tallied. For instance, on July 24 came this report from a Park Service employee hiking the Iceberg Ptarmigan Trail:

Blond adult grizzly with medium brown cub. Red Rock outcrop—Iceberg Trail. Several sightings of sow and cub. Numerous diggings. No aggressive behavior. Bear habituated. Bear off trail. Trail closed.

Hmm. "Bear habituated," "Trail closed." Was this grizzly mother teaching her cub to be indifferent toward humans? Just like another grizzly mother might have taught her chocolate-legged daughter?

On September 17, two visitors to the Park reported a blond adult grizzly with three blond cubs near the Ptarmigan trail:

> *Two visitors stated that they were bushwhacking and sow came down above them and ran past them. Sow then came near visitors.*

Back in early July, a blond adult grizzly was reported by the Many Glacier horse concessioner to have acted strangely in Cracker Flats:

> *Bear crossed back and forth along trail. Remained in area approx. 45 minutes. Encountered 3 times by 2 different horse parties at one point. Bear ran off into bushes. Back and forth along trail, coming within 30 feet of lead horse, then finally ran.*

Whatever else might be implied by follow-up analysis of available reports, it's certain that blond grizzlies were not at all uncommon in the Many Glacier Valley. Neither were blond grizzlies uncommon who appeared to be habituated, indifferent, or disdainful around humans. Chocolate Legs—if she was indeed guilty of certain transgressions—appeared no more, no less, a product of her environment.

To a sharp-eyed golden eagle soaring wind currents over the divide between Beaver Woman Lake and the head of Pinchot Creek on that late July day of 1983, the first thing to catch the eye might be the helicopter's slow-turning rotors. Circling lower, the bird would soon spot the men, though they might squat or sprawl unmoving amidst the white-blossomed plenty of a showy beargrass field. The blond bear with the dark legs, though she also lay unmoving, would also be noted by the eagle.

"Okay," the smaller black-haired man grunted, "she looked

up. Time to get the hell out of here."

The lankier one began walking backward, sidehilling around to the waiting helicopter. The suntanned pilot watched the rangers gather the cargo net and throw it in his chopper's storage compartment, then hop into the machine. In a moment, the rotors accelerated, thumping louder and faster.

The thumping of the helicopter frightened the groggy young grizzly, as did the overpowering odor of humans—close and permeating. Never before had she feared the smell, now....

The bruin pushed to her feet and staggered up the hill, eyes still unfocused. She collapsed and rested for a few minutes on her side, then rolled upright and pulled her right front leg beneath. The effort turned her dizzy and it took the bear a full two minutes to again get command of her faculties. She made no effort to turn her head to peer at the helicopter; her ears, even though lying flat against her skull, told her the crazed thumping noise was coming from up the hill. With an effort, the bear pulled her left leg beneath. Now she was ready to launch. With a jerk, she lurched upright, only to have her hind legs fail.

Chocolate Legs roared and leaped up again only to stagger a few steps and crash into a boulder. The helicopter accelerated and lifted from the ground as the bear at last whirled to confront her tormentor. She caught only a glimpse of the machine as it sailed over the ridge.

Gaining strength by the second, the golden bear whirled and careened down the hill like a runaway locomotive, crashing through fields of waving beargrass stalks and stunted alpine fir and limber pine. She galloped unseeing across a snowfield, losing her balance and rolling and sliding and scrambling until she reached the bottom and fell from the four-foot leading edge of the retreating snow with a thump.

Bruised and battered, the young bear leaped to her feet and rushed across the tiny basin, splashing pell-mell through a marsh and a creek and a second snow field, until she zoomed downhill again, this time through an old-growth forest of Englemann spruce. The young bear's tongue lolled and she gasped and panted from the headlong dash, but her eyes were at long last taking focus and finally she slowed, then stopped at a tiny brook.

Chocolate Legs turned her head to stare back the way she'd come, blinking slowly, not at all understanding what had happened, but not caring, either, as long as she was far away from the thumping engine and her newly burgeoning hatred for the man smell. At last she lifted her snout to the breeze, to a host of familiar smells in an unfamiliar place: to the sharp tang of saplings bowled over and broken off in her reckless downhill dash; to the fetid smell of decay beneath a tag alder tangle—not unlike the smell of her familiar quaking aspen thickets.

Again, the young bear took stock of her surroundings. A huge boulder, five times her height towered at her shoulder, moss hanging down the side. She took a savage swipe at the moss and felt sufficient pleasure as a large section cascaded to her feet that she reared to reach more. Then the bear dropped to all fours and bent to the creek to slake her thirst.

She drank for a long time, then crossed the creek to climb a finger of a small ridge where she scooped out a shallow depression and sprawled into it. Soon Chocolate Legs slept.

The chatter of a pine squirrel awakened the blonde bear, a sound to which she'd long been accustomed. The bruin ignored the squirrel. What wasn't to be ignored was the sound of a heavy animal tromping across the brook where she'd stood and pulled moss from the boulder. Chocolate Legs tested the breeze and found the currents drifting the wrong direction to get a sense of the approaching creature. She gathered her front feet beneath, ready to flee in an instant.

The palmated antlers came over the knob of her hill first. She saw the antlers just as the intruder's scent reached the young bruin—the smell was not unfamiliar, nor was the animal exuding it. The moose hove on into view, ambling around the hill and crashing through tag alders as if they weren't there. He stopped in his tracks as the young bear's scent drifted to him, then turned and seemingly in slow motion, looking behind, took a step back the way he'd came, then another.

Chocolate Legs' spirits buoyed at the big moose's retreat, although she would have difficulty articulating her feelings in terms we could understand. Until the dart drugs took effect, she'd felt supremely confident in her bear world. True, her mother had turned ugly toward her when the big boar with the scarred features first licked mom's face and nuzzled her body. But the young bear had done fine on candy bars and sandwiches anyway, and why would a big girl like Chocolate Legs need protection?

The dart and the human with the needle had changed all

that. Then came the big thump, thump-machine that lifted her in half-drugged sleep from her home of two years and carried her miles and miles from the only place she'd ever known. Then the needle again; and awakening to another thump, thump of the machine. Then came the wild flight and the strange forest and her weariness. So the retreat of the huge moose shored up her debilitated ego. Besides, she was hungry.

The easiest food to obtain, of course, was to find the road and solicit tidbits from passing motorists. But an hour's travel down the mountain uncovered no road, no motorists, no tidbits. It did, however, uncover a larger creek and an avalanche path that, at the bottom of its fan, contained a patch of cow parsnips with tasty stalks, and a nearby sun-struck slope with huckleberries just beginning to ripen.

Chocolate Legs was a survivor. To some degree the young bear accomplished this through a predisposition to roll with the punches; by quickly grasping there was no profit in pitting inferior assets against superior forces, whether man, machine, or mother. Besides harboring a young bear's normal reluctance to push boundaries, she discovered she was already in an area of natural bounty. So she tarried near the head of Pinchot and Stimson Creeks for a few days, then began a slow drift down from the high, rocky land that had been her temporary home, descending first into a sparsely forested land of sharp ridges and shallow ravines. To her delight, huckleberries were even more abundant as she wandered around the shoulder of Mount Pinchot, until she struck her first sign of human activity since the helicopter huffed from her ridgetop.

Chocolate Legs paused behind a screen of tag alders to study the four spruce blocks freshly cut from a tree that had fallen across the trail. Satisfied at last that the blocks presented no immediate threat, the young bruin lifted snout to the breathless air. She identified a faint human odor—nothing alarming there. So the bear pushed through the tag alders, paused to sniff a menzesia bush where one of the trail crew members had urinated, smelled each of the spruce blocks individually, then turned to follow the day-old human tracks up and over a surprisingly low pass into Marthas Basin.

In all of Glacier National Park there are but few places one can get such a sense of solitude and majesty as in Marthas Basin. Maps list the basin's two shimmering gems as Beaver Woman

Lake and Buffalo Woman Lake. They're the centerpieces set as jewels in a perfectly round cirque measuring over two miles from lip to lip. Beaver Woman snuggles hard against the barren cliffs forming the north wall of the mighty amphitheater, while Buffalo Woman occupies its southwestern curve. The outlets of each lake join as they rush from Marthas Basin to form the head of Coal Creek, a major stream flowing south and west from the southern heart of Glacier.

Ramparts surrounding Marthas Basin like turrets on castle walls are Mount Pinchot to the north, Eaglehead Mountain to the west, and Peril Peak to the south. Pinchot and Eaglehead both top 9,000 feet, Peril Peak is 8,645. To the east, where the pour-spout for Marthas Basin gapes, rears cone-like, 9,500-foot Mount Phillips. The last is a mountain that seems poised to slide as a stopper into the basin's decanter throat.

It was through the narrow defile of Surprise Pass, between Mounts Pinchot and Phillips, that Chocolate Legs moved on the evening of August 7, 1983. Perhaps for no other reason than the work crew had taken the trail fork into Marthas Basin, the young bear turned right, splashed across the creek, and padding silently along the forested path, passed the humans' tents, then waded into Beaver Woman Lake for a swim she'd not had since her bearnapping from her Many Glacier home.

The following morning, one of the members of the trail crew whistled softly when he spotted Chocolate Legs' tracks where the youthful bruin had skirted their camp during the night. He called his two companions. The young bear was, by then, lying on a forested swell of ground midway between the two lakes, oblivious to any consternation she might have caused. It was with heightened senses that the trail crew broke camp, slung their packs, and continued on their assigned rounds down Coal Creek and eventually to a coming weekend of fun and frolic at the sawdust-floored saloon in Kalispell.

Later that afternoon, Chocolate Legs patrolled through the deserted campground, looking for discarded tidbits. There were none. So she turned to the plentiful huckleberries, criss-crossing the basin between the two lakes—until she bumped squarely into an ugly male grizzly with an evil disposition to match his malevolent appearance. The young bear took flight with alacrity, speeding around a timbered shoulder of Peril Peak into yet another, smaller cirque. From there, she climbed up and over a steep ridge and dropped into yet another basin. She liked what she saw in the third basin because here was the mother lode of all huckleberry patches. There were no signs of humans there—no trails, camps, footfalls, or cigarette butts. Most of all, there were no other bears to contest it. Chocolate Legs settled in to succulence and solitude.

Struggle to Adapt

"All ri-i-ight! I've got her," the biologist said, fiddling with dials on her receiver. The pilot gave a thumbs up and put his Cessna into a sharper turn, staring far below at the tiny cirque clinging to the south shoulder of Wolftail Mountain—and at the sawtooth peaks surrounding it that groped uncomfortably at the Cessna's soft underbelly.

Radio monitoring was spotty back during the earlier years of electronic wildlife tracking. Pioneered on grizzly bears by the Craighead brothers in Yellowstone back in the late-60s and early 70s, then refined by Herrero in Canada and Jonkel in Northwest Montana during the 70s and 80s, and advanced by the technological explosion in the 90s, radio tracking is recognized as a master method for monitoring wildlife movements. The method was—and still is—thought particularly suitable for staying on top of "problem" bears. Like Chocolate Legs.

The first fly-over designed to track Chocolate Legs occurred just two days after her translocation and continued for the next two days. With assurance that the young bear was moving normally, responsibility for overseeing her movements fell to routine flights monitoring the frequencies of all radio-collared wildlife in Glacier.

Her location was fixed three more times in August: 15th, 18th, and 30th; seven times in September: 7th, 13th, 17th, 19th, 21st, 23rd, and 27th; and twice in October: 7th and 12th. Apparently, as subsequent flights proved, the latter mid-October date recorded the last movement the young bear made in 1983. Thus sometime on or before October 12 Chocolate Legs entered her den for the long winter's sleep.

Those fifteen 1983 site-fixes recorded for Chocolate Legs after her relocation was considered startlingly condensed: Pinchot Creek for a brief period, Marthas Basin, and the smaller basin to the south and west.

Except for that one quick foray over the Continental Divide....

Life was good for Chocolate Legs for the last half of August and most of September. It was a bumper year for huckleberries and her isolated basin-and-range province was a fine place for a lonesome bear to find a full dinner table. Gradually the young bruin recovered her confidence after the earlier twin debacles that shattered life as she knew it: her mother's rejection, then the sudden awakening in an unknown land sprinkled with unknown bears.

The place where she took up residence differed in many ways from Marthas Basin—smaller, higher, mostly mountaintop terrain. But her chosen living room was open to the late summer sun and proved more than adequate for her needs. True, it was high—nearly 7,000 feet on the basin floor, but if she cared, the view of surrounding mountains beggared Switzerland's most famous tourist retreats. From Dunwoody Basin on the south to Peril Creek on the north, the place she called home might more properly be termed a high, wild, stair-stepped plateau. Each of the streams flowing from that *au naturel* land plummeted down mountainsides to cascade like bridal veils into Coal Creek, well downstream from Marthas Basin.

Day after sunlit day, Chocolate Legs gorged on ripening huckleberries, stuffing herself during the critical period known as "hyperphagia," when all bears must put on sufficient fat to carry them through their long winter's sleep.

Autumn rains came and went, along with several frosts and a couple of dumps of heavy, wet snows. Those early snows, frosts, and pelting rain devastated lush berries clinging in speckled blue profusion to leafless bushes on the open slopes. But the first storms of early autumn occasioned no hardship for the young bear who merely moved into the forest where other huckleberries were protected by the sheltering evergreens until late September.

On the 25th of September, a blowing, drifting snow from the

Canadian Arctic struck the continental spine, bringing plummeting temperatures and overnight collapse of her huckleberry bounty.

Bears have for millenniums faced changing seasons. But nature usually provides a transitional period for young bears where their home ranges tend to overlap that of their mothers while the young creature is forced into independence. Gradually, as the years progress, young bears periodically shift the boundaries of their home range farther and farther from that of their mothers until eventually there may not be any recognizable parallel. The advantage of the transitional overlap is that the young bear has some basis of experience in coping with seasonal changes and shifting food sources.

Chocolate Legs was, of course, denied this transitional period by relocation. And the collapse of her huckleberry bonanza quickly brought hunger. As a result, she followed the course instinct led and left her foster home, traveling from Dunwoody Basin, over the ridge to the east and down into Coal Creek. But Coal Creek, too, was an unknown for the young bear and though some forage was certainly available, she found no place familiar. So she continued on, across Coal Creek, climbing the slope beyond, around a shoulder of Mount Phillips to cross the swell of land into the headwaters of Nyack Creek. It was here the circling aircraft caught the bear's radio signal on September 27th.

Drifting north, down Nyack Creek, the young bear found some forage in late-clinging russet buffalo berries and showy red clusters of mountain ash. But a second arctic storm struck on October 2 and again hard times befell the young bear. She toughed it out for four days, then pointed her nose at the mountain wall to the east, clambering up, up, through chest-deep powder, over the Continental Divide at Dawson Pass, then contoured down the mountainside to the north and east, to the shores of Young Man Lake. There, on October 7th, the search plane again picked up the lonely bear's signal.

"There's no doubt she's moving," the biologist said. "Can we get lower and spot her?"

In reply the pilot put the Cessna 182 into a tight spiral and only moments later, the biologist screamed loudly enough to rattle the wings, "I see her!"

Chocolate Legs paused on an open, windswept point west

of the lake to peer up at the droning aircraft. A gale-force wind buffeted the plane and shuddered the ruff across the bear's neck and hump, and her chocolate-colored legs had never stood out more clearly than against the skiff of windblown snow where she was rooted. "Isn't she pretty?" the pilot murmured, banking the Cessna in the opposite direction to give him a better view.

"One thing is clear," the biologist said, "she's headed out of her relocation home."

A third major winter storm grounded the plane for four days. On October 12, when the plane could fly, Chocolate Legs' radio transmitter pulsed from the northeast slope of Wolftail Mountain, near where the rangers had transplanted the wayward young bear.

"October 12 is too early for a bear to enter her den, Roland," the biologist said. "Especially a young sow."

The usually reticent guy grinned as I tried to interrupt by pointing to Chocolate Legs' location data.

"You see," he continued, "a young bear might take on a lot of huckleberries. But just simply growing bones and muscles and body mass requires that much of her first years' food goes to something besides storing fat for winter." My repetitious tapping of the data sheet cranked his grin wider as he droned on with, "I've never heard of a bear going to bed that early."

But my data thumping got to the man in the following silence as he braked his pickup for an icy stretch of road. "Read me what it says again."

"It says the first recorded date in her den was October 12. And let's see, she was still at the same site when first recorded on March 8, in 1984."

The biologist raised an eyebrow and shrugged. "That says it, I guess. But that seems awfully early to me."

Dan Carney is everybody's idea of what a bear biologist should be: reserved, competent, with an inquiring mind and an inclination to speak the truth as he sees it. He cut his teeth researching grizzly bears in the Mission Mountains of western Montana, then worked at trapping, radio collaring, and monitoring the great beasts in southern British Columbia for Chuck

Jonkel's Border Grizzly Project.

Carney took a three year hiatus to pursue his master's degree at Virginia Tech. While there, he studied black bears in Shenandoah National Park. With masters degree in hand and a wealth of credentials as a veteran bear researcher, the guy successfully applied for the position of wildlife biologist for the Blackfeet Nation. When we discussed the bear Chocolate Legs, Dan had served as Blackfeet biologist for thirteen years. Since the Blackfeet Reservation abuts Glacier National Park on the east, he often works with Park rangers and biologists in the monitoring and management of wildlife. Dan Carney and Chocolate Legs, as their lives unfolded, became inextricably entwined....

"Want to know my analysis of why Chocolate Legs denned so early in 1983?" I asked.

"Let's hear it."

"Okay, she was dropped off at the head of Pinchot Creek—a pretty traumatic event coming on the heels of the earlier trauma of being kicked from the nest by her mother. Memory served up nothing to help the young bear in her new home. She was, however, relocated at the choicest time of year when a smorgasbord of natural foods was ripening. But Pinchot Creek was not the richest place for bear food. So she wandered away from the headwaters high country and wound up in food-rich Marthas Basin.

"But Marthas Basin proved too big and too rich to not be occupied by other grizzly bears who may have resented an interloper bear, so she wandered on over a ridge or two into Dunwoody Basin.

"It was a great huckleberry year and there were no other bears in this smaller place. Chocolate Legs was doing fine clear through the rest of August and most of September. Then the first big snow fell and her ready food source crashed. The young bear wandered for a few days, but found nothing better as a second snow fell. Finally she returned to the only location she knew where memory served peace and happiness and carved out a den.

"Finally, a third snow dumped on her basin in mid-October and with no other suitable alternative, the bear crawled into her den and went to sleep."

The biologist nodded. "Sounds plausible." Then he shook his head, musing, "But that would've meant she was in her den for a long time."

5

Settling to the Wild

During the prematurely shortened first year in her new range, Chocolate Legs—except for the brief eight-mile dash to the top of Continental Divide in late September—explored a new home-area approximately two miles east-to-west, eight miles north-to-south. The bulk of her time during the last half of 1983 was actually spent in an area two miles by three. Fortunately it was a banner year for the great ursids, with abundant natural foods. In addition, her new home was an unaccustomed wild place with few trails and little chance for encounters with humans—which fit her new mood quite well.

The young bear had been aware of the trail crew in Marthas Basin and two groups of hikers on the Nyack Trail. But by the time of her arrival on the forested slope above Nyack Creek, September was waning, with fewer human travelers—a development to gladden the heart of a young bear who'd lost any desire for contact with the foul-smelling bipeds.

Other bears undergoing similar experiences to Chocolate Legs have been known to leave their relocation area and travel many miles, surfacing in other strange and unknown places. Still others, sometimes transported to a new home dozens of miles from their old territories, return by the shortest possible route to the places they know so well. One so called "nuisance" bear, trapped near Whitefish, Montana, was transported over two hundred road miles and dropped near Benchmark, just outside the southeast corner of the Bob Marshall Wilderness. That bear made a beeline for her home country, next surfacing over eighty rugged mountain miles away, at a campground off the northwest corner of the Bob Marshall, only fifty air miles from Whitefish.

In recent years, the practice of relocating problem bears has been discredited among some circles. "Why should we transfer the problem from one place to another?" a biologist recently wrote.

Instead, gaining favor at the turn of a new era is "aversive conditioning," which teaches bears who might've lost their natural wariness around humans to fear them. However, the principle of aversive conditioning is itself undergoing refinement. The ultimate goal, some biologists say, *should* be to teach wayward bears not so much to fear humans, but to fear the result of their own inappropriate actions around humans—an important distinction to which we'll return later in this book.

For whatever reasons, Chocolate Legs chose to remain in her adoptive territory rather than beelining back the mountain miles to Many Glacier, the only home she'd ever known. Humans anthropomorphically assigning their own species' traits and actions to wild animals might believe the bear had "learned a lesson" in her relations with people.

Perhaps. Or perhaps she was simply hungry. Or adventurous. Or curious about this new country. Or she might simply have been too tired for a long journey. Ripening huckleberries certainly did supply dietary needs for much of the summer of 1983. Similarly, the high wild place with few people and fewer other bears may have supplied a psychological need—at least until the harshness of winter began to grip the land.

Or it might have been that her original Many Glacier home, with its abundance of bears and hordes of humans, wasn't all that great a place for a young bear to grow up.

On the surface, Chocolate Legs' new 16-square-mile home might seem ideal. But the high, wild territory contained one fatal flaw: it was too high and perhaps too wild, containing almost no early spring and late autumn habitat. Perhaps this was the very reason Chocolate Legs left it during that first season and pushed across the Continental Divide to the edge of the Two Medicine Valley.

The Two Medicine Valley is, in some ways, a miniature of the spectacular Many Glacier country where the young bear was born. And had it not been gripped in early winter's icy hand, Chocolate Legs might have chosen to remain. But when the young blond bruin returned to her isolated mountain basin, instead of venturing further down the valley of the Two Medicine, researchers' hopes were buoyed that she really had given up her penchant for roadside beggary and human habituation. Thus, preliminary opinion was that her relocation proved, at the least, a qualified success.

It was instinct and recollection that compelled the young bear to clamber over multiple ridges and traverse steep slopes in her return to Wolftail Mountain. Finally she struck a game trail filled with fresh tracks of migrating elk. Instead of following the animals, however, Chocolate Legs followed their backtrail until she paused to sniff at the base of a large, old whitebark pine. There, at the 7,400-foot level, she started to dig.

The den Chocolate Legs excavated for her use on the north-facing slope—the first ever accomplished alone by the young bear—was not finished in one, two, or even three days. Twice she left off digging to wander about in a torpor as her body began shutting down for the season. Each time, she would return to dig deeper and deeper until the only sign of the blond bear with the dark legs was in the "porch" of gravel and soil pushed out of her hole, and in occasional puffs of debris flying from the opening.

The young bruin barely beat the real onslaught of winter—a bitter Arctic blizzard developing savagery while still centered in the Mackenzie Delta and pouring south across the borders of Yukon and Alberta and into Montana. The storm finally built sufficient vertical to spill over the Continental Divide and smash into Wolftail Mountain late in the afternoon of October 10.

With blowing, drifting snow cascading across the steep, sixty-degree slope where her winter bedroom was located, Chocolate Legs hurried to gather a few branches for a bed. Then the animal clambered into what, to any but a bear, would seem unusually tight quarters.

God followed by sifting her chamber's entry door closed before morning.

Of that, the young bear knew nothing.

Radio signals pulsed steadily from Chocolate Legs' den on March 8, 1984 when the years first survey flight was made over her mountain fastness. But it was not until seventy-three days later—on May 20—that Chocolate Legs' location was again pinpointed. In between, it was as though she'd vanished from the face of the earth.

It's not unheard of to occasionally lose the signal from a radio collared animal; especially one traveling some of the most rugged real estate on the North American Continent. The narrow canyons and sky-scratching peaks often hide or block or reflect sound waves, especially to anyone but a highly trained radio operator in the aircraft. And it often takes teamwork—pilot skill and skillful operation of the radio receiver—to ferret out the location of an animal who is quite content to lay unmoving in a tiny declivity all day. Even expert surfers of collared animals' differing frequencies are often challenged by the terrain. All the more so when the radio receptions are handled by beginning or inexperienced operators.

Too, the weather can deteriorate on a scheduled flight day—and the spring of 1984 turned out notably inclement.

And finally, funding for research can sometimes be fuzzy and erratic for federal agencies subject to differing priorities that may depend on bureaucratic emergencies and alligators and swamp depth. Overflights for radio frequency monitoring of collared animals are expensive and "go" or "no-go" may be decided with little or no prior notice.

Take your pick of hypotheses for the two-and-a-half month gap. Or choose all three.

It was an all-white world that greeted the disheveled blond bruin with the chocolate-colored legs as she burst through the drift covering her den's exit hole.

The young bear's fur was matted with muddy clay and imprinted with spruce and pine needles—Chocolate Legs still had much to learn about where and how to locate her den, and how to properly line it.

The day was clear though, and because the sun was high in the sky, it was also bright and cheerful. A Clark's nutcracker had spotted Chocolate Legs breaking through the snow and called. The young bear plopped her butt on the steep slope, front legs bracing to keep from sliding or rolling, and stared up at the flitting jay. Another bird joined the first; the bear looked past them to the sky, then turned her big head and stared up the hill.

Instinct told her to head down. Down into the basin just

beyond the south ridge where she spent an idyllic month the summer before. It was a basin of rocky benches and treeless plateaus that, at this time of year, were barren and devoid of life. Below awaited a gentle, welcoming forest, rich—as far as her memory served—with berries and grass and soft breezes.

Each of her previous three springs Chocolate Legs had emerged with her mother from their den onto landscapes that looked much like this. Each time they'd traveled into lower valleys where skunk cabbage and cattail roots and water lily bulbs could be had for the digging, swamp grass and sedge grass taken for the grazing.

The bear swung her head to gaze in a torpor downhill, then sprawled atop the snow and slept. When Chocolate Legs awakened, it was dark, the jays gone. But for an animal who moved as easily at night as during the day, the dim light posed no problem. Besides, with nightfall, the snow surface, softened beneath a burning spring sun, had begun to freeze making for much easier travel. She picked her way over the south ridge, then started down.

The young bear moved steadily for an hour. She paused only for a moment in Dunwoody Basin, saw it was gripped in ice and snow, and dropped down, down, into the narrow valley below. She thought about crossing Coal Creek and climbing up and over the next divide into the Nyack drainage in the hopes mountain ash berries would still be hanging as they were late last fall. But an inner sense told her she must continue down these mountains in order to reach levels where spring might be more robust in emerging. She turned to follow the rushing creek. Finally, in late afternoon she paused to lie up on a high bank and sleep some more.

Chocolate Legs was up and moving within an hour, driven by hunger and a strange impatience she'd never before known. Down, down, through the ever-present, gloomy forest. The stream she followed was joined by others, then others, until it became a raging torrent. The snow depth was lessening and bare spots began to show on nearby south-facing slopes. Down, down, until the narrow canyon widened and she burst out onto the edge of a series of beaver ponds.

The ponds were free of ice though their banks were still covered by snow. More important, the dried stalks of cattails sprouted from the water near the stream's tiny entry delta.

Chocolate Legs paused to sniff a beaver slide, where the industrious animals had been out harvesting willow branches for breakfast, and where their pungent scent still remained. The bear considered lying in wait near the trail but hunger drove her on into the water and out to the cattails. In a few moments the bruin stood to her belly, tearing below the water's surface at the interlocking roots.

Except for the bear's splashing at the pond's inlet, and except for the broad, smooth pouring of water across the top of the dam, quiet reigned as all other nearby creatures stayed in their burrows or quaked in their dens.

It was while the bear tore at the cattail roots when the Cessna passed overhead. "Hold on Ray," the passenger said. "I just got a pulse from something."

The pilot put the Cessna into a lazy turn as his passenger muttered and watched his needles and listened and finally shrugged. "Guess not. Sorry."

The pilot grinned. "Don't worry about it, lad. But as much trouble as you're having, there might be something wrong with your machine."

"Or with Chocolate Legs' radio," said the technician.

"That I could believe—if we weren't having so much trouble receiving the others, too."

Meanwhile, far below, Chocolate Legs worried the interlocking root systems of the cattails. When she loosened one and broke it from its entwined grasp, she'd then thrust her head beneath the surface and come up with the tuber, dripping water from its smaller roots. Chew and swallow, dig and bite. And so it went. An hour went by. Two. Chocolate Legs paused and stared at a beaver house only some thirty yards away. The house had no snow atop its roof of interlaced limbs and mud.

One time, she remembered her mother had torn into such a house in an attempt to reach its succulent occupants. Try as hard

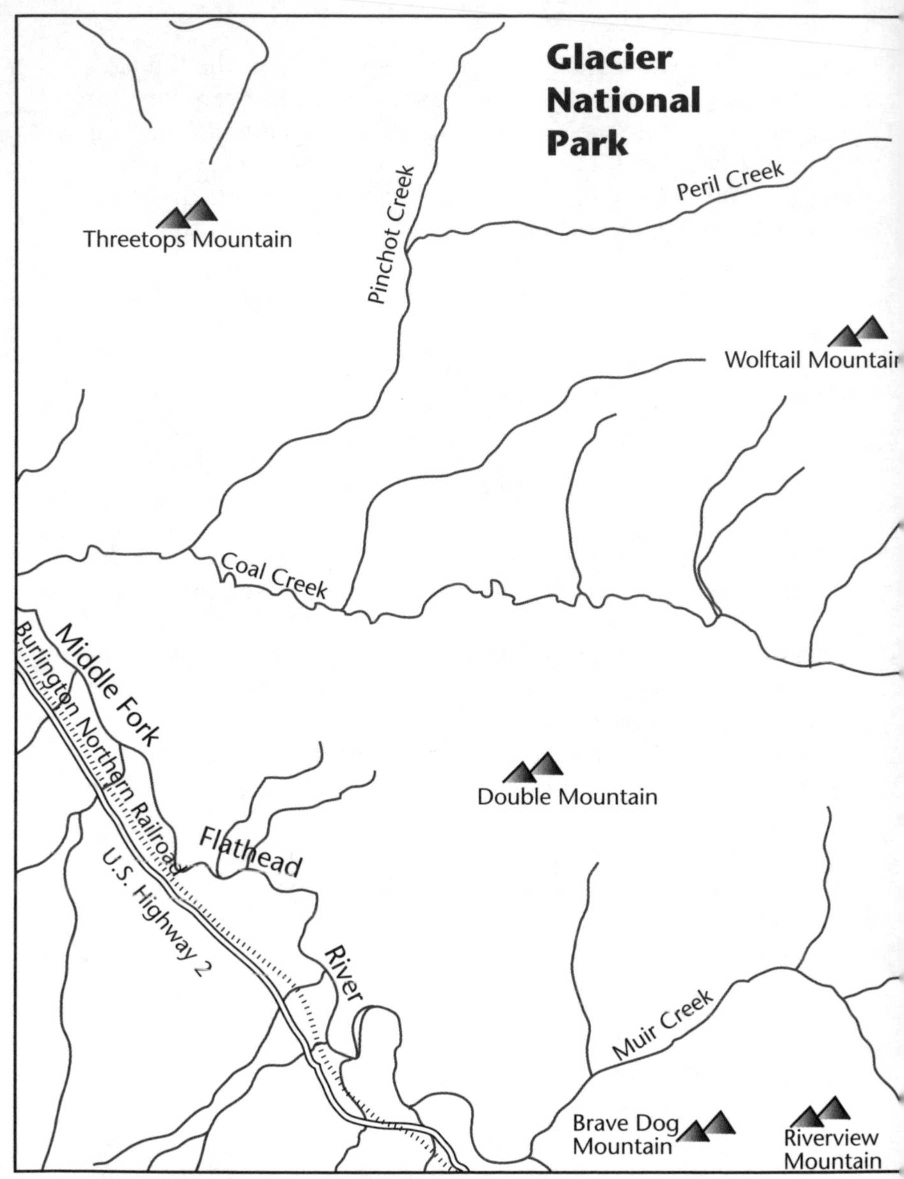

Nearly 150 miles of national forest wilderness to the south and east. Nation park wilderness to the northeast. It's bear country and deer country and e country. Moose and mountain goats and bighorn sheep live here, too. So do an mals who prey upon them—cougars and coyotes and yes, even wolves. It's perfect place for wild animals and half-tamed people.

**This map and others within these pages were produced in part through a DeLorme (Yarmouth, M system that, in turn, used U.S.G.S. quads as their base. Detail–1:50,000*

as she might, the young bear couldn't recall her mother's labor resulting in any tangible food. Still, a gentle pond breeze brought the beaver's odor from the lodge. So she waded toward it. The water was much too deep for wading, however, so the young bear turned the other direction, past her cattail roots to swamp shallows where marsh grass thrust from the water. There she grazed for an hour more before returning to the cattails to dig and eat until she could hold no more. Unfortunately the roots torn from the mud were old and woody, not yet charged with the new growth that would be theirs in another month. The roots and marsh grass were filling, yes, but only a little nourishing.

At last the bear waded back to shore and scooped out a daybed in the packed snow.

Night had fallen when Chocolate Legs next awakened. The pond was glass smooth. The young bear waded toward the beaver lodge, then began swimming. She pulled herself onto the lodge and sniffed all over the top. The huge rodents' odors were intoxicating, so she began to tear and dig, throwing off branches and sticks and mud.

Finally the bear broke a pail-sized hole through the top of the lodge and thrust a clawed front foot inside. She felt nothing, so she returned to dig with renewed vigor until finally she could thrust her head inside. Although the lodge interior was too dark for her to see, a deep sniff told her the beavers had fled. It was while she still had her head inside the beaver lodge, hind-end wriggling in anticipation, that a mighty "Whap!" came from the water behind.

Chocolate Legs jerked her head from the hole and whirled, slipping and sliding on her perch. Spreading rings told where her enemy had surfaced.

When the angry beaver next slapped the water with the flat of his tail, it was from the lodge's far side and it was Chocolate Legs' turn to grow angry. She leaped across the hole she'd torn into the lodge roof to again confront only concentric rings spreading across the water. And when a mighty "whap!" came for a third time from her rear, she whirled and splashed into the center of the newest rings.

But this pond belonged to the beavers, for whom water was a front yard, and all the young bear could do was thrust her head below the surface and swim in circles. Minutes later, when thoroughly bedraggled, she waded ashore, another "whap!" came from near the beaver house to punctuate her humiliating encounter.

Chocolate Legs spent another day at the cattail marsh. Much of that day and the following night was spent lying in ambush beside a muddy beaver slide. But when at last she moved off downstream in search of more sustaining food, the beavers—animals she'd not once spotted during her sojourn in their domain—had nearly completed their lodge repair.

Near the confluence of Pinchot Creek and the much larger Coal Creek, Chocolate Legs stumbled onto the elk carcass. It lay in a driftwood tangle amid willows and red-osier dogwood that had been "broomed" back to stubs by unusually heavy browsing. Apparently a small band of elk had been trapped in the stream bottom by a late-winter snow. Eventually most of the elk had managed to beat their way from the stream bottom up onto a south-facing slope where ceanothus and mountain maple were abundant. But one calf did not; it was death by starvation.

Chocolate Legs' nose detected the carrion from some distance and she stalked the odor on the breeze. The dead calf had "ripened" under the gentle wind of a warming southwest chinook. The young bear studied the tangle, the gravel, the surrounding forest, and the calf for some minutes before approaching. When at last she'd assured herself that she was alone, the blond bear shuffled near, raked the decaying calf onto the gravel and began to feed....

Much later, the young bruin lay atop a low knoll, keeping an eye on the remnants of her bounty. It may have been fortunate she was in her daybed and watchful when the big male grizzly forded the larger stream. With ears pressed tightly to his head and water cascading from his silver coat, he strode straight to the elk remains.

Chocolate Legs scooted backwards from her knoll and, keeping the rise between her and the big male, galloped downstream.

6

Ursid 101
Moving to Secondary School

Four hours later, Chocolate Legs returned to where the big sil-vertip had taken over her elk carcass. Only a little hair and a few crushed bones remained.

True, she'd left little for the big male bruin to appropriate. But the rotted elk calf had afforded the best meal for the starving young bear for over six months, so it's understandable that she wanted to make certain nothing edible was left.

At a loss now about where to forage, the young bear sniffed along the older bear's trail, more or less following it without reason. Instinct, of course, whispered that other, older bears who were more familiar with the territory might locate food sources unknown to her. Soon the scent she followed crossed the rushing Coal Creek, then came out on a Park Service trail heading back up the drainage. Dusk was just beginning to descend when Chocolate Legs heard the older animal ransacking a patrol cabin.

She took a vantage point between the trail and a hitchrail where rangers tied their horses, then waited. The bear she followed had apparently stood on a remnant snowdrift and torn a corner from the shingled roof of the cabin, then clambered through the hole. Tumult followed.

Just as daylight tinged the east, the older bear's head appeared at the entry hole. When he hit the snowbank, he paused to sniff the breathless air and a growl rumbled from deep inside. The young bear tensed for flight. But the big ursid turned to lumber off up-trail, heading God knows where.

Chocolate Legs remained hidden for one, two, three hours, then trotted to the snowbank and clambered through the hole, into the cabin. The stovepipe had been knocked aside and soot lay an inch deep throughout. Most of the cupboard doors were askew and the contents—dishes, pans, even shelves—had been

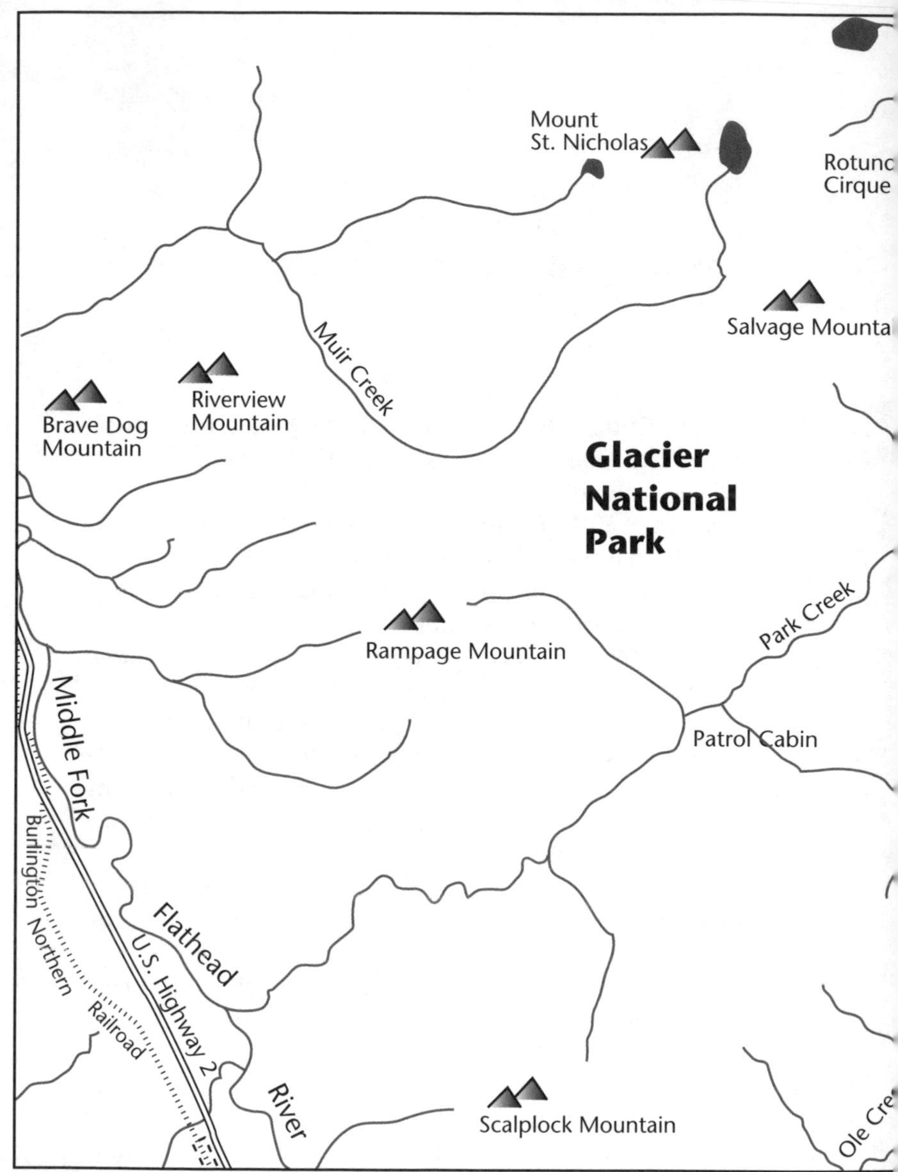

Few sectors of Glacier Park qualifies as "off radar" as much as the zone beyo the Middle Fork of the Flathead. Why? Because the area isn't sufficiently de into the interior to attract attention from the muscles-in-the-eyebrows set. Yet t view from Scalplock Mountain is spectacular. And don't forget the most pron nent landmark in all Glacier—St. Nick.

**This map and others within these pages were produced in part through a DeLorme (Yarmouth, M system that, in turn, used U.S.G.S. quads as their base. Detail–1:50,000*

jerked out into the room. Holes had been punched in every can of food stashed within those cupboards.

The big silvertip had been thorough, but he'd left enough for an enterprising young bear. She licked flour mixed with soot. She worried the tins and each morsel of remnant food was sucked out. She finished off the dish soap the other bruin had disdained and discovered a box of raisins he'd overlooked.

It was high noon when the young bear crawled through the opening into bright sunshine and, with nose to the ground, again took up the trail of her benefactor.

The silvertip had again crossed the creek, sticking to the broad Park Service path, then crossed back a little more than a mile from the cabin, taking a trail fork south. Chocolate Legs followed. The new trail climbed sharply into deeper snow, the going hard because of the thawing mid-day crust. So she rested until evening, then took up the trail again, down into Muir Creek, up that drainage until its bend to the north, then, still on the Park Service trail, climbed over yet another ridge and dropped into Park Creek.

She discovered another cabin on Park Creek, and so had the other bear. But there was less snow surrounding that cabin, affording no easy access to the roof for the second-story bruin.

By the time Chocolate Legs crossed Park Creek, the trail she followed was dim. But without rhyme or reason, the young bear pressed on along the Boundary Trail up and over yet another low ridge. It was atop the divide between Park Creek and Ole Creek that she slept for several hours.

Hunger drove her on. In Ole Creek the blond bear struck the fresh scent of other grizzlies, this time a sow with two cubs. The new animals seemed to be going the same direction taken by the big male, so the blond bear followed, climbing through yet another low defile until she came to a third patrol cabin.

She circled the latest building three times, finding only deep scratches left by the big male in window shutters. While here, the odor of elk drifted in, carried by a gentle breeze from the east. The scent made the young bear's taste buds salivate, so she climbed Elk Mountain.

Elk Mountain provides an open-face sandwich for the big ungulates, offering an excellent range of forage plants interspersed with scattered evergreens providing shelter from the worst storms. The mountain lies in the snow shadow of higher upwind ranges and its open, food-rich slopes are turned to catch the gentle southwesterlies.

All the above may have escaped Chocolate Legs, just as did every single one of eighty-seven head of elk grazing on the mountain that day. But what didn't escape the young bear were the spring beauties and desert parsley thrusting from the newly bared pea gravel slopes in an array of whites and yellows. Soon the mountainside looked as though it was under siege by an army equipped with garden tillers. Those tasty bulbs provided the third good meal Chocolate Legs had since emerging from her den. And she was content to remain on the mountain for a week.

Much happened during that week. Elk drifted back to the exposed slope of a mountain rich in both nutritious browse plants and the first greening bunch grass of spring. Theirs was a working arrangement with the blond bear who swiftly learned that energy wasted in fruitless pursuit was energy needed for survival. Ground squirrels began chirping from their mounds, rock chucks and pikas from beneath boulders and in the middle of rockslides. Even a mountain goat peered down from the crest.

From her first day on Elk Mountain, Chocolate Legs heard the traffic: autos and pickup trucks and buses and 18-wheelers traveling the busy highway far below. And she heard the railway trains as they puffed their way up and over Marias Pass, or as they coasted down the Rockies' Pacific slope—dozens of huge diesel engines each day and throughout the night. Those engines pulled hundreds of freight cars loaded with compact automobiles from Japan for distribution throughout America's heartland. And they were loaded with corn and wheat from that same middle-of-the-country breadbasket for eventual shipment across oceans.

The highways and automobiles and sometimes pickup trucks, Chocolate Legs knew a bunch about. At Many Glacier she'd learned they carried people who, in turn, were guardians of tasty candy bars and sandwiches and sometimes an apple. But she knew nothing of 18-wheeler trucks and jake brakes and drivers gearing up and down and keeping pedal to the metal while speeding up and down the highway at seventy-miles-per.

U.S. Highway 2 was two air miles distant and some three-thousand feet lower in elevation—well beyond reach of a bear's weak eyes. But the noise of their constant passage was there, as was the slam of doors from the homes in the valley below. The bear was more in the dark about the huge unit trains plying the rail tracks—phenomenons triggering no memories. Those trains were, however, only a mile distant and they sometimes snaked for a mile or more, so she could indeed see them. And she often paused in her digging or grazing to peer down the slope at the long snake—locomotives and box cars and chemical tankers and grain hoppers. All were beyond her ken.

What wasn't beyond her ken was grizzly bears. And during her week on the mountain, two more silvertipped beasts ambled through. Those bears headed north, instead of south, however. Where did they come from? Finally, curiosity and the fact she tired of grass shoots and spring beauty bulbs got the better of Chocolate Legs, and she strolled down the mountain for a closer view.

Her timing couldn't have been chancier if it had been choreographed—she arrived at the double sets of railroad tracks just as three helper engines coasted by on their way back to their Whitefish Division point. One minute the young bear cautiously sniffed the steel ribbon and the next minute this steel monster bore down upon her. When she next paused to catch her breath, Chocolate Legs was half-way back to her Elk Mountain grazing pastures.

The second time she regained sufficient courage to approach the tracks, she waited screened by a patch of willows until one of the long, jointed beasts had puffed up the mountain, then had to run like hell to escape another grain train on the way down!

Clearly, these steel ribbons and huffing monsters were not something a young bear should loiter near. So Chocolate Legs charged across the double tracks and loped off downhill, down a dirt road, past a farmhouse and a summer home, to the highway.

"Damn," the biologist muttered, twisting her dials.

"Say something?" the pilot asked, flashing a mouthful of chalk-whites at the woman in the seat beside him.

"Yes. It's been almost two months and still nothing from 251. Where was it you said Frank thought he had a signal?"

The pilot shook his head. "Dunno. Somewhere over Coal Creek, I think. We can be there in a couple of minutes, but we'd better hurry, the cumulus nimbus over in that direction looks chancy."

Ten minutes later the biologist shook her head. "No, nothing. I would've expected Chocolate Legs to move down Coal Creek from her den. But she could be in Missoula by now."

"Okay, so what now, boss?" the pilot asked, eyeing the oncoming anvil clouds.

"I'd like to run down to Highway 2 and follow it to Marias Pass," she said, "but those thunderheads look a little too close for my comfort. What about you?"

In answer, the pilot put the Cessna into a sharp bank and headed through Dawson Pass for safety.

It was nine o'clock in the morning when the blond bear stood near the asphalt ribbon hoping for a handout. Instead, a Peterbilt shot by at seventy miles an hour, its airhorn blaring from the time the driver rounded a far-off bend and spotted her.

After two automobiles and a United Parcel truck blazed by honking their horns, Chocolate Legs got the message that auto traffic along this asphalt was not at all like she'd remembered at Many Glacier where a smorgasbord of snacks awaited her pleasure. So the young ursid turned toward meadows and a swamp downstream from a nearby guest ranch. Around the edges of the marsh, yellow heads of skunk cabbage pushed beneath a canopy of spruce and pines. The young bear, ever watchful fore-and-aft, stopped to feed.

It was around noon that the thunderstorm burst upon her, followed by buckets of rain. The young bear took shelter atop a finger of land covered by lodgepole pines, where she scooped out a shallow pit, settling her bulk into it to wait out the storm.

Chocolate Legs emerged from her daybed to again feed on the skunk cabbage. Darkness descended. Even so, she spotted the cow moose and her yearling calf the moment they waded into the marsh; knew when a band of elk hurried by on a game trail; and spotted the black bear boar as he edged up to her patch of skunk cabbage. Chocolate Legs had ignored the ungulates, but when the black bear—who might have outweighed the young grizzly by a hundred pounds—edged too close, she laid her ears back and popped her jaws in a display of anger.

The ebony bear stepped back, then turned and trotted a hundred yards away, curling up behind the decaying stump of a fallen white fir, occasionally peering around in watchful respect at the blond bear with the dark legs.

When Chocolate Legs had at last fully gorged on skunk cabbage, she splashed into the swamp, charging playfully at the moose. The cow and calf fled, spraying water fifteen feet on either side.

The black bear was already digging skunk cabbage when Chocolate Legs waded back to shore. She shook herself and stood as a statue for a full five minutes, watching the black who warily eyed her as he worked. Finally the young sow scooped out a small depression and sprawled in it, continuing for over an hour, head on paws, to study the ebony ursid. Then she pushed to her feet and ambled toward the skunk cabbage, ears flattening as she neared. The black returned to his bed behind the fallen white fir.

Snowbanks were in full retreat on Elk Mountain when next the young bear wandered back. But spring beauties and parsley were still abundant. And what's this—glacier lilies? Though Chocolate Legs didn't know the flowers by their human names, she did know their bulbs were sweet and rich by ursine standards. As a result, the young grizzly again spent days rototilling the richest white- and yellow-flowering hillsides.

At last the young bear began adding sufficient calories to halt the precipitous loss of fat that had actually accelerated after leaving her den. And with her spring hunger abated, the young bear headed toward the only home she now knew.

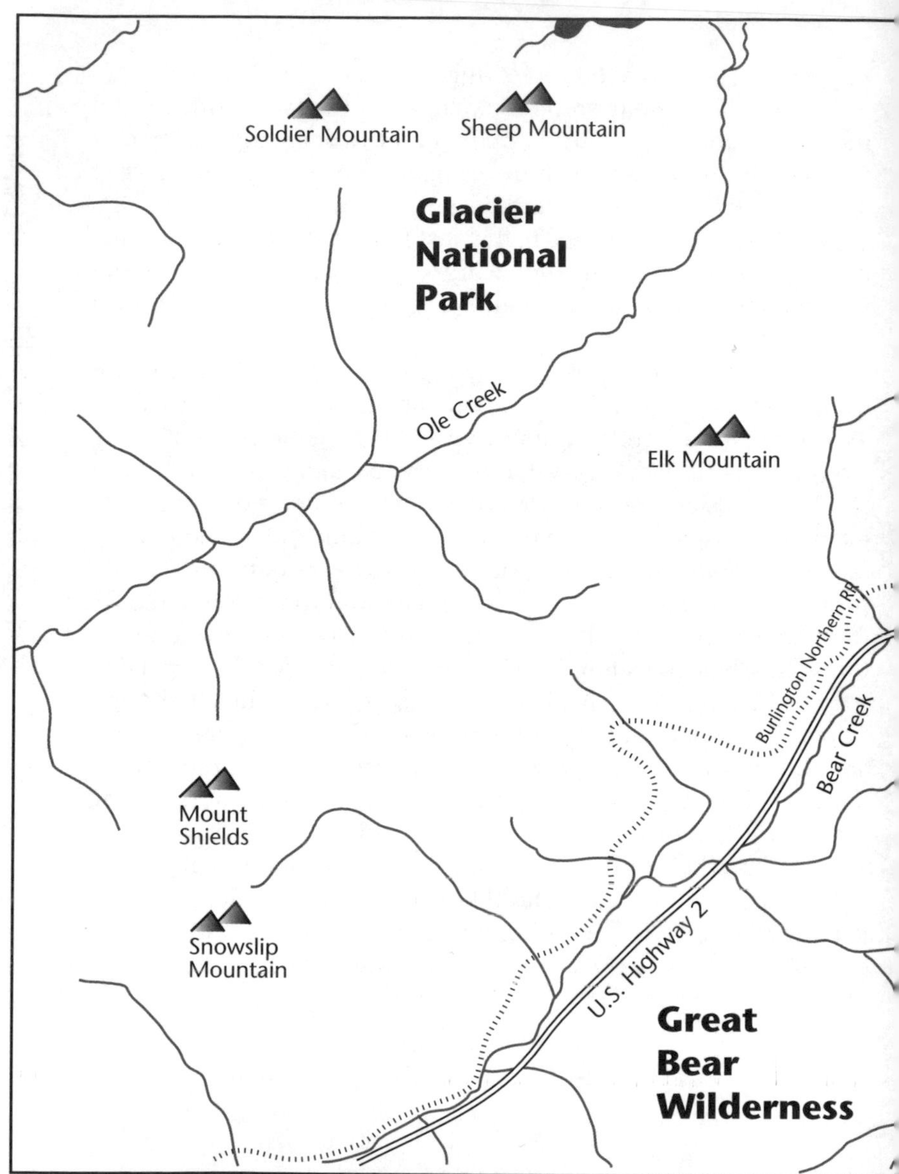

With one of the busiest trans-continental rail lines in America and the norther most transcontinental highway both running along Glacier National Park southern flank—well, it's a busy place. Then throw in a couple of campground a neighborhood bar, a guest ranch, and several summer homes and you have potentially lethal mix for grizzly bears.

**This map and others within these pages were produced in part through a DeLorme (Yarmouth, M system that, in turn, used U.S.G.S. quads as their base. Detail–1:50,000*

7

Tough Love—the Continental Crest

By the end of the third week of May, Chocolate Legs was again occupying the range biologists hoped she would adopt when they relocated her to the heartland between Nyack and Coal Creeks:

"My God! I've got Chocolate Legs!" the biologist screamed. Ray, the pilot, took his hands from the controls and clapped. "Where?"

"Down by Nyack Lakes. Probably along a shoulder of Mount Phillips, to the south." Her excitement was infectious. "Where, oh where have you been little girl?"

It had been a slow journey north during the peak of spring snow melt. The intensity of spring run-off was compounded during the second week of May by the onset of unseasonal deluge. With two inches of rain in a mere two days falling throughout the rain forests west of the Continental Divide, the danger of water crossings intensified. Each had to be accomplished at the risk of running flood tide in the wake of oncoming debris. Entire trees cascaded into streams to be swept down the flood. Only non-aquatic animals with the brute strength of bears, or the natural, hollow-hair buoyancy of deer or elk or moose could dare undertake such crossings.

Muir Creek was bad enough, but the straight-gut, fast-drop channel of Ole Creek proved nearly too much for the young bear. And Park Creek! Two times through Park Creek and the bear had yet to find anything to recommend it! But when she ambled up to the raging torrent of Coal Creek, the young bruin decided to forego an immediate attempt to get back to last year's sanctuary on Wolftail Mountain. Instead Chocolate Legs worked along the south and east bank of Coal Creek until she reached Mount Phillips and its exposed southwest slope.

Soon she'd traversed the mountain until angling through Surprise Pass, this time heading north. And the young bear wound up just above Nyack Lakes when the spotter plane circled overhead.

Most of the snow had disappeared from the major streambottoms by the time Chocolate Legs ventured into the Nyack drainage. Though Nyack Creek drained even more square miles than Coal Creek, the valley was broad and the stream's gradient more gentle. In addition, Nyack Lakes—perhaps more properly termed marshes—spread across the valley bottom, acting as surge controls over the torrent cascading toward it.

It was at Nyack Lakes that Chocolate Legs discovered the field of sedge, mostly inundated, but still accessible. And she chomped her way through a couple of haymows full of the square-stemmed energy builder before she tired of it, swam the lake, and went touring into the mountains on the other side.

The young blond bear trailed other animals who, following ancient patterns, migrated uphill behind retreating snow. To her surprise, Chocolate Legs discovered mountainsides where, at higher elevations, grasses were farther advanced than that of the riverbottoms. Here, too, she began to hear the chirp of ground squirrels and the piercing whistle of hoary marmots. Just as she'd found a month earlier at lower levels, spring beauties and glacier lilies followed on the immediate heel of melting snowbanks.

She found alpine depressions containing greening sedge grass and open slopes where bluebunch wheatgrass shot from the life-giving soil, and she grazed on the energy-giving plants until moving on to another mountain and another valley.

On one occasion she watched a cinnamon-colored black bear ambush an elk calf and moved in to steal the kill after the calf's mother quit making bluff charges at the gorging bruin. But when Chocolate Legs approached, ears flat and head swinging low, jaws clacking, the cinnamon, held her ground, also flattening ears and clacking teeth until the grizzly was a mere ten feet away and gathering her feet for a charge. Then the cinnamon black raised her head and looked away, stepping back.

It was the age-old dominance show and there was no need

for the young grizzly to charge and do battle in order for her to seize the dead calf as her own. Finally the cinnamon bear backed farther away and, whining softly, left the area.

The calf was but one meal. But it was a good one of fresh, red meat and it left Chocolate Legs hungering for more. Marmots and ground squirrels were abundant in this high country and the young bear, driven by a taste for meat, turned zealous in a bull-dozing quest to overturn boulders and excavate hillsides in pursuit of the annoying creatures who always seemed to pop from holes behind, or off to the side, or just out of reach of the young bear.

Thus, it was in a basin near the mountain where Pacific Creek, Atlantic Creek and Hudson Bay Creek all begin—the one place on the North American Continent where streams flowing from one mountain eventually reach *three* oceans—that on June 4, the spotter plane again found the young bear. And on June 12, Frank again picked up her signal, this time squarely atop the Continental Divide east of Razoredge Mountain.

"Look at her standing there like she owned the place," the Pilot said, buzzing low over the ridgecrest.

"She may, some day," Frank replied, scribbling on his report sheet, "provided she keeps her nose clean and stays in the Park."

"Sort of like a doyenne, you mean?"

Frank nodded, thinking. "Maybe the term could apply to a grizzly dame after she's had her litters of cubs. But there's many a slip between the cup and the lip."

The following morning, the future doyenne still toiled with fury and industriousness after marmots. She'd just pulled a squirming fat rodent from its hole, dispatched it with a bite and, with the carcass still hanging from her jaws, spotted another blond grizzly up-slope. The new bruin descended at an ears-laid-back trot. Chocolate Legs eyed the oncoming bear in surprise, then spotted the three furry blond balls bouncing behind. She fled.

Later, Chocolate Legs returned to peer from a screen of limber pines, watching the new sow and her cubs digging for their own marmots. She took some satisfaction that they seemed to be no more successful in their quest. Finally, because the little family toiled a good hundred yards away, the younger sow moved from her hiding place to sit and watch without obstruction. The mother bear looked up, flattened her ears and huffed a warning,

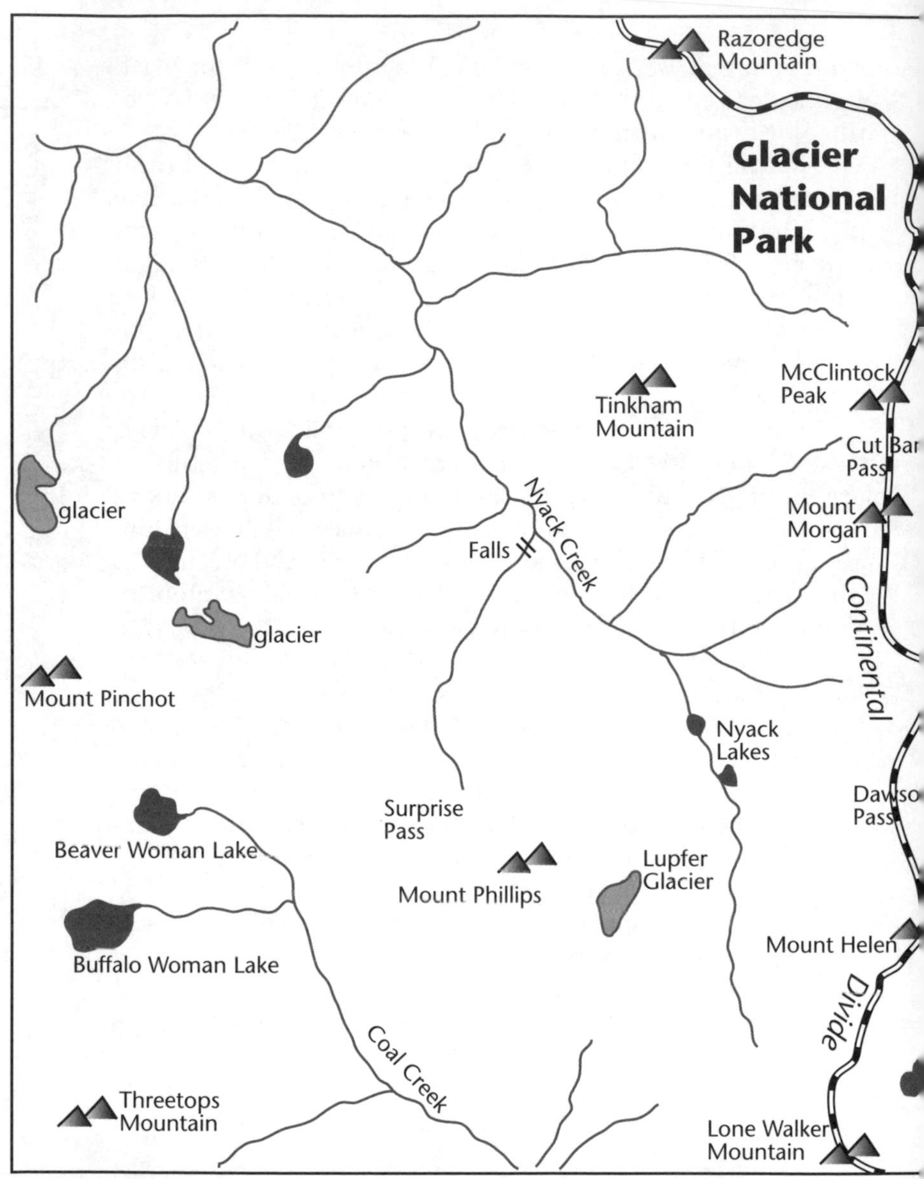

The center of Chocolate Legs' home territory after the young bear was reloca from the Many Glacier Valley. It's a tough, beautiful, fragrant, bitter-sweet, tryi food-productive, starvation land of towering mountains and quiet basins. But it u home—the only one she knew—during the middle years of her life.

**This map and others within these pages were produced in part through a DeLorme (Yarmouth, ME) tem that, in turn, used U.S.G.S. quads as their base. Detail–1:50,000* then returned to her digging. And when the family, tired of the hard work and few rewards, wandered away to the south, the young bear trailed along a hundred yards behind.

Flood waters had receded despite two other drenching rainstorms when in late June the blond bear with the chocolate-colored legs next reappeared along Nyack Creek. Again, she tanked up on sedge grass, then crossed through Surprise Pass and took a quick swing through Marthas Basin. On July 2, the Cessna caught her radio signal at the base of an avalanche chute on Mount Phillips, then again, on July 9, from the edge of Lupfer Glacier, above the marshes on Nyack Creek.

She returned to the Mount Phillips avalanche chute in time to be caught by the spotter plane on July 16. Then, fifteen days later, was recorded three miles north, again on the steep northeast-facing slope above Nyack Lakes. And a week later—on August 8—the signal from the blond bear with distinctively colored legs beeped from the 7,000-foot level on a hillside above Medicine Grizzly Lake, near Triple Divide Pass.

This latest telemetry reading marked Chocolate Legs' first 1984 appearance east of the Continental Divide and the northernmost point reached since her relocation. But only nine days later, this traveling bear with the distinctive markings was back in what was rapidly developing as her favored Mount Phillips avalanche chute. And she was still there four days later, on August 21.

The question, of course, is what was the young bear doing when she bounced back and forth from her Mount Phillips home to wander along the continental crest? It's always late-July before berries begin ripening, even down at the 5,000-foot level around Nyack Lakes and upper Nyack Creek. Sedge grass grows plentifully in openings all along the Nyack bottoms. And to bears, the stalks of cow parsnips usually turn succulent beginning in July, and they're plentiful on moist-site sidehills throughout the Nyack-Coal Creek bottoms. Cattails, of course, grow in the marshes making up the two Nyack Lakes. And there are several types of swamp grasses there, too.

But still, why did Chocolate Legs' radio transmit four times from a Mount Phillips avalanche chute, beginning July 2 and ending August 21? Why was she at the 7,000-foot level above Lupfer Glacier, on the northeast face of a mountainside still locked in snow on July 9th? And why did she seemingly patrol several miles north, along a ribbon of the Continental Divide that included Triple Divide Peak and Razoredge Mountain and later reached as far south as Flinsch Peak and Dawson Pass?

Surprisingly, the lower levels of the Mount Phillips avalanche chute, though on a mountainside, is still lower than the Nyack Valley bottom where the blond bear took up partial residence. At least the locations the young bear was logged at varied from 4,400- to 5,200-feet in elevation.

As for the July 9 reading from Lupfer Glacier? Perhaps that was logged in while the young bruin was crossing Mount Phillips to reach a Nyack destination. And as far as being on the glacier itself, perhaps Chocolate Legs would've rather been someplace else.

June 4 atop the continental spine is a chancey proposition, too. What in the world could she have been doing up there? And she was still there a week later!

I can understand a young bear's wanderlust—I'm stricken by the same curse, even after having made the leap from puberty to medicare. But that the youthful animal was hanging to the same vicinity a week later tells me there's much more to the story than my own fitful early June experiences along mountain crests have thus far provided. That's why I had her digging glacier lilies and marmots and ground squirrels.

So let's take a look now while I use my own experiences, as well as experiences of others, to pull together a plausible scenario explaining the remainder of Chocolate Legs' movements throughout the July-August period.

There's nothing carved in stone about its onset. Only nocturnal creatures knew precisely when it began and of those, none were capable of writing for posterity; none fluent in a language we understand. The bears knew when the snow began, of course, particularly grizzly bears; of all creatures inhabiting the northern Rockies, grizzlies are alone in having no reservations when moving about—daylight or dark, rain or snow, frigid cold or blisteringly hot. Therefore some of them, at least, saw the first flakes fall. It began as bits of eider down floating earthward from lowering heavens, and when the gray light of dawn settled over the mountain peaks of Glacier on that late-September morning in 1983, flakes the size of postage stamps zigzagged their way to blanketed an all-white world.

To Chocolate Legs, it was the snow that set off inner alarms and triggered her to vacate what until then had been her place of idyll. Plummeting temperatures and subsequent snowfalls arriving one on the heels of another drove her restlessly over entire mountain ranges and finally back to her high, windblown, Wolftail Mountain den site.

The blond bear was not the first animal to hole-up for the winter; marmots and ground squirrels had long since sealed their underground residences and pine squirrels curled within their nests. Other animals migrated from the higher mountains, while still others adapted via physiological changes that helped them cope with the coming sledgehammer storms of Arctic gales from the frozen north.

Save for one. *Oreamnos americanus*, the mountain goat.

Across the Coal Creek Valley from Chocolate Legs' Wolftail Mountain home rises a solitary, heaven-scratching colossus. Mount Phillips is unique in having withstood the great ice-age glaciers alone, singularly forcing ice sheets around its flanks to gouge and carve downstream, downwind, down south.

Mountain goats roam the flanks and twin summits of Mount Phillips. If any animal can be said to represent a landscape, the mountain goat is the defining symbol for Glacier National Park. It is said the snow-colored ghost is the most perfectly evolved year-round mountain dweller in the entire world. The small herd of Oreamnos who consider Mount Phillips their own certainly belong in the running for mountaineering blue ribbons.

Home environments for the white mountaineers spark a continuum of superlatives from we two-legged intruders: rugged, beautiful, brutal, serene, dangerous, inspiring, demanding, fulfilling, ad infinitum. When the tilt of the earth's axis leans Mount Phillips more directly into a blazing sun, and warm equinoctial breezes brush the mountain, life is good for the goat. True, there are summertime risks: ambush from predator or parasite, injuries in contests with other goats, falls from the cliffs and ledges of their living rooms. But compared with winter's deadly onset, every morning during the green months begins an Oreamnos holiday. When gale-force winds blow in from Baffin Island, however, bringing white-outs and sub-zero temperatures, it's a different story.

Not that the goats themselves let on there's a thing to worry about. Ensconced in their balmy double-layered coat of long white fur designed to collect radiant solar warmth, plus equipped with a metabolism that generates heat via a ruminant digestive tract, the snow-colored creatures have been observed lying on the crest of ridges in raging blizzards, contentedly chewing their cuds.

So goes one storm, two, three. Until half a winter has passed. Three-quarters. Then it's March—the month known as the "Hunger Moon" to several American Indian tribes. As with most other hoofed animals inhabiting northern climes, fat reserves are largely depleted by March. In addition, easy to reach forage—lichens, moss, twig ends, grass clumps, conifer needles, and dried forbs—have been picked over, then picked over again.

Mountain goats can, due to their bulky forequarters and wide-padded hooves, move massive amounts of snow in order to get to succulent forage. But access to energy-giving foods can also be energy-consumptive. And even with such rugged, niche developed creatures as *Oreamnos americanus*, the end of a long winter is when the spirit is willing but the flesh is weak. As a result, it's when the clock ticks down that wild animals, just as with we human animals, can be prone to mistakes.

With the bitter cold and deep snows of early October, winter had only begun. More snow fell throughout November, so much that it lay three-feet deep in the valley bottoms and ten feet deep in the coulees and along the lee side of mountain ridges.

The first godsend came for wildlife in mid-December with a warming three-day chinook. The warm wind and rain settled and compressed the dry and powdery earlier snow, even baring a few windswept ridgetops and precipitous slopes. But the godsend turned to nightmare when those three days were followed by yet another savage blizzard with temperatures falling to 30-degrees below zero. And the subsequent freeze-up laid a sheet of ice across the still-deep snow.

The freeze was a mixed bag for mountain goats. For one thing, the icy surface would sometimes support their weight, permitting access to bush stems formerly out of reach. But the downside was digging grass and forbs became difficult to nigh impossible.

Then came another dump of snow. And another. High winds brought buckets of driven particles to Mount Phillips from the Canadian Prairies that piled in great cornices on the lee sides of the mountain's ridges and promontories. Eventually there came the 24-hour January thaw to which natives to the region are accustomed, followed by more bitter cold. Then more snow. Most of the Mount Phillips goats finally migrated down-mountain into the thin strips of timber between avalanche chutes where they fed on fir and spruce needles. Amid the trees, however, they were more vulnerable to predation from the big cats.

Cougars, while superbly efficient predators, aren't even in the ballpark when it comes to causing mountain goat mortality. Nor are golden eagles who are their most visible predator. Nor bears or wolverines or coyotes or wolves. The greatest killers of mountain goats are snow avalanches. In fact, avalanches kill more goats than all other causes combined.

Mountain goats are, of course, sensitive to rock and snow and ice avalanches, and the dangers from same. But the kinds of places they live see frequent snowslides and their very frequency can breed a sense of complacency in the white mountaineers.

Observers have watched goats from afar while the mountains talked to the animals. Those observers all tell how the goats seemed finally to pay little attention to the "whomps" of releasing snow and the booming of its cascades. Those observers have studied Oreamnos shrinking against a rock outcrop while an avalanche cascaded down one side, then another, sometimes even spewing ice and snow and debris over the top of their hiding place. They've also watched goats flee, ears back, tails up, to avoid being overtaken by the onrushing white death.

One researcher told me of watching the animals even trigger avalanches as they walked across slopes. And so it was during the early March day when a little band of three nannies and four kids chose to cross near the bottom of a "bowl" that fed like a funnel into an avalanche chute. The goat band's apparent objective was to reach a tree line on the other side of the chute.

When the uppermost nannie and her two yearling kids plowed into the bowl, a fracture line zigzagged across the slope and the slab beneath it slipped away with a "whomp." The nanny who triggered the fracture and her kids whirled to flee back from whence they'd come. It was good that they did because the jar of the first fracture released the upper two-thirds of the bowl's snow load.

The preliminary slide paused when it hit the neck of the funnel into the chute and the lead nanny and her kid managed to flounder out to high ground on the other side. But the second family didn't make it, overwhelmed as the first slab funneled down upon the two helpless goats with all the subtlety of a tsunami heading for a bathing beach.

Then it was into the chute with the upper slab, with tornado-like winds at its face, toppling and snapping trees before even reaching the forest. Huge blocks of snow packed into house-size ice-boulders tumbled down the slope, picking up limestone slabs and telephone pole-sized timber to jackstraw into a huge turning, tumbling, crushing maelstrom that rushed down the mountain with the force of a fleet softening an island for tomorrow's invasion.

A minute went by. Two. Then a hush descended over the mountain. Far below, the avalanche had run out onto the Coal Creek bottom in a fan that approximated the size of the Mount Phillips bowl where it'd all began.

Buried somewhere in the fan's middle was a tiny yearling goat without a single body bone left unbroken. His mother lay somewhere upslope beneath thirty feet of jumbled ice and logs and rocks and snow.

Chocolate Legs busied herself digging out the carcass of the kid when the Cessna flew overhead on July 2. She'd passed the huge blocks of ice and boulders and jackstrawed trees in late May and sensed no bounty within. But instinct and a modicum of experience told her no self respecting grizzly bear ever passed an avalanche without at least checking it out for bounty. And when she'd wandered past, heading down Coal Creek during the middle of the previous night, an unmistakable odor led her unerringly to her find of the season—the leg of a young goat dangling from a huge block of melting ice. The leg was only the beginning.

Two hours later the young bear had her manna free and carried it to a streamside red-osier dogwood thicket, where she consumed it in one long, drawn-out, gourmet meal.

Chocolate Legs spent two additional days exploring the rest of the avalanche from fan to bowl. But up above, at the 5,200-foot level, where the funnel poured into the spout, the residue of ice and snow was still locked in winter's twenty-foot-deep embrace. So the blond bear wandered over the mountain, taking a swing by Lupfer Glacier on the off-chance this ice field, too, might yield a bonanza. There, as she circled Lupfer for a last time before ambling down to the Nyack Lakes marshes for another bellyful of sedge grass, the spotter plane recorded her July 9 location.

Unable to forget the juicy meal of young goat, Chocolate Legs again returned to her Mount Phillips avalanche path in time for the Cessna to circle overhead on July 16. Again the thick ribbon of ice failed to deliver a hint of its second bonanza to the hungry bruin.

So Chocolate Legs wandered back through Surprise Pass, crossed Nyack Creek and returned to the Continental Divide at Triple Divide Pass. As it turned out, the second great huckleberry crop in succession was ripening nicely on exposed south and west slopes. Therefore, it wasn't a food shortage that turned the young blond bear with the distinctively colored legs from her Medicine Grizzly Lake visit so much as a recollection of the fine dining she'd had on the slopes of Mount Phillips. And by the 17th of August, when the Cessna next circled lazily over Mount Phillips, the avalanche had given up its second great gourmet feast of the year to the young bear.

Good luck had straddled Chocolate Legs' shoulders during her wresting of the first goat from the avalanche fan in July—no bigger, meaner, uglier bear had chanced by during the excavation and banquet. But the young bear's luck changed after digging the overripe nanny from her icy tomb as the pungent odor wafted around Mount Phillips, down into the Coal Creek Valley, and across to Marthas Basin.

Chocolate Legs did dine, however, for two days from the dead goat and was busy burying the remains when the first raider appeared doggedly following his nose up the avalanche path to her treasure. It was the same dark silvertip she'd encountered the previous year in Marthas Basin—the one with the short fuse and sufficient muscle to make protest useless. She stayed long enough to fluff up the guard hair along her immature hump and huff a time or two at the boar's inexorable approach, then fled.

But the young blond bear returned to hang around and watch the thief sprawl across the carcass of her goat to protect it from two smaller grizzlies and a black bear who circled 25 yards beyond the larger animal's reach.

And it was while the blond bear, head resting on dark-colored paws, studied all four intruders that the Cessna again swung over Mount Phillips and the headwaters of Coal Creek.

"Wonder what she's found down there on that godforsaken mountain?" the pilot asked.

The biologist shook her head. "Whatever it is, it must be good. If she hangs around here through September, I'll bet she dens on this mountain."

The pilot glanced at his passenger. "Where 'bouts? At what level?"

The lady flashed a smile. "Oh no, you don't. You're not getting me into a bet on who guesses the closest." Then she added, "The north side, at about 6,500 feet."

"Coke or beer?"

"Beer," she replied. "But you've got to pick a spot, too."

The suntanned pilot peered out the side window of the circling aircraft. "She denned over there last year," he said, pointing at Wolftail Mountain. "Right?"

When she nodded, he said, "I'll pick that. Same level."

"Whoever's nearest," the biologist said.

He grinned. "I like Heinekens."

"I like any kind—just so long as it comes in quarts."

8

Chasing Bipeds and Rainbows

It was a day after the other bears had gone that Chocolate Legs again ventured out on the remnant ice left from last winter's goat-killing avalanche. This time she thoroughly sniffed the entire length of the funnel chute, then returned to zigzag through the bowl where the avalanche had begun. The only things she found were huckleberries and a colony of ground squirrels that mocked her half-hearted effort to excavate them.

Too, only a few well-chewed bones were left of the nanny after being scavenged by an assortment of usurper bruins. So the young animal wandered away, to Marthas Basin and Beaver Woman Lake. There she came face-to-face with her first humans since relocation.

"He was so big!" the woman exclaimed to the trail crew foreman, still excited two days after the fact. "And mean. He saw us and didn't run, or move, or anything. We got off the trail and hid behind a tree until he walked on by."

"You sure it was a male?" the foreman asked.

"Male, female. How can you tell?"

"Color?"

"Sort of white—dirty white," the man said.

"Oh John!" the woman cried. "He was brown. Remember, I peeked over my arms when he walked by. And I saw the legs. Definitely dark brown."

The trail foreman grinned and quickly looked away. "While his gaze was still averted he asked, "Was he menacing? Did he threaten you?"

"I've never been so scared in my life. He must have passed what—ten feet away?"

"Oh, yeah," the man said. "He was wearing a big white collar. Probably a radio collar. Does that mean he's a troublemaker?"

Had the people not retreated so swiftly, Chocolate Legs would've fled. Perhaps she should have done so. But habits for bears, as for humans, are hard to overcome. Her earliest experiences were that people fled from her mother's approach. And except for the one unpleasant incident when she'd been darted and drugged by the foul-smelling bearded ranger, she'd never encountered situations where humans engendered fear in her ursine heart.

It was that sudden meeting on the trail to Beaver Woman Lake and a moment's hesitation that permitted the humans to bolt screaming back down the trail. To a thoroughly practical bear such as she, Chocolate Legs saw no reason to change her game plan. She simply ambled on. And when she passed the quaking humans hiding in trailside brush, she observed perfectly sound grizzly etiquette by pretending not to notice them.

Thick and fast, more humans came at last. There was the Park Ranger riding the Coal Creek Trail through Surprise Pass to investigate the report of a marauding grizzly. The ranger would've probably missed Chocolate Legs had he not also been equipped with a radio receiver and located the bear feeding on huckleberries on a Mount Phillips' spur.

The ranger warned a party of four craggy-faced men and one wiry, gray-haired lady, each carrying outsized backpacks and climbing gear who were on their way to Lupfer Glacier. The men smiled and gazed into the distance while the ranger warned of a possible "problem" grizzly working the area, and cautioned them because none wore "bear bells" as warning devices.

The woman called impatiently to the men to "hurry up or winter will be here before we get to Lupfer."

The climbing party was out on the leading edge of the glacier when they spotted the blond bear with dark-colored legs as she fed on sedge grass in the valley below. She'd known of the humans when they'd passed up-creek, knew when they mounted the glacial ice, then ignored them as no threat and no consequence.

"That's the one, all right," one of the men said, studying Chocolate Legs through field glasses. "Damn pretty bear."

"Let me see, Peter," the woman beside him said. In a moment, she murmured, "Ye-s-s-s! Isn't she beautiful." Then she handed the glasses back, picked up her ice axe and trudged away, up the glacier.

"She's awfully close to our packs," one of the other men said. "I trust they'll be all right."

"Perhaps we should stay and make sure," the youngest one said.

"Oh pshaw," the one with the beret replied. "They must be fifteen feet high, in the biggest tree on this mountain. She cannot reach them, even if she wanted. What do you think, Peter?"

Peter's answer was to turn and trudge after his wife.

Chocolate Legs could have reached the packs if she'd wanted. The rope securing them was tied off on a broken limb only six feet up on the whitebark pine tree. Had any of the climbing party still been watching, they would've seen her pause beneath the suspended backpacks and study them as if she was confronted with a thorny mathematical problem. Then she walked further into the flat to the very edge of Nyack Creek where a rich growth of sedge sprouted.

Chocolate Legs met the horse party coming through Surprise Pass. She knew she'd erred the minute it happened—a wise bear only travels through low passes during night, especially a low declivity that other animals must also move through. Too, it's possible she shouldn't have been galloping. But when realizing it was mid-day and how exposed she was in this open defile, she'd chosen to get into Marthas Basin as swiftly as possible.

The horse party—four riders trailing two packmules—was indeed a surprise to the young bruin. But she was hardly alone when she burst through a copse of tag alders and nearly skidded into the middle of the horses. It was an incident that certainly lent credence to the name "Surprise Pass."

Unfortunately there were no veterans among encounter participants: neither Chocolate Legs, nor the four white-stockinged Tennessee-walking show horses, nor the matching three-year-old mules, nor either of the gray-fringed, white-shirted, straw-hatted men, nor either of the halter-topped, peroxided, mascara-eyed women. One minute the horse party had been shooting group lineup photos, the next minute, with stock rested, they'd started on.

Then the charging grizzly!

The photographer hadn't yet finished buckling his saddlebag flaps when his horse made a lunging leap to the side. The women screamed and both mules jerked free and took off bucking, scattering their loads across half the mountainside. The photographer had no chance. Fortunately he was already so off-balance while trying to buckle his saddlebags that when his horse leaped to the side, he hit rolling, still in the trail. His wife jumped to safety from her plunging show horse, landing in the middle of stunted spruce.

The other lady screamed until her horse, on the track of the two mules, disappeared from sight. Then the woman, haltertop hanging and knees ripped from her jeans, limped back up the trail.

The male rider in the lead was the only one managing to keep his seat, and it was a good thing he did. When he managed to get his 17-hand blooded horse under control, it was up to that horse and rider to round up their five runaways.

What happened to the grizzly? There were no similar stories. But the tale generally agreed on when reporting to authorities at West Glacier was, "He charged right into the middle of our outfit!"

The interviewing ranger clucked. "Incidents of grizzlies charging horses is extremely rare," she murmured. When there was no reply, she asked, "What happened then?"

The horse party's leader smiled and shrugged. "That's a problem. None of us know what happened to the bear. All of a sudden he was there, then he was gone." The man's face reddened. "We were all too busy, don't you see?"

"What color was the bear?"

"Blond," one of the blonds said.

"Ah, no," the photographer said. "He was light-colored over the hump and shoulders was all."

"And how large was the bear?" the interviewer asked.

"Big!" was the unanimous agreement.

"But there was no contact?"

"Unless you count our cuts and bruises and torn-up equipment," the photographer growled. "The lens is smashed on my Nikon."

The grizzly bear encounter report was passed up the line at Park Headquarters, then shunted down for review by the bear managers. "That's Chocolate Legs," the biologist said. "It was her at Beaver Woman Lake, too. And at Lupfer Glacier. All she was doing was hurrying to get through that pass and down into Coal Creek. Five will get you ten, she's found a patch of Nyack or Coal Creek huckleberries by now."

The research biologist was wrong. The encounter with the horses had so unnerved Chocolate Legs that she decided to quit such a perilous country, traveling all the rest of that day and most of the night, dropping into Coal Creek and circling Mount Phillips to reach the head of Nyack Creek, then traversing up to the Continental Divide crest near Mount Helen. It was there, out in the open, a thousand feet below the peak, that the Cessna caught her on the 4th day of September.

"Looks like 251 might be heading into the Two Med," the radio operator-biologist said as she fiddled with her receiver controls.

"Hey," the pilot chortled, "that means you can buy me a Heineken."

"Let's wait and see. She's got a couple of months before dentime."

The biologist's optimism was justified when they flew their course ten days later and discovered the young bear had moved but a half-mile north and dropped further down the mountain toward Nyack Lakes.

They hung on the bushes like barbells in a workout gym, big and heavy and with a blue as dark as an ocean deep. With the season's first frost, the berries turned as sweet as the preacher's daughter at an apple bobbing. It was the second great huckleberry year in succession. With autumn's onset, the plants had shed their leaves and the berries so speckled the slope that it looked as though the entire mountainside had the measles. So lush were the berries Chocolate Legs could almost wander aimlessly among the bushes with her mouth open to take on nourishment. Or lie sprawled, raking the berries and stems and remnant leaves and bushes and bugs into her mouth.

Other bears passed up or down the mountain and through the patch the young blond bear had homesteaded. But this single huckleberry field was but one of hundreds—nay thousands—

spreading throughout northwest Montana that banner year. Nor was it just a banner year for huckleberries; currents and rasberries, elderberries and thimbleberries, both red and black twinberries, hawthorne and serviceberries were so widespread and luxuriant in their crop that no bear need defend, or even feel selfish, about one particular patch of berries.

At times, Chocolate Legs grazed only a hundred yards from others of her kind, with each bear, giant or yearling, male or female, studiously observing proper etiquette by not overtly recognizing the other's presence.

With such a concentration of high-energy food available almost without demand, the ursid population of the south-central region of Glacier National Park waxed fat and—as far as bears can exhibit such behavior satisfactorily to humans—complacent.

Chocolate Legs left her red- and purple-specked mountainside for a diet change, drifting a mile northeast to the marsh at Nyack Lakes. The spotter plane caught her there on September 24, grazing once again on sedge grass. Two days later, however, her transmitter beeped from the steep northeast slope of Mount Phillips and two days after that the young bear still lolled in the same place.

"Same place?" the pilot said. "That's steep country. Lots of cliffs. Why's she there?"

"Lots of goats, too," the biologist said, staring down at the mountainside below. "It could be that a golden eagle knocked a kid from a cliff. Or there was a natural accident. The important point here, Ray, is that Chocolate Legs is going to den up there somewhere and you're going to owe me a quart of beer."

His only reply was a broad grin.

The full moon at the end of September fell on a crisp clear night. The temperature tumbled forty-five degrees from a daytime high of shirtsleeve-sixty down to a midnight low of fifteen above zero. The subsequent freeze knocked out the entire open-slope huckleberry crop.

The freeze was of little consequence to the bear, Chocolate Legs. On the first day of October, the Cessna toured overhead while she stared across the Nyack Lakes marsh at a cow moose and her calf who stood to their chests in the water, spending much of the time with their heads beneath. Naturally curious, the young blond bruin struck out swimming across the marsh.

Both the cow and calf spotted the bear when she first emerged along the far shore. They watched as she watched and they watched as she swam to the shore near them. Then first the yearling calf would thrust his head beneath the water as the cow watched. And when the calf raised his head with plants from the marsh bottom hanging from his mouth, the cow would thrust her head beneath the surface.

Chocolate Legs was intrigued. She grazed on sedge grass, then waded a short distance out and picked over some cattail pods. She returned to shore and sprawled in the sun to concentrate on just what it was the moose were doing. She dozed. She awoke. She pushed to her feet, then sat on her rump like a puppy. Suddenly she exploded from her perch, galloping into the lake, splashing water to each side, then swimming strongly, head up, straight for the moose.

Both the cow and calf turned, standing side by side, regarding the approaching grizzly as some sort of strange phenomenon. They stared until she swam within twenty-five feet, then they whirled and taking great strides with stilt-like legs, simply ran away from the swimming bear who was left to circle, occasionally thrusting her head beneath the surface wondering what in the world the moose could have fed upon.

For their part, the moose reached high ground and stood as Delphic oracles regarding a far-off pilgrim. And when Chocolate Legs at last turned and swam their way, mother and son trotted off a short distance along the shore, then waded into the marsh and out to their original spot.

A half-hour later, all was as it was—except for one very wet and confused blond bear who sat on her haunches watching two moose who, a hundred yards away, fed on lake bottom vegetation.

Later, as night fell, the young bear foraged her way through the dense spruce forest along the Nyack Creek bottoms where the deep frost of three nights before had not reached its icy tentacles. There bucket after bucket of rich, dark huckleberries still clung to their bushes. So sweet and so plentiful were the berries that the bear, filled to the brim, left their plenty to range up the mountain to the east, heading once again for the Continental

Divide.

Chocolate Legs was recorded only four hundred feet below the ridgecrest at Dawson Pass on October 5 by the Cessna crew.

"Hot dog!" the pilot exclaimed. "She's left your mountain and I'm going to win the Heineken yet."

The biologist regarded him thoughtfully. "Didn't you pick Wolftail Mountain as her den site?"

"Yeah, I think so."

"Then has it occurred to you that Wolftail Mountain is on the west side of my choice of den sites and the bear is moving east? If she keeps on the way she's heading, even if she dens in North Dakota, my site will be nearer than your site and it is you who will have to buy me a beer."

Again, the pilot grinned.

Chocolate Legs was looking for whitebark pine nuts. Gnarled old trees were plentiful but degenerating with age and disease. Just as every serious orchardist discovers, aging trees must be replaced with vigorous young stock in order to ensure regular crops. And due to man's questionable influence, twin calamities were striking whitebark pine regeneration and nut production.

The first of those calamities was our well-intentioned but ecologically disastrous control of periodic wildfires, the tool nature utilizes to create the conditions favorable to seed germination and young tree development. The second calamity was the introduction of white pine blister rust, a European export that arrived on the shores of the new world some time around the turn of the Twentieth Century and devastated North American white pines of many different strains.

Grizzly bears and black bears evolved throughout the mountain regions of much of North America dependent in some degree on whitebark pine nuts as seasonal food sources, just as they have huckleberries and cutworm moths and winter-killed wildlife carcasses and, in some cases, fish runs up cascading streams.

Chocolate Legs learned of whitebark pine nuts from her mother, just as her mother learned from *her* mother. So it went throughout the age of bears. But what no mother passed on to their offspring was that fewer whitebark pine trees exist today than in the 1920s and that fewer nuts are produced by those trees than was produced in the 1950s. Still, there were *some*. And grizzly bears, young and old, who evolved using the nuts as a primary food source, still moved to the alpine high country in the fall in search of same. Such was Chocolate Legs brief sojourn along the Continental Divide in early October. And the lack thereof was the reason the telemetry recording team caught her back in the bottoms near Nyack Lakes on October 9.

It was four weeks before the Cessna flew again. They marked the blond bear with such distinctively colored legs in her den on the 5th day of November, at the 7,400-foot level, off the northeast shoulder of Mount Phillips, near Lupfer Glacier.

"You know, you're uncanny," the pilot said. "You pegged her den site back in August." He looked at his passenger. "I don't stand a chance with you—hell, I'd be a fool to gamble with you again."

A faint smile brightened the biologist's angular face as she leaned back in her seat. "One thing is for certain, Ray. Chocolate Legs has staked out her territory. We can pretty much draw a line around it. Let's see ..." The lady bent over her maps. "... it looks like an area about seven miles long by four miles wide." She glanced out her window at the snow-covered mountain peaks marching beneath their wings, then added, "As the crow flies."

The pilot nodded. "Plumb predictable, ain't she?"

Well, not quite. There was a large blank spot on Chocolate Legs' chart from March 8, the last date they had her in her 1983-84 den, until May 20—two-and-a-half months later—when she was next recorded. That constitutes a vast void in the world of grizzly bears. Where did she go? What did she do? Those are valid questions that can only be answered by conjecture—just as it is with the lives of each free-ranging grizzly bear.

But the sideboards on those guesses can be narrowed by studying what is known of her history in the Many Glacier area where she first surfaced, as well as the available radio location data in the Continental Divide country where she was relocated and the Two Medicine region where she would, a dozen years later, make history. Those sideboards can also be narrowed by analyzing what is known of her relations with humans and other grizzly bears.

And in order to build an objective comprehensive profile relative to an individual bear, as incomplete as the data may be, we need to analyze her options for seasonal food selections, density of competing bears, mating seasons, the onset of winter, spring, summer, and fall.

Later on, we'll need to consider the effects of motherhood, aging, increasing habituation around people, management changes, biological research, political developments, and the growing human infatuation with a mega-animal with the charisma of grizzly bears.

Between her early October locations and her choice for a 1984 den site on the side of Mount Phillips, Chocolate Legs may have been seeking food such as mountain ash and buffalo berries, digging roots and grazing on sedge grass. But it's much more difficult to guess what the young bear might have been doing for two-and-a-half months in the spring.

I'll confess to speculating, taking the golden bear with chocolate-colored legs as far south as Elk Mountain and Ole Creek. Yet there's nothing from the record to prove that hypothesis. I can only offer that my speculation is logical, even defensible. But it's also arguable.

Or, in polite circles, debatable.

9

Learning the Land

As the amount of daylight faded in the fall of 1984, the young blond bear with the dark-colored legs was much better prepared for a winter's sleep than had been true the autumn before. For one thing, she chose her den site more carefully, with a definite north and east aspect and a high elevation to ensure there would be no unseasonable thaws. In addition, she began excavating her winter's sleeping quarters in mid-October, working sporadically between forays down into the Nyack Lakes' meadows to graze on sedge, or up along the mountainside below Dawson Pass for the last of the mountain ash berries and buffalo berries. She uncovered squirrel caches of pine nuts, and dug lomatium roots along the rock terraces so prevalent throughout that limestone country.

Those forays were not at all like last year's desperation quests, driven by hunger in a new home and no memory bank from which to draw. Instead, when Chocolate Legs left her still-under-construction den in late October to ramble, it was for leisurely top-off-her-tank food gathering excursions in still-delightful weather.

Already roly-poly fat with a two-inch lard layer over her back and shoulders and butt, the young bear had fortified herself well for the coming ursid darkness. All she needed now was to maintain weight and bide time until receiving the mysterious biological signal to close her bedroom door and crawl between sheets. Finally, on the first day of November the young bear completed her den excavation and spent the next two days lining her sleeping chamber with soft boughs from alpine fir and tough-bladed bear grass clumps.

Her body began shutting down despite the unseasonable bluebird weather and her motions became slower and more mechanical—she was falling into a torpor. Then a moist storm front moved in from the Pacific Ocean and snow began falling heavy and deep across the northern Rockies. Ski enthusiasts chortled and rubbed their hands with glee. Hardware and supply stores stocked up with snow blowers and snow shovels and snow plows.

And on a lonely mountain near the crest of Glacier Park's Continental Divide, a young blond bear crawled into her den and went to sleep. Within hours, her entry hole had drifted closed.

No one except a lady biologist circling overhead during a brief lull in the storm (who was later to receive a gift-wrapped quart of Olympia beer) would ever have guessed that an almost four-year-old blond grizzly bear with chocolate-colored legs was fast asleep on the northeast quadrant of Mount Phillips.

It's not known how long Chocolate Legs slept the winter of '84-85, but it's certain that reserves developed from banner food choices of the previous summer and fall allowed her more options than she'd had upon emerging from her '83-84 den. Since the first date recorded for the young bear through telemetry in 1985 was May 7 at Nyack Lakes, and knowing other grizzly bear sows usually exit their dens sometime during the month of April, it's possible to assume Chocolate Legs was out of her den as much as a month earlier. If so, she could have ranged much farther than merely to Nyack Lakes; she could have crossed around Mount Phillips and descended Coal Creek to its junction with the Flathead River. Or, for that matter, simply descended Nyack Creek to its mouth, then wandered back up the Nyack bottoms to Nyack Lakes prior to the onset of spring run-off.

I'm inclined to make book on her descent of Nyack Creek for the simple fact that though her home seemed where her heart was, she'd already demonstrated a penchant for pushing the envelope, especially when food was in short supply. Descending Nyack Creek would be a natural for a young bear looking for edible cornucopias.

It's a long run, Nyack Creek, flowing twenty-five miles before merging with the Flathead's Middle Fork, only four miles downriver from Coal Creek's entry. During those twenty-five miles, the creek's descent is steady, but gentle—from 4,800 feet at Nyack Lakes to 3,400 feet at the Flathead River. During most of its course, the creek winds serpentine-like down a gentle U-shaped, glacial-carved valley. Meadows and willow thickets and marshes are common.

Nyack Creek and its surrounding hillsides are favored ranges for elk, deer, and moose. Below its giant falls, cutthroat trout and mountain whitefish flash in its waters, and the shadows of lunker bull trout drift leisurely along the bottoms of deep pools.

There are no highways or roads up Nyack Creek, merely a trail. That trail can only be reached by long journeys requiring frequent water crossings. Nyack Creek really is a long way from anywhere.

Winter looses its grip early along the lower reaches of the Nyack bottoms—at least as early as any drainage along the southern boundary of Glacier Park. Certainly Chocolate Legs would drift downstream in search of skunk cabbage and sedge grass and cattails and the first glacier lilies.

In short, the Nyack drainage is a great place for bears—which might be considered its only downside for a young bruin trying to find her place in the world. Naturally a lot of bears already used those food rich bottoms. How far Chocolate Legs might have descended Nyack Creek is anybody's guess, but it would have entailed running an ursid gauntlet.

Would she have done so?

Certainly. Her Marthas Basin/Coal Creek/Mount Phillips/Nyack Lakes homeland wasn't exactly devoid of bears. In addition, the young bruin's childhood was spent in the Many Glacier region, where one of the greater ursid concentrations in Glacier Park gather. While it's true bears tend toward solitary habits, some social interaction between the great beasts is the norm, rather than an exception.

As with all other types of wildlife, grizzly bears fill available habitat. Individuals who fall through the cracks are ones who cannot fit in. And Chocolate Legs has already demonstrated credible survival instincts.

With the infinite patience given all wild animals (but long-gone in the puny tame variety known as humans), the blond bear with the deep brown legs stood silent and immobile as a lichen-covered boulder, staring through willow stalks speckled with budding leaves and hanging heavy with pussy-blossoms.

Her vision was limited, adequate for a hundred yards, or two, but problematic for more. However, the young bear's hearing was acute, and her sense of smell need be subordinate to no other creature's. And right now, any single one of those senses would've sufficed.

A hundred yards away, at the far end of the meadow, a mountain lion crouched over the carcass of a whitetail doe. The lion was snarling. So was the subadult grizzly that edged toward the cat and his kill. The bear, a mud-smeared and filthy silvertip, could not be even as old as Chocolate Legs, and certainly had not dined as well before its last denning. The bear did seem aggressive past his years, however, head lowered and swinging from side to side, teeth clacking.

Neither was the cat without its powers of intimidation, laying its ears back tight against its skull, yowling hideously, right paw raised, claws extended, slashing the air with blurring speed. The feline would make no pretense, of course. Were this an adult grizzly, the cat would've abandoned his recent kill with alacrity. But this bear was little more than a child, probably kicked out by his mother shortly after they'd emerged from hibernation.

Besides the mountain lion, a full-grown male, outweighed this youngster bear by fifty pounds. So he held his ground and yowled and bared his incisors and slashed the air with his exposed claws and the young bear hesitated, then began circling the cat.

Chocolate Legs stepped into the clearing. The other animals paused to take stock of the newcomer. Then the stand-off began anew as the muddied silver grizzly swung his head and clacked his teeth and edged nearer and the mountain lion yowled and slashed the air and kept his perch atop the still bleeding doe with the broken neck.

But with the blond bear's entry into the scene, it was no contest and when she drew within thirty feet and lowered her head and began swinging it from side to side and clacking her teeth and slapping at the ground with her front feet and huffing, the cat sprang away and loped into the forest.

It was then that the muddied silver bear raised his head and ears and stalked up to the carcass to be met by an angry huff and a sudden charge from this latest competitor. He backed away, growling and leaping up and down in anger.

But five minutes later, when Chocolate Legs had already torn into the doe's soft underbelly, and her mouth and snout and half her head dripped with blood and gore, the blond bear didn't even look up when the silver youngster began worrying at the deer's head and ripping great chunks from a front quarter.

Three hours later there was nothing left of the deer carcass except great patches of hair, a blood spot or two that had soaked into the ground, the hooves, part of the spinal column, and the half-digested contents of the doe's stomach paunch. Whiskey jacks and ravens, dismayed that so little was left for them, put up a din from nearby trees and the season's first ants marched to the picnic table.

So Chocolate Legs pushed to her feet and wandered away, soon striking the broad Glacier Park trail where she turned left, down valley. And when she became aware the small silver bear followed at a discreet distance, she charged back up-trail with such a rush as to put the fear of death into the newcomer. That evening, however, when she dug cattail roots in a marsh, the silver bear edged out of the forest a hundred yards away, waded into the marsh, and began digging cattail roots, too. When he emerged hours later and shook himself in the moonlight, he looked like a silver ghost, water droplets flying like gnats from a hatch.

One day turned to the next for Chocolate Legs. She met elk and deer and moose wending their way upstream. And she encountered bear after bear after bear: blacks in both ebony and cinnamon color phases; grizzlies so dark they might be mistaken for *Ursus americanus* except for the size of their head and claws and hump along their backbones. She never knew when the young silver bear dropped from her odyssey, but strangely there may have been a twinge of regret when he no longer trailed her a hundred yards to the rear.

The further downstream the young bruin journeyed, the more bears she encountered—testifying to the richer vegetation found at lower levels and the concomitant advance of spring. Eventually the young bear retraced her steps upstream, pausing to harvest different bulbs, graze on different sedge or cattails or glacier lilies.

When occasion warranted, she wandered away from the valley bottom up steep mountainsides looking; searching for she knew not what. She was there on sunny southwest facing slopes when the first chirps of ground squirrels sounded. She was there when pine squirrels opened up last fall's nut caches, and there when rock chucks whistled from boulder fields.

Avalanche paths were aplenty where mountainsides ran down to, and fanned out on, the flat valley bottom. And Chocolate Legs checked out each one for such secrets as the melting ice and snow of late winter snowslides might reveal.

As far as carrion was concerned the young bear was disappointed. But she would've been disappointed even more had unwary ungulates been trapped within the jumbled blocks of ice because other bears patrolled the same avalanche chutes and fans looking for the same bonanzas.

What she did find, however, was a mother lode of tubers enriched by soil deposits carried down the mountain by those slides, and the steady drip, drip of irrigation meltwater to those tubers.

What the young blond bear largely avoided in her spring, 1985 journey, however, was the frequent perilous crossings encountered in her southerly 1984 odyssey. True, she crossed and recrossed Nyack Creek, but always in flatwater stretches and her two-direction travels up and down Nyack Creek was accomplished before 1985's spring run-off really began.

There were sedge grass meadows and entire fields of spring beauties and sidehills of desert parsley and swamps full of biscuit root. Even the sweet bulbs of blue camas.

She slept some and roamed much. And it was a good life; hard but fair. If the young bear harbored any longing for the Many Glacier land of her birth, it would've no longer been apparent to observers, or even to the young grizzly. If this was the land of her future, so be it. At the very least, this strange new land with the huge trees and the dark forests lacked the one commodity that had really made life uncertain for the young bear during her brief span—people. And God help her, that very lack was a boon indeed.

And thus, Chocolate Legs returned to Nyack Lakes on May 7, in time for her radio collar to send signals overhead to the lazily circling airplane.

"Wonder how long she's been out," the pilot said, staring

down into the deep valley below. His passenger shrugged, so he returned to concentrate on the controls, then added, "Still a bunch of snow down there."

Finally the passenger looked up from his radio receiver dials. "And where was it she denned?"

The pilot dipped a wing and pointed to the mountain gliding by on their right. "Halfway down on Mount Phillips. Off the edge of that big snowfield we're coming to. That's Lupfer Glacier. Pretty stiff country where she picked to hole up."

The technician nodded, then returned to his dials, scanning through the radio's frequency range for other signals.

The pilot studied him for a moment, then asked, "How is it you got picked for this duty?"

The technician shrugged. "Right place at the right time. They needed somebody and I've worked a little with radio tracking before. It's an opportunity."

It was the pilot's turn to shrug. "Where to now, sport?"

10

Choosing to Roam

The first light brushed surrounding peaks as though God threw a celestial switch. The golden bear with distinctively dark legs paused in mid-stride, seemingly to gaze upon distant scenes for which her weak ursid eyes could not reach. Still, Chocolate Legs remained rooted, testing the gentle morning breeze wafting through Dawson Pass, only a quarter mile south and 500 feet up the mountainside.

Gradually sunlight crept down the peak to her north, then was blocked from reaching the statue-like bruin by the ridge above. At last she moved, ambling along stunted alpine firs and limber pines, padding softly at the edge of a snowdrift. The drift had been deposited by gale winds rising in Asia and rushing across the Pacific to dump its precious snow load on this very mountain spine where it would be held safely for redistribution through early summer.

Chocolate Legs paused over a network of vole tunnels exposed by the retreating bank and sniffed. Then the bear raked her claws through the soft and muddy soil. A vole, outweighed a thousand times over in the confrontation, lost the match-up and disappeared. She raked again and another vole went down the hatch. It was a couple of hours later, after a warm spring sun had beat its way over the ridge and upon the young bruin's back when she tired of her snowbank patrol and moved into the scraggly, still snow-laden forest for a nap.

"What in the world is Number 251 doing up there?" the technician mumbled to himself, leaning over to stare out the Cessna window as the plane swept through Dawson Pass.

"Is that Chocolate Legs?" the pilot asked. "Have you got Chocolate Legs?"

The technician nodded and the pilot pulled back on his

yoke to gain altitude and circle. "It sounds like she's in that line of trees just north of the pass." the technician added. "But what's she doing up so high in mid-May?"

The pilot started to say something flippant, then remembered he didn't know this new guy well enough to joke with him. So the man clammed up and concentrated on doing his job.

But when they flew the course the following week and actually spotted the young bear ambling along the rocky ridge thrusting as a finger between Old Man and Young Man Lakes, the technician and pilot connected as buddies in an instant.

"My God, she's beautiful!" the technician cried, clapping his companion on the back. "You said she is and she is."

The pilot eased his wheel forward, descending ever so slightly into Young Man Basin, swinging around the ridge-finger into Old Man Basin, cutting in a tight "U" and back again, almost at eye level with the blonde sow. "Well, looky there," Ray murmured. "She's laying down."

For her part, Chocolate Legs at first ignored the passing plane. She'd already had a hard day's night crawling up and out of Old Man Basin and was still infected by an urge for wanderlust. Therefore she decided to rest where she was for a few minutes, then see what edibles might be located elsewhere. While she rested, that *thing* buzzing first one side then the other began to annoy her.. Did it remind her of that other *thing*, the thump-thump one that evoked so many unpleasant memories?

As if responding to her complaint, the annoying thing quit buzzing around Old Man and Young Man Basins and motored away into the distance. Chocolate Legs dozed.

The blond bear with distinctively colored legs was not the season's first grizzly to explore the shores of Upper Two Medicine Lake. In fact, she wasn't the only *Ursus arctos horribilis* to do so on the days she was there—the same day humans in the valleys below were laying sprays of flowers on loved ones' graves. A silvertip sow not much larger than Chocolate Legs, with a dark cub of the year snuggling hard against her side, and a rangy light-colored boar, both dug for glacier lily bulbs from the hillside above the north shore of the lake. But most of the mountainside was such a riot of yellow that one might think a giant hand had dashed it with a mammoth bucket of lemon paint. Thus, neither sow nor boar paid the slightest attention when a young blond bear with dark legs crept from the forest and took a digging claim along the mountain's far edge.

The bear was still in the same location when the Cessna buzzed over on the first day of June. This time the biologist worked the radio. "She's right down at the lakeshore," the lady said as the pilot dropped his flaps and brought the plane into a slow turn.

"Can't see her though?" the pilot asked.

The biologist shook her head.

"You should have been here last time out. She was laying on a ridgetop, right out in the bright sunlight. God, she was beautiful."

"I'd rather have been here than where I was." The lady said, "I'm getting to the point where meetings don't hold the infatuation for me they once did."

"Isn't that another bear over toward Pumpelly's Pillar?" the pilot murmured.

The biologist nodded. "Has a cub, too." Then she glanced up at the sky and said, "Let's not go down any further. If those clouds get any lower, we're going to have to break off the flight."

"We may have to go out down-valley now in order to stay under them."

"Maybe we should. I'll check with my office to see when we can finish doing the grid."

Thus it was on a bright and sunny June 4th morning when the Cessna's crew began their radio monitoring where they'd left off three days before. "Well, Number 251 is still at Upper Two Medicine," the biologist said. "This time further up-slope. Hmm, about middle of the lake and around the six-thousand-foot level—there she is!"

The pilot eyed her in admiration. "You're good with that radio. A bunch better than your replacement."

The lady never took eyes from the golden bear, twisting to watch below as the Cessna putzed by at near stall speed. "Frank is all right. Just a little green behind the ears." When her companion said nothing, she glanced at him. "He's getting better, isn't he?"

The pilot shrugged. "You'll have to be the judge of that. He

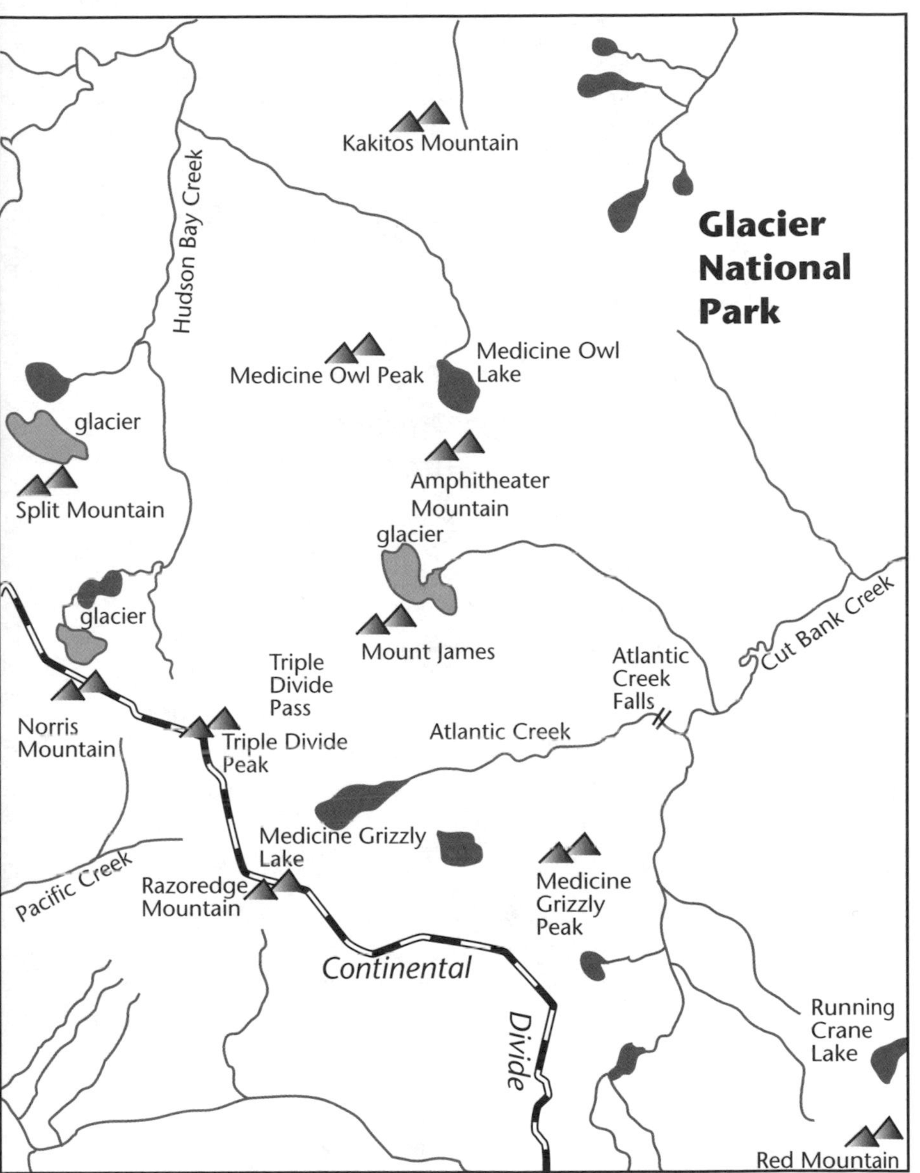

There's no doubt in a lot of minds that a September bluebird-weather hike to Triple Divide Pass ranks right up there with ice cream, first love, and a good country back scratching as one of life's great delights. And to top it off, the view from Triple Divide isn't the least bit perishable. But, come to think of it, neither is my first love.

**This map and others within these pages were produced in part through a DeLorme (Yarmouth, ME) system that, in turn, used U.S.G.S. quads as their base. Detail–1:50,000*

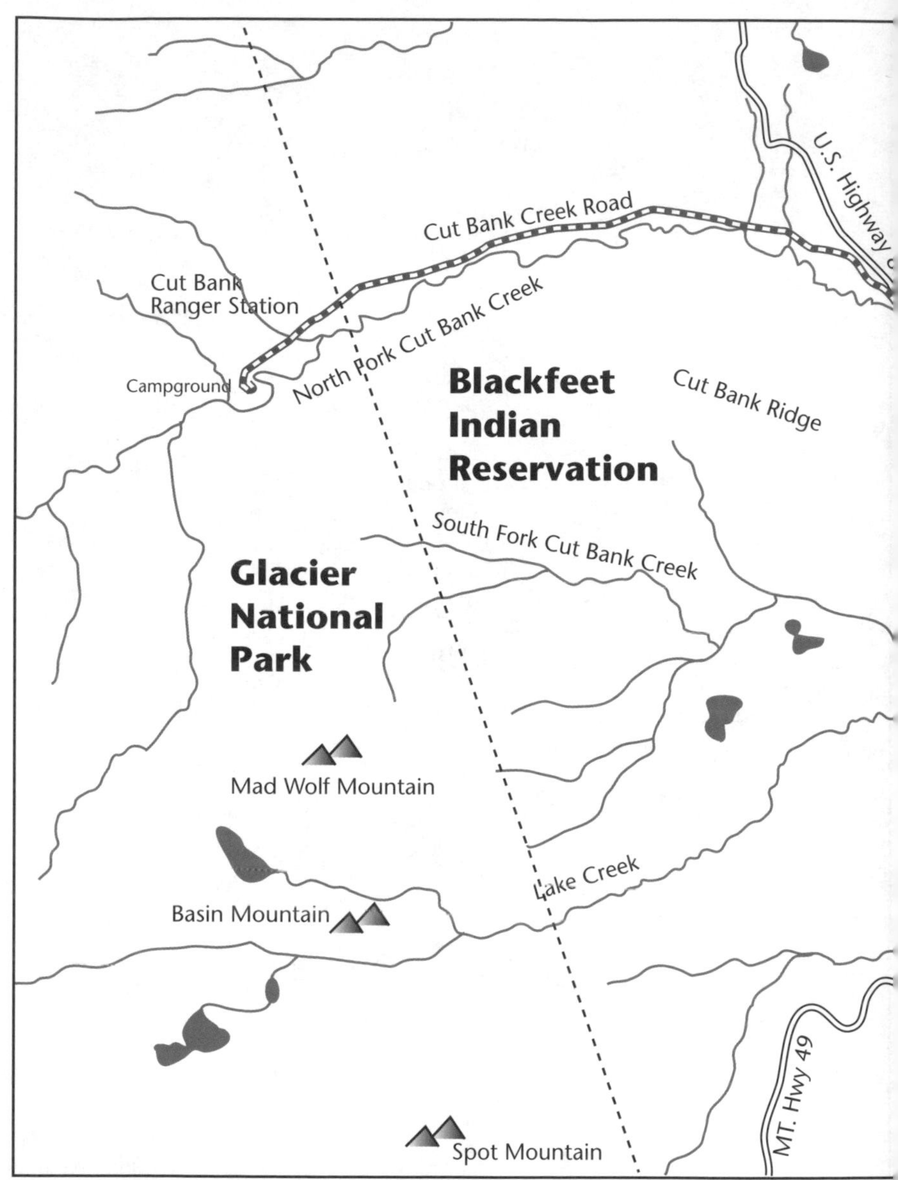

Cut Bank Creek and environs are usually thought of as the ugly cousin of Mary's, Many Glacier, and Two Medicine drainages. But the truth is, the nativ know better. Later, we'll talk about places like Triple Divide Peak, Pitamak Pass, and Morning Star Lake. Now, however, we'll content ourselves with telli you, Cut Bank Creek is a great starting place.

**This map and others within these pages were produced in part through a DeLorme (Yarmouth, M system that, in turn, used U.S.G.S. quads as their base. Detail–1:50,000*

can't pinpoint locations like you just did if that's what you mean."

"Experience. Frank just needs experience, that's all."

The pilot nodded and nudged up the throttle for more altitude. "Okay, here we go over the top. Which one are you looking for now?"

"Number 186. I'm betting we'll find him somewhere up Red Eagle. But he could be heading for Mount Logan high country by now."

They fell silent as the Cessna headed north and west over Cut Bank Pass and Pitamakin Pass and Triple Divide. Then Ray asked, "Where will she den this fall?"

"What? Where will who ... oh, you mean Chocolate Legs."

"Yeah you'll have to give me a chance to get even."

The biologist laughed gaily. "Whoever said anything's fair about love and war and where grizzly bears den?" She returned concentration on her radio receiver, then murmured, "Besides, the collar might not last that long."

The pilot watched her work with the scanner dials, then asked, "What do you make of her move to Two Medicine?"

The biologist shook her head. "What makes you think she has? Where she is now isn't all that far from where she's already established a home range. It's not unusual for bears to test their boundaries." When the pilot only nodded, she added, "Ray, that bear could be back in the middle of her home range tomorrow."

Which was where Chocolate Legs was when on June 10 the tracking plane next flew—on a north shoulder of Mount Phillips, with easy access to both Surprise Pass and Nyack Lakes.

The pilot shook his head. "You beat anything. You predicted she'd be here last week. How do you do it?"

The biologist studied her chart. "It helps to have worked with the animals for a dozen years. And," tapping her chart, "it helps to have previous records to go by. And," she smiled, "maybe it helps to be a woman predicting what another woman will do."

"Okay, so where will she be next week, boss?"

Again, the biologist bent over her chart. "You're stretching my occult powers, Ray. But here it says that last year she was up by Triple Divide Peak in mid-June. So, yes," she said, placing a forefinger to chart, "I'll predict she'll head that way soon."

Seven days later, the Cessna putzed lazily over Medicine Grizzly Lake—a mountain gem snuggling like a sapphire bead at the south base of Triple Divide Peak, amid some of the most muscled-up mountains in all America. The pulse from Chocolate Legs' radio came from somewhere below.

"You did it again!" the pilot said in awe to the woman occupying the passenger seat next to him. "You called it again."

He put the Cessna around the only mountain in the world from which water drains into three oceans. Clearing the cliffs on the north, the pilot cut his throttle and trimmed the Cessna into a glide, circling almost noiselessly down, sweeping just above ground level through Triple Divide Pass, then lifting flaps further to push the plane into rapid descent until leveling out 500 feet above the lake surface. It was but 6:30 in the morning and the young golden bear looked up as the shadow of the giant bird swept over the mountain, the cliffs, the waterfalls, and the bear.

Concentrating now because of the narrowness of the canyon and potential vagaries of wind, Ray still had time to murmur, "One thing for sure, you have that bear on a leash."

Untroubled by spruce trees flying by at a gallop and groping at wingtips as they passed, the biologist stared at her chart. "Probably back to Nyack Lakes next time out. The sedge will be maturing now, heavy in protein. And she'll be marking time, waiting for berries to ripen. That'll happen first...."

She looked out the window as the pilot fed power and flap to the Cessna while exiting the narrow Atlantic Creek canyon into the much broader Cut Bank drainage.

"... on the west side of the divide. First with red twinberries, then currents and thimbleberries. The first huckleberries will be on by the end of July. After that, she'll be able to go wherever she wishes, but why would she want to?"

Able now to relax as the Cessna gained to mountaintop altitude, the pilot looked at his passenger. "Why is she spending so much time on the mountaintops?"

The biologist spread her hands from the chart lying across her lap. "That, my friend, is a good question. I've been wondering myself. If there were moths out now, the answer would be simple. But it's too early. Most bears don't start moving after moths until July and they normally won't really hone in until August."

She peered out the window at the still-snowcapped peaks, unseeing. "I can't believe she's getting the kinds of food-intake she needs from mountaintops this time of year."

The biologist wasn't the only one thinking the blond bear with dark legs wasn't finding sufficient foods needed to maintain weight and replenish energy—Chocolate Legs had doubts on the same subject. But instead of returning to Nyack Lakes as the lady biologist had guessed, the young bear followed the route taken by the airplane: down Atlantic Creek to Cut Bank Creek.

She paused not a whit when the Medicine Grizzly Trail hooked up with the Triple Divide Trail, continuing down to the junction with the trail to Pitamakin Lake and Cut Bank Pass. Right or left? Turn right and she could, by morning, be in lands she knew: Cut Bank Pass and into the Nyack drainage, Old Man Lake, the Continental Divide ridgetop she'd learned so well.

Day blinkered out while the young bear stood in indecision. Day? Night? It makes no difference to a bear who has no fear of darkness—nor of fear itself. She turned left. Two miles down Cut Bank Creek Chocolate Legs stumbled into a meadow and marsh. Sedge also grew here, as did cattails and lilies. It was also a marsh and meadow rich in wildlife: ducks, beaver, muskrat, moose, elk, whitetailed deer. The young golden bruin discovered there were other bears, too. Before morning she found herself splashing wildly across Cut Bank Creek, pursued by a slobbering, cantankerous beast who outweighed her by four hundred pounds and carried a chip on his shoulder.

A breath of wind came with daylight, causing the aspens to chatter like high-toned women at a church social. Sun-up found Chocolate Legs scooping out a day-bed on a promontory of land covered with a scattering of lodgepole pines and with a view downstream and up.

The young bear knew all about the two groups of hikers who traveled the across-the-creek trail. And she knew about the Park Ranger on horseback—though she hardly knew the woman was a Park Ranger. But she missed the cantankerous grizzly with the chip on his shoulder as he passed down-valley, moving off-trail, screened from casual view by the deep forest, trailside brush, and windthrown trees.

It was midnight and a full moon shone like a spotlight on a drug bust when the young bear next made ready to move. She crossed the creek and padded onto the trail, still heading east, down-valley. She'd not gone far when the trail turned into an old road and the road turned into meadow and the meadow turned into a campground at its edge.

Memory served the young bear pleasant recollections of campgrounds, so she crossed the meadow in full moonlight, tiny beams shimmering by the thousands off each golden hair. But what's this? There were no tents or camper trailers in this campground—just some kind of huge hunk of metal sitting on wheels by the entrance. The fragrance of rotted meat came from the contrivance. So did the overpowering smell of bear. Chocolate Legs edged nearer out of curiosity.

Suddenly a mighty roar blasted from inside the culvert trap and the cantankerous animal who'd chased her downstream struck the jail-wire screen near her end with a full body-check from an enraged 600-pounder. The trailer-born culvert trap shifted three inches in the graveled road and was still rattling as the young blond bear fled the campground, the road, and the entire North Fork of Cut Bank Creek drainage.

When she stopped running, Chocolate Legs headed up another Park Service trail that snaked into the higher mountains between the North and South Forks of Cut Bank Creek. It was on the 22nd of June when the Cessna crew picked up her signal from a tiny basin along the north slope of Mad Wolf Mountain.

"It can't be 251, Frank. The lady said she'd be over at Nyack Lakes."

"I don't care what the lady said. This is the signal from 251."

"Why don't you try it again?" the pilot said, putting the Cessna into a tight turn.

Five minutes later, the technician said, "I don't care how many times you take this damned plane around, it'll still be the transmitter from 251."

"Where's the signal coming from?"

"Mad Wolf Mountain."

"Yeah, but where on Mad Wolf Mountain?"

The technician held out the chart and pointed to the spot he'd just X-ed.

"You're sure?"

In return, the technician's lips pinched and he reached out to switch off his radio.

"Okay, okay. Where to now?"

11

Taking the Plunge, Surviving the Risk

The warm, bright, diffused air of earliest morning presaged a blistering day. The bear prepared for it by scooping out a day-bed beneath the close-to-the-ground limbs of an ancient, but stunted, Engelmann spruce. The spruce was surrounded by a gaggle of aspen and lodgepole pine serving as courtiers to their king. The spruce—the only one of its kind for miles—spread atop a tiny knoll only a hundred feet from the shores of a ten-acre pothole lake. A dawn insect hatch over the pothole brought trout out in a frenzy, their splashes making bull's-eyes all over the tiny lake's surface.

Chocolate Legs crossed Glacier National Park's eastern boundary sometime during the previous night. She knew nothing of the boundary, of course, and wouldn't have cared if she did. She only knew she'd stumbled upon a rolling land chocked with meadow and marsh, laced with rivulet streams, rich in succulent roots and bulbs and shoots and rodents, and spotted with copses of aspen and pines for shelter and security.

The morning's first breeze brushed across the little lake, announced in advance by aspen leaves waving and clapping frantically to attract attention. The bull's-eyes disappeared with the breeze, as did the insects who'd brought about the bull's-eyes in the first place.

The breeze also brought something else—an odor Chocolate Legs had never before sensed. She dozed. She awoke to the raucous cries of passing Canada jays. She dozed. She awoke when a pair of nesting mallard ducks raised a ruckus over a coyote's stealthy advance. She dozed.

She awoke with something bawling just beyond the brow of a nearby hill. The scent she couldn't identify was overpowering now. Something else was there, too. She came to her feet in hesitation, then sank back into hiding as the first Hereford cow pushed around the hill to her lake.

That first Hereford was followed by a dozen more of her kind, cows and calves. Two dozen. They crowded to the pothole to drink, then began to graze the sedge grass the young bear fed on earlier. More cattle crowded around the knoll. They were followed by men on horseback. The riders were young and so were their horses, spirited and high-strung. The riders wore big hats and silk neckerchiefs and striped white shirts and batwing chaps. The feet of each were clad in pointed-toe boots that also packed spurs with three-inch rowels. Each man's Levi jeans were held up by belts with huge, six-inch oval, silver mounted buckles. And each rider carried a Winchester rifle slipped into a saddle scabbard that was tucked muzzle down, butt forward, partially beneath his right stirrup fender.

One rider tried to urge his pony into the lake, only to have it spin and dance and crow-hop a little. The man's laughter floated across the lake to Chocolate Legs.

The bear lay in deep shadow, with spruce limbs sheltering her from view. Only her eyes moved. Cattle milled and lowed and grazed along the far shore, then halted and bunched. The men rode their horses together and one cocked his leg around the saddlehorn, fishing in his shirtpocket for the makings. The other whipped off his hat and smoothed back sweaty, raven-black hair. "Hot," he said.

The first man cupped a paper between thumb and finger and sprinkled tobacco into it. Then he stowed the Bull Durham sack in his pocket and carefully rolled the smoke, finishing it by licking along its leading edge and twisting the ends. A match flared and smoke drifted away as by magic. "This far enough, Snook?"

The other had watched his partner roll and light his cigarette. Now he grinned at the question and stared at the cattle. "Good enough for me, but they're your cows."

"The old man's, anyway. And it looks like they ain't int'rested in going further. It looks good enough for me, too."

Snook glanced down at his hat. It was a Resistol, black felt with a high crown and wide of brim. The brim had been stylized, with a roll on each side and the ends made to droop in order to shade the eyes and the back of the man's neck. Its owner put a little more curl in one brim, then gently set the hat back in place, slapping it one time for good measure. "Why them cows not grazing around the lake?" he asked, eyes passing over Chocolate Legs hiding place.

"Too wet, maybe. Maybe there's a bear."

Both men laughed at that, and the first uncurled his leg from around the horn and tucked the pointy-toe boot into the stirrup and they jammed spurs into their ponies' flanks and rode back the way they'd come, laughing.

After the men had gone, Chocolate Legs continued to study animals with whom she'd had no experience. For their part, the Hereford-Red Angus cows and calves remained bunched-up at the lake's far end. The sun was at its zenith and cooking the land. With rising temperatures, the steady sink of cool nighttime air had reversed itself and ground-level air now rising up across the foothills, created a steady breeze that took the bear's scent to the cattle.

The smell of bear was not at all alien to these animals. The older ones had grazed these same foothills for years and grizzly bears had grazed them for millenniums before that. The very nature of the landform—its marsh and meadow and tree-copse mix, the plentiful water, cool nights and warm sunny days—made for great pasturage for both bears and cattle.

Bison once roamed into the foothills here. And grizzly and black bears patrolled the mountain front for winter-killed carcasses, or for sick or maimed animals in dire need of carnivore attention. The advent of man's firearms had upset the age-old prey-and-predator balance, eventually eliminating the bison altogether and substituting his own vision of white-face hump ribs and rump roasts.

The switch was easy enough for grizzly bears to make. Herefords were easier to catch and fatter to chew. And silly man! He even penned their buffalo replacements so grizzlies could help themselves without need to chase miles after migrating creatures.

There was only one flaw. No one had cared how many bison the grizzly took. But everyone seemed to go into apoplexy if even one bison replacement served as ursid tablefare. The learning curve proved difficult—and costly—for grizzlies. They died. They were poisoned, trapped, brought to bay by dogs, shot on sight. Old habits die hard, but gradually the great beasts learned that cattle are to be left alone.

Men learned, too. Some learned that a mountain without a grizzly is a body without heart, a head without thought. Among the Blackfeet are those with great reverence for the grizzly, holding the animal as spiritual. Other tribespeople view the bear as a talisman proving their land still remains as the Great Spirit made it. Still others among the Blackfeet have little regard for grizzly bears or, indeed, for the land or its other non-human—or even human—occupants.

The two young cowboys who moved their cattle on summer pasture held grizzly bears in awe. There would be no thought of spying one from a distance, then stalking and shooting it. But they feared the great beasts, and feared for the lives of their Hereford-angus charges. They also carried rifles in saddles scabbards. And an armed and frightened human is hands-down the most dangerous creature on earth. So it was in her ignorance that some sixth sense whispered to the young golden bear to hold tight to her place of concealment. And it was a different sense that told the cattle a grizzly bear was nearby.

Grizzly bears had, however, been nearby to each mature cow during previous years. Grizzlies had crested hills, swam in lakes, fed in marshes, even walked through meadows where cows grazed. Somehow, almost ethereally, the animals had come to a mutual understanding delineating their space. The cattle watched the bears, feared the bears, avoided the bears where possible. The bears pretended not to see the cattle. It was a workable arrangement.

Of this arrangement, Chocolate Legs knew nothing. Neither did she fear the bovine creatures. However, there was nothing in her experience that dated back to her ancestors' dependence upon bovine burgers to tide them through the winter. So she remained in her daybed and studied the cattle and the cattle remained bunched on the pond's far end and studied the place they'd identified as the source of bear scent. Until both grew hungry.

And thus the cattle began drifting back the way they'd come, foraging as they went. And Chocolate Legs stood, stretched, ambled from her lair and began feeding on the nearby sedge her mere presence had ensured would be left untouched by the Herefords.

And it was on June 28 when the Cessna found her within a mere half-mile of U.S. Highway 89, far out onto the Blackfeet reservation. Open, windswept Cut Bank Ridge lay at her rear, the pothole region to her south and west.

"She keeps moving this direction," Frank muttered, "she'll be out on the prairie before breakfast."

The pilot grinned, but kept silent. His job was to fly airplanes, not to second-guess the grizzly bear second-guessers.

As luck had it, the radio monitors caught Chocolate Legs at her farthest advance into what for her was uncharted territory. Though the land was intriguing, much of the best vegetation was being eaten or trampled by hordes of the white-faced, cloven-hoofed creatures and their stench was not at all like the pure mountain country she'd left behind and remembered so well. Besides, other grizzly bears—quite a few grizzly bears—also roamed this country. And among them rode men on horseback, or men on ORVs, or men in 4-wheel-drive pickups.

Thus when the Cessna buzzed overhead a mere five days later, the young blond bear with distinctively dark-colored legs was well inside the Park, moving west through a remote region without trails.

"Well, I don't know about you, Frank," the pilot said, grinning at his companion, "but I feel better knowing she's back in Glacier."

The technician nodded. studying his chart. "Looks like she's moving up Lake Creek. Let's see, that'll probably take her to Running Crane Basin, or maybe to Lonely Lakes. From there, who knows? She's on a route for home, way it looks. But it's hard to figure a bear that moves as much as she's doing."

Ray nodded. "All's I know is your boss-lady is going to have a lot to answer for about this one."

It was raining on the day America celebrated its independence. Chocolate Legs crossed a spur ridge and followed the land's contour around just another mountain peak. The rain was unfortunate because wildflowers were just beginning to take hold in the high basins nearby. In the following two months flower arrays to boggle man's imagination would seemingly flow up and over the high country. Not that bears particularly care. That's man's province.

But man is not the only species to cherish wildflowers—cutworm moths also have an affinity for God's gaudy blossoms and fly hundreds of miles to reach them. And while grizzly bears might not appreciate the visual attractiveness of wildflower arrangements, they do cherish the taste of cutworm moths. A chapter, "Surviving on Insects" in the book *Learning to Talk Bear*, details the importance of the cutworm moth/grizzly bear association. From page 65 of that book:

> *Much of today's fertile analysis of cutworm moth/grizzly bear connections comes from several mountain sites around Yellowstone National Park. To understand the essential nature of those connections, it is first necessary to understand something of the dynamics of cutworm cycles—just now becoming understood.*
>
> *Each fall, adult female moths lay their eggs throughout the Great Plains in the soil at lower elevations. Cutworm larvae emerge in early spring, feeding on leafy plants, including commercial crops such as wheat, barley, oats, sugarbeets, alfalfa, etc. Cutworm depredations are often so severe that pesticides are utilized to reduce crop damage. After feeding for several weeks, the larvae enter a beneath-the-soil pupal stage, emerging as adult moths in early summer. Shortly after surfacing, they migrate en masse, sometimes for hundreds of miles, to distant alpine habitats where they spend summer nights feeding and pollinating a variety of wildflowers.*
>
> *During their summer-long stay, cutworm moths convert flower nectar to body fat—from 30 percent of abdominal body fat when they first arrive in the mountains to 70 percent by fall migration. That high fat content produces high energy, compared to other available bear food.*
>
> *The moths are entirely nocturnal, feeding on wildflower nectar during the night and taking shelter from heat, rain or snow under various rock formations—usually talus from nearby cliffs, cols, or aretes—while metabolizing nectar. Research indicates that moths tend to aggregate in large clusters, distributed randomly throughout the talus, gravel, and boulder fields. Those moth concentrations serve as pot roasts to a host of predatory*

pillagers: black bears, coyotes, ravens, American pipits, mountain bluebirds, owls, bats. And, of course, systematic excavations of the cutworm army's bivouac by grizzlies.

There are several known cutworm moth sites in Glacier National Park. As fortune had it, the route chosen by Chocolate Legs up and over this particular mountain was up and over one of those migratory cornucopia destinations. As bad luck had it, though the golden bear made her journey at night when the moths might have been most active, it also proved to be a time when alpine wildflowers were just beginning to bloom and moths were just beginning to arrive. In addition, the driving rain served to inhibit arms-wide petal displays, foraging excursions by moths, and scent distribution of moth clusters—had there been moths there in the first place. Instead, the young bear followed the ridge south, then turned west, and by daylight took a bed among lodgepole pines, on a promontory near the east shore of Pitamakin Lake.

And three days later, when the Cessna lazily circled overhead, Chocolate Legs was a mile to the west of the Continental Divide, lying just off the Pitamakin Pass Trail....

12

Jousting with Eagles

Down in the Nyack Creek bottoms, Chocolate Legs soon dis-covered 1985 was not going to be a good year for huckleberries. Heavy frosts hit the crop soon after berries were beginning to form, wiping out nine-tenths of the year's production. By ranging fast and far, the young bear discovered the frosts, while general in scope, still skipped occasional pockets where berries clung, ripening slowly. The problem was, other bears searched for those places, too, and Chocolate Legs lacked seniority or size or temperament to wrest what few patches she found for herself.

So she roamed even farther and faster, living on always abundant sedge and less than tasty swamp grass and less than enough gophers and voles and ground squirrels. She dug lomatium roots from dry-site hillsides and glacier lily bulbs in north slope basins. She excavated for mountaintop marmots. She chewed her way through bales of cow parsnip stalks. She even went fishing with little success in a feeder stream to Nyack Creek and chased elk calves on the mountainsides above Nyack Lakes.

The Cessna picked her up atop the Continental Divide, west of Upper Two Medicine Lake on July 15, then two weeks later, on July 29, found her on a favored shoulder of Mount Phillips, near her favorite avalanche path.

While more experienced bears were moving toward energy-enriching cutworm sites in the Two Medicine and Cut Bank lands she was only beginning to learn, Chocolate Legs headed into territory she knew from earlier days: the Dunwoody Basin and Wolftail Mountain lands that had produced life-saving berries two years before.

"Poor girl," the biologist said, snapping off her earphones and leaning back in the bucket seat, "she's having to struggle to find enough to put on weight."

"You think that's why she's moving like a yo-yo?" the pilot asked.

"I don't know, Ray. I haven't got the foggiest idea what took her out on the Reservation in early summer, but I do know there's not much of a huckleberry crop where she is now."

"She's about back to where her radio tracking began, right?"

"Right. That has to mean she's searching hard and hasn't yet found what she's looking for."

"Can she be looking for something besides food."

"At her age? Not a chance. Food is the only thought on her mind. Food to put on fat. Food to lay away for winter. We're just lucky she didn't get into livestock out on the Reservation." Then while the Cessna headed south for Marias Pass, the biologist added, "She's lucky, too."

The pilot glanced at the chart spread across his passenger's knees. It was marked 8/5/85. The "X" was placed in a basin just east of Peril Peak. He turned back to his controls. "Are you worried about her?"

"Oh, not really. This is her third season. She's been pushing the envelope, but she has to be getting a feel for her territory now. Nyack Creek, Coal Creek, Two Medicine. It's good productive country. Two Medicine worries me a little, but outside of a couple reports of contact with people at Surprise Pass and in Marthas Basin, there's been nothing on problems between her and people." The woman settled the earphones into place and switched on her receiver. "I think she's got a good chance."

"If she stays in the Park?"

"If she stays in the Park."

The airplane had just passed over, then buzzed into the distance when Chocolate Legs came to her feet and wandered on to the Pitamakin Trail and on down to Nyack Creek. She made her way to the Upper Patrol Cabin and spent much of the early afternoon trying to figure out how the dark grizzly had torn into another cabin in another year. At last she abandoned her study program and wandered back the way she'd came. It was a good thing she did because a Park Service trail crew arrived soon after she left. The trail crew planned to spend that night and the next

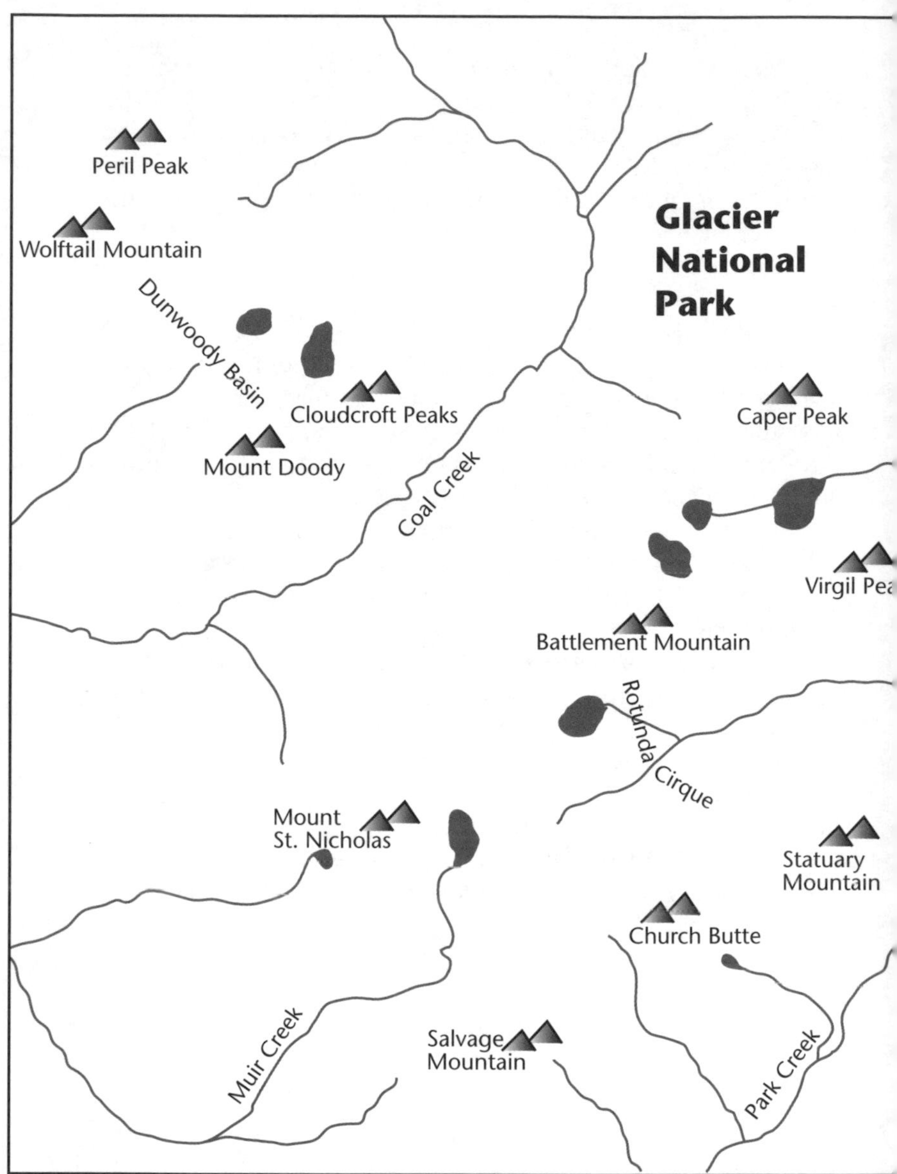

Probably the wildest, most isolated region in all Glacier National Park. Two or three trails up creek drainages—the only way to reach the interior is crosscoun-try. Bushwhack. And if you'll stop and cogitate for a moment, you'll readily see that's not easy. What is easy is to believe that anyone—animal or otherwise—who get inside this country is tough!

**This map and others within these pages were produced in part through a DeLorme (Yarmouth, M system that, in turn, used U.S.G.S. quads as their base. Detail–1:50,000*

two at the cabin while working the Pitamakin Trail and both directions on the Nyack Trail. Then they would move on for Surprise Pass and complete their Nyack/Coal Creek circuit.

Chocolate Legs heard the trail crew arrive at the cabin, heard them chattering like magpies, heard them splitting wood—for she was but a short distance away, much engrossed in quicksilver flashes darting about in the pool below the first falls on Pacific Creek.

The bear squatted behind a boulder to study the water. After a few minutes the quicksilver flashes and the shadows caused by those flashes drifted back into the pool and to the falls. One of the flashes leaped into the tumbling water. Chocolate Legs could not resist—she leaped into the middle of the pool. It was as though she'd thrown a handful of spruce needles into a whirlwind, so swiftly did the quicksilver disappear.

But an innate sense told her to remain motionless and few animals have the patience to remain as motionless as a bear when it wishes to do so. Soon the trout began drifting back, tickling the hair on her legs. One made another lunge at the falls and Chocolate Legs made a lunge for the trout. It was her first and only success.

"I didn't think she knew I was there," said the trail crew member on summer hiatus from the University of Illinois while recounting the tale at dark. "I spotted her from the trail and stayed up on the bank to watch her playing in the water for, oh, a good half-hour. Eventually she walked out of the pool and climbed up my bank and I froze. Then she stopped and turned her head and looked right at me. I nearly died!"

"What then?" the trail foreman said.

"Then she just swung her head back and walked on up trail like she didn't care that I watched at all."

"What did she look like?"

"If I'da been her, I wouldn't want anybody watching, no better at fishing than she was."

The rest of the crew laughed.

After putting the member of the trail crew in his place for the rudeness he'd displayed in studying her while fishing, Chocolate Legs topped off her tank on sedge at Nyack Lakes, then climbed to the Continental Divide in a fruitless search for berries—the buffalo berry and mountain ash plants still had far to go before fruiting. Back in the Nyack Bottoms, the bear did come upon a few twin berries—both red and black. River hawthorne were also ripening. And on the south- and west-facing lower slopes, service berries were coming into season. At last, the young bruin returned to her old Mount Phillips stomping ground.

The golden bruin with dark legs couldn't have expected her avalanche path to produce mountain goat pot roast as it had the season before. But one of the ledges above did.

As it happened, two golden eagles had teamed up the morning before to knock a yearling mountain goat from a ledge. The young goat had broken a leg in the fall and it had taken the eagles most of the rest of the day to harass the kid from beneath overhangs and from taking shelters in rock crevasses until they could repeatedly dive upon him, and strike him, and finally stun him. Death was inevitable.

The eagles had taken their fill and finally sailed away in darkness to perch on the cliff above their bounty. Meanwhile cold night air had begun to settle down the same mountain where a blond grizzly bear with unusually dark legs searched an avalanche path to no avail.

It was just before dawn when the bear paused while padding along a game trail to lift snout to the breeze. Slowly she began climbing, eventually clambering onto a system of ledges and terraces, following her nose. At last the bruin paused and reared upon hind legs, nose searching the ledge above, front paws hanging limp just as, in miniature, a ground squirrel might appear to do upon emerging from his hole.

Chocolate Legs tried to climb the cliff face, but could not. So she padded along the ledge she was on until she could go no farther without slipping into the chasm below. Retracing her steps, the young bear picked her way along the ledge in the opposite direction. At last she discovered a break in the cliff angling up to the terrace sought. In a moment she'd climbed onto the ledge where the carcass lay.

There was no way her approach could be construed a stalk. After all, no scent of another bear flowed on the breeze—only the goat, along with another scent she couldn't identify—so there was nothing to fear. She was only a few feet from the dead goat when

Chocolate Legs was struck a mighty blow on the head! The young bear staggered and whirled but saw nothing. She turned back to her banquet and was struck another blow, this one glancing. This time she spotted her assailant as he sailed away. Then there was another blow from the rear.

She roared and swatted at the eagle who'd last struck her and thus saw the next assailant sweeping in from the sky. She reared attempting to grapple. The second eagle veered at the last instant and here came the first eagle out of the dimness. He, too, veered.

Chocolate Legs turned for the carcass, spinning away as one of the birds dived toward her. She tried to grasp a leg and pull the goat nearer the rock face but was struck a glancing blow for her trouble. Again she reared, this time remaining silent. The birds dived and dived and dived, just out of range. Each time the bear dropped her head to eat, an eagle dived upon her.

And so the standoff went, two golden eagles and one golden bear in silent and deadly battle as a pink sky turned to pastels and a blazing sun rose over the mountain ramparts to the east, turning the land below to shades of grays and reds and browns and greens.

Finally the birds circled together in an eagle caucus and Chocolate Legs managed to grasp a leg and drag the carcass until she backed directly against the rock wall with the goat remains raked within her two front paws.

Now with her rear protected and eyes on the watch for danger, the eagles could do no more than feint toward the feeding bear. They made a few more half-hearted dives, then took the day's rising thermals and sailed away.

Finally, in a tiny unnamed cirque south of Marthas Basin, Chocolate Legs found a patch of ripening huckleberries that was, as yet, undiscovered by other bears. The basin was the hanging kind—meaning it had been glacially sculpted from the side of a high peak while other, larger glaciers carved away at the valley below. Eventually, one of the larger glaciers so scraped the mountainside where the unnamed cirque lay that its exit was bulldozed into sheer cliff with a cascading waterfall and difficult access.

The cirque lies at 6,000 feet and opens to the northeast. When the killing frost struck most of the region's huckleberry crop at its most vulnerable period, snow still shrouded the unnamed cirque. There, huckleberries bloomed later and fruited later and were just beginning to ripen when Chocolate Legs clambered to it in early August. Her entry was just in time for the Cessna to circle overhead and the biologist to bemoan her lack of food sources.

She's an intelligent bear, Chocolate Legs, and after she'd picked a few earlier-ripening fruit, she filed the basin away in memory, climbed up and over Peril Peak to Dunwoody Basin, toured it, then returned to the more friendly confines of Mount Phillips.

She was again clambering around on the ledges where she'd discovered the latest goat remains when the Cessna returned on August 13.

"See what I mean, Ray," the biologist said, pointing to the bear they could clearly see out the side window, "her searches for food is growing more desperate."

But a week later, when the Cessna returned and again found her across Coal Creek Valley and wandering the unnamed cirque, the pilot said, "If she's so desperate, why would she return to the same place where she struck out before?"

The biologist flashed a toothy array impressive enough to make an orthodontist beam. "Perhaps we aren't as smart as we think—is that what you're trying to say."

They matched smile for smile. "So where do you think she'll den this year? I want my beer back."

"Oh no you don't. This time you have to pick first."

"Okay, I pick Mount Phillips. Now it's your turn. The closest to the site is the winner."

The biologist studied her map, musing, "Okay, the best choice for me would be to choose across the canyon on either Nyack or Coal Creek. Which one?"

"That's what I asked, which one?"

She put her finger on a spot just off the Pitamakin Trail. "I'll choose here, below McClintock Peak and Cut Bank Pass."

"Done," the pilot said, holding out his hand.

She took it and pumped to seal the bargain. "Only this time I want the Heineken. You get the quart."

He laughed.

Far below, the subject of their wager was not suffering as much as the biologist suspected. Two weeks of hot August weather had worked wonders on the unnamed cirque's huckleberry crop and the young bear busied herself gorging. Though it was not an exactly tiny cirque, there were limits to its crop producing capabilities and a week of intense tanking up by an underfed grizzly bear largely stripped the place of its fruit crop.

Fully fed and wonderfully rested, with youth and wanderlust jerking at her muscles from head to toe, Chocolate Legs, in just one night, left the unnamed cirque, crossed Surprise Pass into the Nyack Drainage, swept past Nyack Lakes without pausing, clambered through Dawson Pass and wound up at the head of Upper Two Medicine Lake by daylight.

"What in the hell is she doing there?" the pilot muttered.

"She's got to be somewhere," the technician said. "That looks like a pretty good place to be."

"Not if she dens there. You don't suppose your boss-lady's put a bug in her ear?"

"Say what? Why does it make any difference to you where she dens?

"Beer, my good man. Beer. I bet she'll den on Mount Phillips, the lady picked the Divide near Cut Bank Pass."

"Ahh, now I see." The technician laid the points of a pair of calipers on his chart and said, "You'll still win if she doesn't move further north."

"I've heard of people hazing grizzly bears in Alaska with an airplane," the pilot said. "I wonder if we could do that with her."

"You're joking."

"Of course I'm joking. Not only that, I'm not suicidal. Where to from here?"

13

Matriculating with Honors

The prairie wind can pick up a snowflake falling on the McKenzie Delta and lift it to Montana without hitting enough barbed wire to wear its edges. It can blow 90 miles an hour at Duck Lake, 110 miles an hour at Browning, and pick up speed when it hits the mountain front to turn frantic trying to pick a way through its passes. But when it blows boxcars from Burlington Northern tracks near Browning, it hits from the southwest.

Bears are not supposed to be afraid of anything on earth—except bigger, meaner bears. But Chocolate Legs was a little afraid of the wind that took her over the Continental Divide at a gallop on the first day of September, 1985. She crested the Divide and immediately plunged at breakneck speed for the shelter of upper Nyack Creek.

But a funny thing often happens with prairie winds pounding upon mountain walls from the east. As soon as those savage wind gods break through the ramparts into the western side of the Rocky Mountain Front, they often pause in bewilderment and gentle down like barbarians at Sunday School.

A hundred vertical feet below the top, Chocolate Legs likewise paused with the wind—or lack thereof—and began sniffing around for something for supper. Another 500 vertical feet down, she discovered her first ripened buffalo berries, and mountain ash soon after. A thousand feet further descent and her harvest turned phenomenal—the same growing conditions that had decimated the huckleberry crop produced rich harvests in the hardier buffalo berries and mountain ash berries. She settled in for a stay.

That's why, a week to the day after she'd been recorded at Upper Two Medicine, the Cessna crew caught her just above Nyack Creek, two miles upstream from Nyack Lakes.

"Hot dog," Ray beamed, "she's signaling that I'm sure to win a quart of the brewery's best."

"Don't you think you may be premature?" Frank asked. "It's still a couple of months until denning time."

"Sure I'm premature. But a loser like me has to gloat whenever he has the chance. You want in on this bet?"

The technician laughed. "No way. A third year college student doesn't make enough money to throw it away betting on something as uncertain as *this* bear."

Now it was the pilot's turn to laugh. He reached over and patted the radio receiver. "Just stay south, little girl. And you'll make ol' Ray happy come Thanksgiving."

Chocolate Legs had been putting on weight now for almost a month. Though filling out with fat, the young bear was not yet large by most *Ursus arctos horribilis* standards—a mere 185 pounds. She looked larger, of course, all bears do except when wet. With the luxuriant coat of youth, exceptionally long guard hair provided by genetics, and a natural color that exacerbated the appearance of size, most newcomers to grizzly structure would guess another hundred pounds.

With sufficient berries in seemingly inexhaustible supply, supplemented with still succulent sedge grass at Nyack Lakes, and the occasional small mammal out of luck and in her path, the young bear felt both comfortable and satisfied. So much so that she again wandered over the Continental Divide during a clear night and a rising moon.

"Hell she was right there two weeks ago," Ray blurted. "Why's she back there again?"

In reply, the biologist asked, "Can you take the plane down a little, Ray. Maybe we can spot her—she's out in the open at the upper end of the lake. I'd like to see what she's doing."

They'd not spiraled far before the biologist murmured, "I see her. She's just off the dead far end. Not far from where two fishermen are standing. I wonder if they see her?"

Almost as if in response, the fishermen both began running along the shore of the lake. Ray said, "Look, she's going down to the water. Do you think she's following them? Or is she just going for a drink?"

"I doubt it's either one. I think she's eating their fish. Can you get closer?"

The pilot shook his head. "I can get real close if you want. But we won't fly out. Your bosses will never forgive me if I don't bring you home to your daddy."

It was while the plane clawed for altitude at the outlet end of Upper Two Medicine when the biologist mused, "I wonder if this will be reported as a grizzly encounter? I didn't see her threaten those anglers, did you?"

"Nope." The pilot relaxed enough to lean back in his seat. "It would have been interesting, though, to see what might've happened had they stopped long enough to pick up their fish."

The season's first high country snowfall blew in the next day. Four inches of wet fluff blanketed the Divide when Chocolate Legs clambered over the top during the following night. Dropping below the snowline, the young bear immediately was into more buffalo and mountain ash berries.

Again she gorged.

After a few days, her feet turned itchy. This time the young bear climbed Mount Phillips, returning to the ledges where she'd confronted the pair of golden eagles. If the birds remembered, they held no grudge, contenting themselves with circling high overhead and occasionally loosing a piercing scream.

The snow had pretty much melted by the time Chocolate Legs arrived on the ledges, especially on the exposed southwest slope she traversed. But if she expected a second succulent beast-the-color-of-winter, she was disappointed.

In addition, all remaining hoary marmots and rockchucks had fled the season's first snow to their underground bunkers, as did the Columbian ground squirrels. Wedges of ducks and geese flew overhead. Mountain bluebirds fluttered through on their way south along the Continental Crest. Elk had drawn together for the rut and mule deer bucks were eyeing each other for bragging rights when the right swaggle-hipped doe chanced by.

The Cessna circled overhead while Chocolate Legs stood on a ledge weighing her options. "Might as well pay me my quart now," the pilot said to his passenger.

She chuckled. "Counting your eggs already, Ray? Don't you know this bear has a way of converting saucy airplane pilots to broken wannabe hecklers of advanced science."

He laughed. "Wiggle and squirm all you want, ma'am. I'll be drinking your beer while you try to explain the quart on your expense account."

After the Cessna disappeared into the sunset, Chocolate Legs chose to descend into the Coal Creek bottoms. She'd not been this far downstream on this creek since emerging from her first lonely den in Dunwoody Basin two seasons before. Down, down she shuffled, digging roots and feeding on a few clinging berries. Down, down until she came to the cabin the dark grizzly had broken into and she eyed the corner where she and he had entered the cabin; where workmen had repaired the roof and strengthened it with heavy planks and metal strips.

And at last, the blond bruin with distinctively colored legs turned to retrace her steps back up Coal Creek, disappointed that she'd found little on her foray but bland dried grass and overripe cattail pods and roots and stalks.

Twice she blundered into elk boudoirs and interrupted the mating process to the distress of bulls overtaken by the fury of the rut. Once a bull even charged her, head lowered, antlers outthrust in anger and madness and she, one of the earth's most fearless creatures, ran in jackrabbit terror from a process she neither understood nor, at an early age, condoned.

And finally, on September 26th, she paused at a deepwater pool below a logjam on Coal Creek and peered into the water to see more quicksilver flashes and shadows the size of her mother's forearm drifting lazily along a graveled bottom no more than two feet offshore.

She leaped. The shadows shot away. And after she stood immobile for fifteen minutes, the shadows slipped slowly back, edging toward plate-sized redds full of eggs and roe. A quick dip of her head and the young bear splashed to shore with a 23-inch bull trout flopping in her jaws.

Fifteen minutes later, night had fallen and Chocolate Legs again stood among the redds, awaiting the shadows' return. Fifteen hours later the Cessna putzed overhead and the pilot chortled. "Give up?" he said. "She's moving my way, not yours."

"Almost," the lady biologist said. "But not quite. She's still five or six weeks from denning."

The pilot laughed. "Maybe so. But it looks to me like the only thing you've got to hope for is that the collar drops off. Then I suppose you'll call it a default and beat me out of my just desserts."

"Remember, Ray, all is fair in ..."

"... love, war, and where grizzly bears den," he finished.

Down below, Chocolate Legs was tiring of fishing. She'd stood motionless for over an hour in the pool and no big shadow had glided to the 10-inch round depressions where females had deposited their eggs and males had fertilized them by pausing above and squirting them with sperm. She had managed to catch a total of three of the big char and feasted long and well.

A wolverine had loped by while the blond bear stood in the pool and an otter glided downstream from above. But neither animal had caused the bruin to move so much as a muscle, though she was as aware of the two creatures from the family *Mustelidae* as they of her. The otter spotted her just as he was about to wash over the logjam and did some tall scrambling—and enough splashing to set fishing back for another hour—before escaping back upstream. The umber-colored wolverine merely paused in his ground-eating lope to regard the bear through beady black eyes for nearly ten minutes. Then she continued on her bouncing way, still as puzzled as when she first paused.

Upon the retirement of the largest member of the weasel family, Chocolate Legs moved; she raised a paw and dragged her claws through the redd. She cocked her head at sight of a baker's dozen bead-size, orange fish eggs popping to the surface. Playfully she poked a claw at one, then bobbed for another like a giant bobbing for crabapples. The taste was great, though hardly satisfying, and she looked for another. But the eggs, released of their sand and gravel retainers had whisked swiftly past the bear with the downstream current.

Chocolate Legs turned to another redd and this time was ready when the eggs popped to the surface.

A day later and fully two miles of bull trout redds plowed and scraped until there was no eggs left in them, the young bear ambled upstream. That night she passed through Surprise Pass, and the following day climbed the Pitamakin Trail feasting on mountain ash berries along the way.

On the fourth day of October, the biologist murmured to her

pilot, "Hey, Ray, I've got bad news for you."

"Don't tell me—you got Chocolate Legs?"

"I have Chocolate Legs."

"And you're gonna tell me she's north of Nyack Lakes.

Still fiddling with her dials, the biologist replied, "She's north of Nyack Lakes."

"Don't tell me she's quite a ways north."

"Umm-hmm.

"My den or yours?"

"You poor, poor man. "She's north of the Pitamakin Trail."

"Arrrgh!"

"Don't cry, Ray," she said. "It's unbecoming for a grown man. Anyway I was merely joking about her being north of the Pitamakin Trail. But she is due west of Cut Bank Pass, close to the Pitamakin Trail."

"Well, where exactly?"

"Cruise a little north by east and I'll narrow it down, but I think she's on that east ridge off Tinkham Mountain."

"Arrrgh, again! What's she doing there? She hasn't been there all year."

"Yes she has. My records show she probably passed through in mid-June."

"Aw, c'mon, ma'am," the pilot said, "you're not telling me she booked in for winter's bedtime then?"

"No, I'm telling you no such thing. All I'm telling you is that you owe me a Heineken. We can debate the reasons why later."

Ray swung the rudder to bring the Cessna's pass over Tinkham around on his side. "Surely you're not saying she's denning now. Hell, there's only a skiff of snow there."

The woman laughed. "Not to worry, sir. I doubt she's denning now. But you do know, do you not, that bears usually move to their denning vicinity sometime around mid-October."

"Ha—gotcha! It's only October 4."

The Cessna swung around under power and now the biologist stared below at the northeast quadrant of Tinkham Mountain. "Wow, that is one rugged piece of real estate."

"Do you see her?"

"No, not even tracks—not that they'd show in only a skiff of snow from this altitude. But she's there. At almost eight thousand feet. Perhaps under a ledge." Then she smiled sweetly at her pilot and added, "Or in her den."

His was a fleeting grin. "Want me to take it down? We can maybe get down another couple hundred feet."

"No," she said, slipping on her earphones, "we'd better get on with it. That afternoon conference at East Glacier isn't going away, no matter how much I'd will it to do so."

14

Falling from Grace Basking in Favor

The bull was hurt badly and climbed the mountain to walk it off, much the same as a carpenter will shake his thumb and shout curses when he smashes it with a hammer, then traipse around the house while waiting for the shooting pains to subside. Only the bull's injury was far more serious than a mere smashed thumb. And it was unlikely that the shooting pains would fade. Two hours before, the bull had been gored by a smaller, younger elk in battle over the lesser animal's harem of five love-sick cows.

The sequence of events leading to the larger elk's mortal danger had occurred four months before, in early June, when his antlers had only begun to grow.

Antler growth for elk begins even before the old ones are shed. A bull's antlers are usually fully formed by late July or early August. The shedding of "velvet" (dried skin covering) begins soon after, usually first undertaken by mature bulls with what is supposed to be a greater stake in the coming rut. As the rut approaches, bulls prod the ground and the forest is filled with loud rattling and crashing as the animal mock-fights with surrounding saplings and brush.

It was a process followed in previous years by the bull central to this story, but largely ignored during this particular season because of the accident....

Along with two others of his kind, both bulls born during the same spring six years before, our elk drifted slowly up the Nyack Valley, returning to summer range from the low country where he'd spent each of his previous winters.

Much of the most succulent new growth, particularly our bull's sought-after favorite—bluebunch wheatgrass—sprouted best on south-facing open slopes. And that was where all three elk grazed, moving slowly up-country through a landform composed of steep sidehill meadows laced with rock outcrops and occasional ledges.

There was nothing frightening about the steep mountainside to the elk; nor was it unfamiliar—they'd grazed through here in each of their previous migrations. Frost wedging in mountainous country of northern latitudes is a major tool of erosion, however. Moisture seeps into cracks in rocks, then freezes and expands to widen the cracks minusculely. And thus, the thawing and freezing process works over a season, a year, a decade, a millennium, to widen cracks until one day the ice pushes a slab of rock free and it tumbles down a mountainside with a mighty roar.

These elk had, of course, heard rocks tumble before. And given their years and their lifestyle, it's probable they'd witnessed snow avalanches and large-scale rockslides. But none had ever had a ledge collapse while he was on it.

It happened when our bull had grazed a rock outcrop only three feet above the ledge where several clumps of bunchgrass sprouted. The elk polished off grass around the outcrop, then simply hopped down to a ledge cleaved in two by decades of freezing and thawing. The cleavage occurred in a vertical crack extending downward, but running diagonally along much of the ledge's length. As a result of the latest freeze and thaw, the outside half of the ledge was poised to collapse outward with the slightest additional stress. The shock of eight hundred pounds of elk landing upon it provided that stress.

There was a tiny "click" and suddenly there was nothing below the bull's two right hooves for fifteen feet—except for a falling slab of rock. He scrambled, eyes wide with fright, then he disappeared, hind-end first, over the edge.

The great stone slab hit first with a tremendous roar. Debris and dust and dirt rose in a cloud, then the slab bounced, slammed into a sapling, then was catapulted down the mountain, bouncing and smashing aside brush and trees and other rocks in its path. The elk struck only milliseconds after the stone bounced away, while dust and dirt and debris was still exploding in a cloud about him.

Elk, particularly bull elk in the prime of life, are powerful creatures with a rugged vitality exceeding that of most hoofed animals. And a fifteen-foot fall, even one of total surprise and under duress, need not be fatal—especially if nothing is broken. In addition, the bull landed on a 65-degree slope, in an area that had just been pulverized by a five-ton boulder. As a result, nothing *was* broken.

Except for the new antler growth on his right side.

The bull lay amid the settling debris for a few moments, stunned by the blow to his head. Blood gushed from the broken antler stub down across the base of his ear and along the jaw line to trickle from his nose. He raised his head once, twice, then leaped to his feet and fled wildly across the mountain until he rejoined his companions.

And that should've been the end of the tale; indeed would've, except for the deformed antler.

The bull's broken-off antler tried desperately to resurrect itself, developing into a sort of a blob with ten-inch point that hung down like a deformed horn on a Jersey cow. The left-side antler, on the other hand, developed magnificently, with seven stiletto-like points off the main beam.

At six years of age, the bull was just coming into prime, a period that should last another two or three years before the animal began to physically decline. And with the quite natural winter's-end shedding of this year's antlers and next spring's regrowth, he would once again be the magnificent, fully proportioned and equipped animal he, having no mirror, presently perceived himself to be.

Bull elk tend to wander apart during summer, often opting for solitary existences. Our bull, being in what he thought was the peak of health and in his prime, wandered into a high basin east of Tinkham Mountain. It was a glorious autumn with one sunny day following another. Food was abundant, his basin without serious predators. Time slipped by. The first frost came and the grass yellowed. Leaves turned from green to red or gold and fell from the brush. Meanwhile our still-complacent monarch ate and slept and kept his own counsel.

Until one day, he woke up. There was this delayed pulsing in his loins and a gleam in his eye. He was surprised. He was shocked. Yes, he'd gone through the ritual of rubbing the velvet from his antlers on small trees and brush. Well, the left one anyway; the right one did not rub as well. But the rubbing process had still failed to kick off his rutting urge. Now the season was late and he was late, and that angered him.

The bull charged from his basin and hurried around Tinkham Mountain, bugling and trumpeting curses and challenges all the way, dropping steadily toward Nyack Creek, where he expected to find others of his kind. Along the way, he passed below a foraging grizzly bear, not knowing she was there. The young bear, recognizing nothing but trouble in noisy, hurrying elk, wisely kept to herself and the bull disappeared down-mountain. Until he found what he searched for—a younger bull without either heft or age or maturity to sport fully developed antlers of his own. What was even more engaging, the smaller bull had rounded up a harem of cows in estrous and either managed to hide them, or fend off challenges from other lesser bulls. But not from an enraged monarch of the size and strength and anger of our animal. The monarch charged into the little glen where the cows were grouped, bugling and grunting and throwing up dirt with his fore hoofs. The lesser bull rushed through his herd to confront the newcomer, scattering the cows.

Among bull elk, serious battle is rare. Usually size is sufficient: size of body, size of antlers. Occasionally two bulls of near-equal heft and glory might square off over mating rights with nearby cows, but in such cases, the two bulls will usually lock weapons for a few minutes of pushing and grunting that decides dominance. Then the weaker bull will cut and run for the exit.

On this day, the lesser bull was so wrought with cows in estrous that emotion overcame prudence. And thus he charged forth for the ritual test of strength.

Our bull believed in himself. He had no way of knowing he was going into battle only half-armed and half-shielded. With antlers swinging near the ground, they locked horns. Only they didn't lock horns. Our bull shoved. But instead of pushing the lesser animal around with impunity as should have occurred, the smaller bull was spun left into our bull's unprotected right side. The smaller bull's antler tips entered just behind our bull's rib cage. Two of them penetrated into his stomach.

The mortally wounded monarch climbed steadily up the side of Tinkham Mountain; up, up, into a skiff of snow, until he found a wooded little knoll overlooking the valley below. There he carefully folded his hooves beneath him and collapsed to wait until the terrible upset to his stomach healed.

There would be no healing. Twenty-four hours later the bull, in agonizing thirst, tried to push to his feet to seek water. He could not. Thirteen hours later he was dead.

Three hours after the bull gave his last sigh, a young golden bear with unusually dark legs padded around the shoulder of Tinkham Mountain amid softly falling snow. She paused to sniff the gentle up-mountain breeze and identified elk. But there was something different about the scent—elk but what else? Ten minutes later she discovered the answer to her dreams.

The snow tapered off, then on again and off again for ten days as the bear lay beside her windfall. For ten days, storms covered them and uncovered them, only to bury and uncover them again, like it was peeking at the mystery of an animal who falls from grace feeding on one still basking in favor.

"Oh my God—don't tell me you still have Chocolate Legs on Tinkham Mountain," the pilot moaned.

The biologist nodded in tight-lipped smugness, jotting 10/9/85 on her chart at a spot off the southwest quadrant from the summit. "At six thousand feet, Ray. That's about right for a den. I think you should give up."

"Is six thousand okay when it's on a southwest slope?"

"I'll admit that seems low for the aspect. But that's really broken real estate down there. She probably is preparing a den on the north or east slope of a ravine, or something."

"That looks like a little knob to me. She could still be getting ready for a midnight dash across Nyack Creek to Mount Phillips—it's just across the valley you know."

"Oh Heineken, oh Heineken—wherefore art thou my Heineken?"

And when ten days later, Chocolate Legs radio beeped from the same place, the biologist shouted, "That does it! She has to be denning. That's her den site for sure."

"Look at the tracks in the snow. They're all over that mountain." Then the pilot's brow wrinkled and he asked, "Can it be she's lost her collar? Last spring you said that might happen."

"Come on, Ray, you're twisting in the wind. Admit it."

"It's still early—that's all I'll admit. The nineteenth of October is early. Come on."

"You are purely twisting in the wind. Besides that, you're trying to avoid pay-off time until the next blizzard hits and it'll be too cold to drink beer."

The pilot flashed his impressive array of sparkling teeth. "I'll wait, thank you, until the other bears go to bed. Then we'll see."

Twenty-four days later, the biologist snatched off her earphones and pressed her nose to the sidewindow glass. "Ray," she said slowly, "our bear is at seventy-two hundred feet, due south of the summit."

"On the south slope?"

"On the south slope. Look at it, there's nothing but an unbroken white expanse out there."

"What does that mean?" Ray asked.

She said it almost as an afterthought, obviously fixed upon something else: "Well, besides the fact that you owe me a Heineken, it means she stayed in one place on Tinkham for an awfully long time, then climbed higher and made her den."

The pilot glanced at his passenger, knew she was in no mood for levity. "Okay, I'll concede on the Heineken, but I guess I'm not quite tracking what you're thinking."

The plane still circled Tinkham while the lady stared below. "Try this: we were right about six thousand feet being too low for Chocolate Legs to den on a southwest slope. But there was something keeping her there—on this mountain—something she was determined not to leave."

The pilot trimmed the Cessna enough to bring them into a closer circle.

"So the bear went up the mountain off and on to dig her den, always coming back to whatever was keeping her there. That something was food, of course. And it kept her in one place for a long, long time. That means it was an animal. A big animal. I should think a bigger animal than a deer or even a mountain goat or a bighorn sheep. Like an elk. Or a moose." She paused, then continued, "But what I don't quite understand is the carcass location." She held out her chart. "Look at this, Ray." Then she glanced out the sidewindow and said, "No, you watch your flying, I'll look at the chart." She was silent for a full minute, studying the map. Finally she muttered, "The carcass—and it must have been a carcass—was in a peculiar place for predation to have occurred. Too high, on a knoll, not really thick vegetation.

"She couldn't have killed a large animal there and probably neither did a mountain lion or another bear—it just doesn't fit. She wouldn't have drug the carcass there, either, though it was a dandy place for her to dine—secure with a good view of all approaches. With storms mostly in from the west and most other animals down in the bottom, it was unlikely any other predator would get the wind. The weather was generally too lousy for birds to fly way off up here, too, so she had it all to herself."

At last the biologist reached for the earphones, saying, "No, it was good, it was big, it was safe, and it was hers. Why wouldn't she dig her den higher up the mountain, at an elevation where the snow isn't likely to melt."

The pilot nodded, taking the Cessna back across the Continental Divide. "What I think I hear you saying, ma'am, is that you'd like to know what that 'something' was, right?"

She nodded. "Yes indeed, I'd like to know what that something was."

15

Off Radar at Last

Radio data from Chocolate Legs is scanty for 1986, providing only three locations until the collar's band weakened from age and dropped from her neck on June 2nd—just as the collars are programmed to do.

Reasons for designing radio transmitters attached by devices with a prescheduled life expectancy are both logical and simple when one turns the mind to it. Radio transmitters are, of course, expensive and the hope is to retrieve them when they no longer provide useful information. The two most prevalent reasons why transmitters cease to provide usable info is: a) battery failure, b) loss of collar. Simply said, if the batteries fail first, the chances of retrieving the radio is nil. If the collar fails first, the device's location can usually be pinpointed electronically and retrieved from the ground. Therefore collar straps are deliberately designed to deteriorate and fall apart after three years. Radio batteries are designed (biologists hope) to last a little longer.

Another reason the collars are designed to weaken after a period is that bears grow—particularly young bears. Their necksize swells and to keep from choking growing bears, the collars will, in time, simply drop off—as did Chocolate Legs' device on June 2, 1986, only a short distance east of the summit of Tinkham Mountain. The collar fell from her neck surprisingly close to where the young bear had spent the winter.

The two prior recorded locations for Chocolate Legs were May 7, low on Tinkham Mountain, almost to Nyack Creek and May 20, midway on Tinkham, only a half-mile southeast of her den site. Three locations, all well within a short half-circle. Without prior information on this bear, a casual researcher could conclude Chocolate Legs to be a bruin with little imagination;

one with scant inclination to travel. Which, in light of her previous known wanderlust, is patently untrue.

May 7th is the date for Chocolate Legs first recorded location after exiting from her den in '86. But there is no record of the date for actual den emergence. True, she went to bed fully fed and well rested and could easily afford the luxury of sleeping longer than normal. But why would a five-year-old healthy young female bear approaching maturity and without cubs want to sleep when an entire world awaited? I choose to believe she emerged in April, as do most other female bears.

So what would she have done between April emergence and her first recorded location on May 7? Wander down Nyack Creek, as others of her kind have done for centuries, just as she had almost certainly done in at least one previous year.

Other bears were down near the confluence of Nyack Creek with the Middle Fork of the Flathead River, of course; it is a place of earlier snowmelt and more timely green-up. But though she was never a large bear, she was rapidly coming of age and not nearly as timid as might have been the case at age two, or three, or even four. Besides, the golden bear with dark legs had learned a very important thing during some of her encounters with other bears, both blacks and grizzlies: each of them usually held some degree of specialized knowledge she might someday put to use.

Such was the case when she parted marsh grass on a swamp that was little more than a slough off the main river to discover it was already occupied by a young male grizzly with no discernible attitude problems. His lack of aggression was why she edged up to the marsh's far side and began grazing on swamp grass. And when the male drifted her way without the normal signs of dominance displays, she stayed put, warily eyeing the young silvertip as he fed. And when darkness fell, both bears were within thirty feet of the other, digging for skunk cabbage that was just beginning to peek from the muddy soil.

It was a week later, to the day, when their marsh grass and skunk cabbage was invaded by a larger, more irascible male grizzly and the two younger animals fled to the fringe of big spruce trees growing between the marsh and the river. That's why they were first to spot the orange-colored inflatable raft as it nosed to shore and saw its sole occupant tie his raft, then creep to the marsh edge and part willows to peer through. They also watched the man tiptoe back to his raft, take out some heavy bags and what could have been a bundle of sticks.

Chocolate Legs' young male companion slunk off into the brush, seeing no profit in staying longer at a marsh dominated by a larger male and now invaded by a human. But except for the one notable experience of the dart gun and helicopter, the blond female had no previous reason to fear humans. Thus she elected to stay hidden and watch.

The photographer set his tripod and a huge front lens, attached a camera and, as the big dark-colored boar fed near the middle of the marsh, began shooting frame after frame. An afternoon sun caught the scene perfectly, snaring a kaleidoscope of colors from water droplets as the big bear splashed about in the water.

Perhaps the man became too absorbed as his subject fed closer and closer to his screen of willows. Suddenly the bear turned his head and stared, ears pricked. Had the photographer remained still, the bear may have eventually dismissed whatever attracted his attention, but the man panicked, snatching up his tripod and bolting for his raft. The bear, ears still pricked in curiosity, galloped forward, water splashing a dozen feet either side. When the bruin burst through the willows, the photographer was just reaching his raft. He jerked the slip knot on his tie rope and leaped for the inflatable, eyes wide aft.

The outsized grizzly slid to a stop, then reared to stand on his hind feet for a better view. What he saw was the photographer still dragging himself into an orange raft that was itself shooting out into a river swelling with spring run-off. Then the man's odor hit the big male, and with that and the strange orange conveyance turning lazy circles as it bounced downstream, the bear wheeled and galloped away.

Chocolate Legs continued to sprawl on the spit of land between slough and river throughout the afternoon, pondering. At last satisfied that the domineering male was truly gone and that the marsh belonged to her for the taking, she pushed to her feet, stalked to the place where the photographer had placed his tripod, and sniffed the ground. Finally she gazed out across the river, then across the marsh. Again she sniffed the ground, moved to where the big grizzly had stood aloft in hesitation and curiosity and finally fear, and sniffed that spot. At last, Chocolate Legs shuffled to the river and sniffed where the man had been. Strange. The human and the bear together. Then they were both gone, apparently frightened of the other. Why?

A week later, the golden female with dark legs wandered through the forest across Nyack Creek from where Surprise Pass Trail came down to the bottom. She began to climb toward Tinkham Mountain and the knoll where, late the previous fall, she'd left bones from her elk bounty.

It was while climbing there that the crew in the circling Cessna recorded her first location during the spring of 1986.

"Want to choose a den site for this season?" the pilot asked.

She laughed gaily, deigning a reply.

So he tried again: "Will she breed this year?

"It's possible. Probably not. Most females wait until they're six before coming into estrous. She's only five. But it has happened and could again."

"Can we tell by her location?"

"Maybe. If she's hanging around males—or better said, if they're hanging around her, and continue to hang around her—I should think we'll have a chance."

With the bones still covered by snow and apparently nothing edible overlooked from her November fare, Chocolate Legs dropped back down to Nyack Lakes and her standby fields of sedge grass. But on May 20, she was recorded climbing steadily up the eastern slope of Tinkham Mountain.

And on June 2, her collar beeped from atop an open ridge only half a mile from where she'd been last recorded.

"Why can't we see her?" the pilot asked, putting the Cessna into a tight turn, staring down. "That ridge is plumb open. We should see her."

The biologist appeared glum when Ray glanced at her to see why she'd not responded. She snapped from her reverie upon his questioning stare, "The reason why, my friend, is because Number 251 has dropped her collar. We have our last location for Chocolate Legs and, with luck, we'll never get another one."

"Huh? What do you mean, 'with luck'?"

She smiled halfheartedly at the man. "`With luck' means that if we never see or hear of her again, she's completely assim-

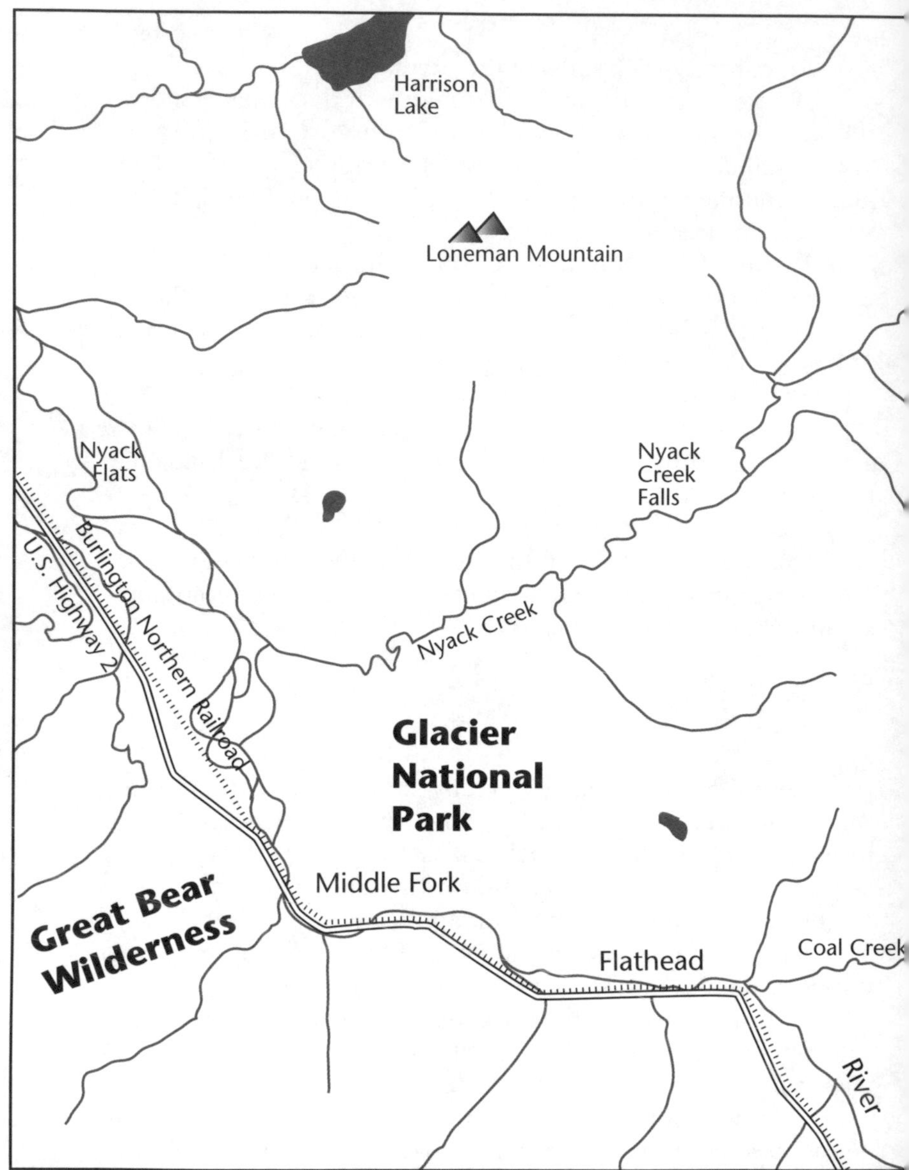

The country north and east of the Flathead's Middle Fork looks beguilingl empty and simple to reach. The truth is that the territory is fascinating, bu tough to access. The bottoms are largely overgrown with mixed forests of pines firs, larch, and spruce. The mountains are there, as elsewhere in Glacier. All on must do is climb. And climb. And climb.

**This map and others within these pages were produced in part through a DeLorme (Yarmouth, ME system that, in turn, used U.S.G.S. quads as their base. Detail–1:50,000*

ilated into the bear world. 'With luck' means her relocation was a resounding success and is a model for future transplants. `With luck' means we're learning something about bears and how to handle them."

Then the lady turned again to stare out the window. "And it means I no longer have an annual beer guarantee, damn it."

The pilot laughed. "I'll buy you one when we get back to ground m'lady."

"No time, I'm afraid. I have a staff meeting."

Five weeks later, a trail crew member armed with a carefully marked map and a hand-held receiver located Chocolate Legs' collar on the shoulder of Tinkham Mountain and returned it to the Ranger Staff at West Glacier. With a new collar band and new batteries in place, the transmitter again entered service around the neck of another blond grizzly sow who worked the boundary between Glacier National Park and private land in the Flathead's North Fork. The sow had been apprehended breaking into unoccupied cabins.

Unfortunately the reconstituted collar was found lying in a deepwater pool on a large creek, near where a U.S. Forest Service road brushes against the stream. The device had its radio transmitter smashed and the collar cut. Of the second blond sow, nothing more was ever heard.

16

Approach to Adulthood

This book now must enter a period of pure speculation. Previ-ously the story tracked the bear Chocolate Legs based in part on data provided by research. Though much of the tale told in the previous fifteen chapters was supposition, it was supposition grounded through periodic recorded locations, as well as knowledge gleaned from the actions of other grizzlies working the same territories. But with loss of her collar, Chocolate Legs disappeared from our radar for ten years before once again surfacing via carrying her second "problem bear" radio collar.

What occurred in the charismatic bear's life during those ten years is conjecture, of course, and my adaptation for story purposes may be merely one of a thousand differing possible scenarios. Certainly the storyline I've utilized could be argued. But I believe that it's *plausible*. And it also continues to be based as much as possible on her known actions both prior to—and after—that ten year lapse.

In addition, the tale is based on probabilities. For instance, only a year after Chocolate Legs dropped her collar, experienced outdoorsman and budding wildlife photographer Charles Gibbs was killed by a blond sow grizzly protecting her cubs. The tragedy occurred on Elk Mountain, only a few miles south of the core area of Chocolate Leg's home range. (See *Learning to Talk Bear*, page 104)

Gibbs was alone when he was killed, but a Canon camera with a 400mm lens was found nearby. Film had been exposed through the seventeenth frame. It provided evidence that the grizzly mother was blond, that she knew Gibbs neared, and that she grew more and more restive and angered by the man's approach.

In light of subsequent events, some individuals have speculated Chocolate Legs might have been that bear. Certainly the location was well within an area she could have had occasion to range. But consultation with biologists knowledgeable on bear behavior, as well as careful evaluation of published photos actually taken by Gibbs of the bear who killed him led me to conclude it unlikely for Chocolate Legs to have been the bear in question.

For one thing, this blond grizzly mother appeared older than a young *Ursus arctos horribilis* of six years of age. In addition, the cubs were yearlings, meaning they were born the year previous, which meant Chocolate Legs would've had to mate the year before that, at four years of age—very unlikely. And lastly, the bear who killed Gibbs had three blond cubs trailing her—improbable for a first-time mother.

Yes, it could have happened. But I don't believe it; say only a five percent chance—not good enough for inclusion in a book whose author is striving for as much accuracy as available information will permit.

The grain spills are something else.

Fermenting corn resulting from multiple railway derailments created a tremendous attraction for bears of all stripes and from a broad area. The corn spills were originally disposed of by simply bulldozing dirt over them—which posed no real problem for industrious bears driven by a taste for the fermenting grain. Since the spills occurred over several years' span; and since they were allowed to exist for several more years; and since collared bears from home ranges far beyond that of Chocolate Legs' core area were observed digging and feeding there, why wouldn't the golden bear with distinctively dark legs have been one of them?

My analysis? There's a sixty percent probability Chocolate Legs visited the grain spills. Hence her visits to the spills are included in a storyline that may well be less accurate were it not incorporated.

Strict, detailed fidelity in following the life a single free-ranging grizzly bear may never be an attainable goal. Certainly some means for tracking the ursid twenty-four hours per day from birth to death would have to be developed. Today there's talk of tiny radio implantation in the animal's body, then receiving signals via satellite. But such arms-length monitoring wouldn't always disclose whether the animal rolled rocks for insects or ate berries to satisfy a sweet tooth.

Satellite tracking of a single animal—even if the data were stored in its entirety and minutely analyzed for behavioral traits in a future doctoral thesis—would hardly provide info on the target animal's interaction with others of its kind, with animals of other species, or with the human animal. Only close field observation, in conjunction with radio tracking, might provide that info—and wouldn't close-quarter field observation be obtrusive in and of itself?

It might also be inherently dangerous, perhaps so dangerous as to be prohibitive.

So trust me. As far as is possible to accomplish with today's available information, I've tried to adhere to the plausible. The storyline is as true as I can make it based on known research, personal observation, and the sound biological judgment of professionals in whom I have faith.

But trust me also not to let limitations of the unknown get in the way of my perception of a rousing good story.

Please continue....

After she'd dropped her collar, Chocolate Legs moved along the crest of the Continental Divide. She stood on the west shoulder of Razoredge Mountain on the 15th of June as the Cessna buzzed lazily overhead. Neither of its two occupants knew the young bear was there, though she stood exposed on a flat, barren ridge thrusting out like the flight deck of the U.S.S. Enterprise—with Razoredge serving as the control tower behind.

She heard, she glanced up, she returned to sniffing for early ground squirrels and marmots. Later the bear drifted down avalanche chutes leading to Nyack Creek. And two days later, Chocolate Legs grazed on always-available sedge grass at Nyack Lakes.

The following week, the young bear, now nearing adulthood, drifted through Surprise Pass and into Marthas Basin. She had a few unpleasant hours when the overbearing dark male who called the basin home followed her scent from Beaver Woman Lake to Buffalo Woman Lake, and back again. But strangely, the ugly tempered demon seemed more curious about the newcomer than disposed to challenge her approach to his domain. Still, she preferred solitude to solicitation and left Marthas Basin to the demon's devices, trotting hurriedly to the Coal Creek Trail junction, thence down it.

Naturally Chocolate Legs tested the cornucopic avalanche chutes on Mount Phillips before ambling on her solitary way. It was too much to ask that the melting residues from the previous winter's avalanches would produce another ripening mountain goat or mule deer or elk. But she still checked before clambering over Mount Phillips and descending past Lupfer Glacier to Nyack Lakes.

It was at Nyack Lakes that she again encountered the cow moose and her now nearly grown calf feeding from the upper lake's bottom. Wiser now, the young bear ignored the moose and browsed her lonely way through a swath of sedge, pausing only occasionally to eye the distant moose, who likewise paused periodically to eye her.

Chocolate Legs drifted through Dawson Pass in early July, and into Bighorn Basin. From there it was but a short jaunt around Pumpelly Pillar to Upper Two Medicine Lake and the hillside above that had served such extravagant banquets of glacier lily bulbs during previous years. But she learned she was too late on the exposed south slope, so she moved to the far side of the lake and the sheltered slope above. There, glacier lilies were in their prime. But other bears congregated, also. Still the young bruin found a niche at the head-end of the lake, usually keeping human hikers and fishermen who didn't know she was there between grizzly bears who did.

Chocolate Legs fished at the tiny falls on Pacific Creek in mid July, but discovered she was too late to intercept spawning trout. So she drifted over Surprise Pass and down Coal Creek to the log jam where she'd fished for bull trout with such success during the previous autumn. But the blond bruin found she was too early to fish for the big chars, no matter how diligently she searched down the stream for tell-tale redds.

The young bear did find her first ripening huckleberries in an old fire-scarred area downstream from the Coal Creek Patrol Cabin. So Chocolate Legs loitered as berries ripened and she began to take on real weight from what appeared to be an abundance of hucks.

Other bears drifted into and through her berry patch, circumstances to which the maturing young ursid grew accustomed. Later, she climbed to Dunwoody Basin and finally crossed Wolftail and Eaglehead Mountains into the Pinchot Creek headwaters where she'd first awakened after her exile from Many Glacier. It was too early in both Dunwoody Basin and Pinchot Creek for huckleberries, but Chocolate Legs did take note that green berries were plentiful throughout the land. And when she dropped into the Nyack drainage, great blue huckleberries hung so abundantly on the low bushes as to make a young *Ursus arctos horribilis* forget she'd ever been hungry.

A bear does not treat huckleberries in the same manner as humans, picking them for pails and pies and pancakes. Chocolate Legs—or any other bear—seldom goes for individual berries, plucking a berry here, a berry there, popping the succulent fruit one at a time into her mouth. Instead, she wanders leisurely through a patch, stripping bushes of leaves, stems, and berries, either going for them with a vacuum cleaner mouth, or using three-inch claws to rake entire bushes toward cavernous jaws.

Sometimes, when her tank is nearly full and the berries very rich, the young bruin might sprawl on her belly and graze nearby plants. Or lie on her back and pull the bushes to her.

And finally, when her cup nearly runneth over, Chocolate Legs might reach out to take an individual berry with her teeth or lips or tongue, then drift off to a sleep induced by the torpor of satiation and satisfaction.

While ursid methods for huckleberry harvesting might produce berries in volume, there are compromises. For one thing a bear's vacuum intake method of filling energy tanks include not just berries for fuel, but woody stems and fibrous leaves. The wood and fiber pass through the digestive tract with but little processing, sometimes carrying undigested berries with it. Purple scat piles left by the animals on trails, alongside streams, or near their daybeds can be enormous, sometimes causing even the most experienced bear researchers or management biologists to falter and peer over the shoulder in fear and trepidation.

Natural caution may have saved the blond bear's life the next time she climbed the Pitamakin Trail, heading for Cut Bank Pass and the Two Medicine country. It was the dead of night and she'd just clambered across a series of trail switchbacks, perhaps a half-mile from the Pass. She was walking steadily on-trail now, passing a copse of stunted alpine fir and whitebark pine, when an odor of blood drifted her way.

Chocolate Legs paused in mid-stride, freezing, lifting her nose to the gentle downhill breeze. Yet something was not right about the wispish wind. The odor had been there, now was gone. To her right, the copse ended about fifteen feet and her senses said nothing lay beyond. Still, the carrion smell came from somewhere. Where? Slowly her right front foot ratcheted down and she poised, every muscle taut.

The monster silvertip exploded from the trees! There was no sound except for the breaking of branches and the throwing of clods and gravel. The monster was almost upon her when Chocolate Legs spun away in panic, blowing caution to the wind, frantically rolling downhill like a runaway skateboarder pursued by a runamuck fire engine.

The race continued for a half-mile down the mountain. It was perilously close for 100 yards and uncomfortably close for 200. Thereafter, Chocolate Legs widened her lead as the energy and interest of her raging, wild-eyed, overstuffed pursuer began to flag. At last, the older bear paused and retraced his steps to the mule deer doe he'd surprised in her bed earlier in the evening.

As a result, it was a week to the day before the golden bear with the brown legs again screwed up enough courage to venture across the Continental Divide, this time far to the north, near Triple Divide, dropping into the basin of Medicine Grizzly Lake. Here, as with elsewhere throughout the land, huckleberries were plentiful.

So the young bear moved casually through the country, down Atlantic Creek, up the North Fork of Cut Bank Creek to Morning Star Lake, and finally up the Pitamakin Trail from the east, heading for Pitamakin Pass. She paused at Pitamakin Lake to cavort in the water amid bright sunlight.

A group of hikers spied her and lined up on the shore with cameras. So she swam across the lake, clambered out on the far side and drifted into the trees, wondering all the while why humans seemed so plentiful during this journey, but bears so scarce. At last, Chocolate Legs climbed through Pitamakin Pass, took the trail fork at the top to Cut Bank Pass, and checked out the copse of trees where she'd narrowly avoided being overtaken by an overwrought and dangerously protective *Ursus arctos horribilis*.

The young female approached the site as if she walked on egg shells, ready to wheel and flee in an instant. She needn't have worried, only the skull and a pelvis bone—neither containing even so much as red stains—were left of the deer. Her much feared aggressor was nowhere to be found.

With most of August gone, Chocolate Legs returned to Wolftail Mountain and the friendly haunts of Dunwoody Basin. Hucks were in abundance there by the time she arrived and so were three other bears, a placid chocolate-colored male grizzly and a female black with one young cub.

Oddly, though outweighed by the adult grizzlies, the ebony sow demonstrated enough aggression in shielding her cub from too-close advances by dominant bears that she more than held her own in choosing where to feast. The placid chocolate bear seemed to care not a whit, which was reason enough for the blond bruin to ignore the mother-daughter combination.

Thus August turned to a September broken only by two passing rain squalls and one end-of-the-month snowstorm that pretty much ended the Dunwoody huckleberries. Chocolate Legs was ready to leave anyway. By now she was a veteran, with a veteran's understanding of her home range and thus expected to find russet buffalo berries and mountain ash berries on the scattered-forest slope west of the Continental Divide. First, however, she should check the logjam on Coal Creek for the big flashes caused by the big bull trout.

The redds were there, she found, but the big fish were gone. So the fattening bear contented herself with vandalizing the redds along five miles of the stream. Then she headed for Mount Phillips, Nyack Creek, and the mountainside above Nyack Lakes.

Within a week, the golden bear with brown legs was excavating a den at the head of Pacific Creek, just off the north summit of Razoredge Mountain. By the time she'd finished, one storm after another had slammed hard against her mountainside from the Canadian North. She made one rapid-transit swing down Pacific Creek into the Nyack bottom, then clambered back to her den and tucked herself inside just as a blanket of white down swathed the countryside on November 12.

17

Courtship and Adventure

Emerging from dens amid blinding snowstorms is something seldom done by grizzly bears, but that was precisely the circumstance when Chocolate Legs exploded from her den on April 12, 1987. A great, white blanket spread across the sloping expanse of Razoredge Mountain. With a titanic "Whuff!" the blanket was fractured by a dirty blond wraith standing—actually weaving—above a surprisingly tiny exit hole.

Chocolate Legs stood in stupor for at least ten minutes gathering her wits and muscles, then laboriously trudged downslope toward Pacific Creek and the Nyack bottoms she knew so well. Six hours later the bear had reached the 4,500-foot level and neared the Nyack Creek Patrol Cabin she'd passed many times before. Snow and wind continued to rage about her. Soon she backed her bulk against a cabin wall and fell into a deep sleep.

Hours later, stars winked above and only the tiniest sliver of moon hung like a sickle in the western sky as the bear pushed to her feet. She stalked around the cabin that was buried in two feet of crusted snow freighted with six-inches of powder. The bruin first tested the window shutters framed with angle-iron supports, then checked the front door, and finally the rear door. Both doors were of sturdy planks, plated with cross-hatched two-by-sixes and beefed up with hinges and hasps forged from steel plating. The doors were secured with heavy brass-plated padlocks.

Chocolate Legs dug deep into the cross-hatched two-by-sixes with her claws and managed to pry one loose from the rear door, but entry still eluded her. Clawing again at the windows, the golden bear with distinctively dark legs finally left the cabin to trudge on down the Park Service trail toward the Flathead's Middle Fork.

Thirty-six hours later, she pushed along the man-made

Boundary Trail paralleling the big river. It was still all-white land, even down at this lower elevation. Pink tinged the eastern horizon. She'd scrounged a little swamp grass and dug for roots in swamps along the way, but thus far the young bear had been rewarded with little of nutritious value.

Surprisingly, too, the young bruin had passed few tracks of other bears abroad in the land. The fact that she was early on the scene may have rewarded Chocolate Legs when she chanced upon a dense copse of red-osier dogwood that had housed a small band of elk—two cows and a calf—during their last days.

Scraps were all that was left after being fought over by other scavengers for weeks—coyotes and ravens and jays. But there were pieces of putrid hide and myriad bones that hadn't yet been cracked for their marrow. Chocolate Legs settled in for a couple of days—at least until she'd cleaned up every last morsel from the ungulates' tragic last resting place.

After six years, the golden bruin was nearing full maturity. At last, she felt no need to flee as precipitously as before from others of her kind. And when finally others began appearing along the river bottom she'd chosen for spring foraging, Chocolate Legs felt comfortable among them. But she was by no means of sufficient size to be dominating and usually gave way when more aggressive animals moved into her cattail swamp or sedge meadow.

April faded and only lingering snow was left. Skunk cabbage shoots began miraculously to peek from wet forest floors. Elk herds began their slow drift along south-facing hillsides, heading leisurely toward their summer high country feeding grounds. Chocolate Legs followed, as did other bears, both black and grizzly.

When May turned into June, the maturing young bear ambushed her first elk calf, still on wobbly legs. She devoured the calf in one quick meal before being ousted from the spot by a larger sow grizzly trailed by three playful yearling cubs.

She shared a field of sedge with three other bears at Nyack Lakes, then went for a patrol through Surprise Pass and along the jumbled, remnant avalanches fanning down from Mount Phillips. Twice she was rewarded. Once she had to yield her bounty almost before acquiring it, when her labors were detected by observant bears of more dominant mein.

The second time was different, however. Chocolate Legs

had worked hours to wrest the carcass of a yearling deer from the clinging embrace of an ice block that was as large as a house. The block was lodged at the bottom of the largest of Mount Phillips' westslope avalanche chutes. The fan opened across Coal Creek from the trail to Marthas Basin and it was no real surprise to the young blond bear when the slow drift of warming uphill air brought her number-one Marthas Basin nemesis unerringly to her bounty.

Knowing she was vulnerable, the young bear had carried the carcass uphill for several hundred yards, finally backing onto a tiny clay flat at the bottom of a dry arroyo. Then she fed as rapidly as possible, peeking over the arroyo's lip from time to time to check her surroundings.

She spotted the big dark-colored male almost as soon as he swaggered to the ice block and began nosing around. So she hurried back to her bonanza, took a few quick bites, then lifted the carcass, trotted from the arroyo and beelined for a narrow strip of trees. Flight was useless, of course. The dark grizzly followed her scent trail up the arroyo, they topped out on its lip to study the strip of stunted firs. With ears pricked forward, the giant began a methodical advance.

Chocolate Legs watched from her screen, alternately flattening her own ears, clacking her teeth, and slobbering in anger. The dark male may just as well have laughed aloud, not even bothering to flash any of the usual dominance displays; instead, continuing the head-up, ears-forward advance.

Chocolate Legs broke and ran when the monster approached to twenty feet. She burst from the strip of firs on its far side, galloped across the next avalanche chute, then paused at the next tree strip to glance behind.

But the dark bear had not even hesitated at the deer carcass. Instead, still with head up and ears forward, he plodded methodically from his own tree strip.

Again, she fled, this time climbing the mountain. The dark bear plodded after. She circled across the mountain, coming down the arroyo. He cut across the circle, peeking down upon her just as she clambered up the arroyo wall to search for him!

Still, the male displayed no anger. And oddly, there was less angst from Chocolate Legs. He stared down, she stared up. Then she clambered on to the arroyo lip and, as if walking on broken glass, shuffled across the mountain to the deer carcass. The dark bruin followed. And when she bent her head to feed, the great beast sprawled beside her, nuzzling her flank and caressing her.

Then in an instant, he bounced to his feet, ears back, head swinging low. Chocolate Legs quailed, but the giant leaped down the hill, crashing through the trees. And an older salt and pepper grizzled bear who'd been steadily climbing through the strip of firs fled down the mountain for his life.

Tentatively, the blond bear again returned to her meal. But this time, when her protector returned, she licked his lips. He, too, pulled up a banquet chair.

The courtship between the giant male and the beautiful blond female continued for almost a week. After the deer carcass was consumed, the two bears wandered a short distance down Coal Creek, then the dark bear herded his compliant young female back to Marthas Basin, and Buffalo Woman and Beaver Woman Lakes. Along the way, they kissed and nuzzled and caressed. At last, the dark male mounted the stunning blond.

The lovers slept together, dug roots together, fed on sedge together, swam together, lay in the sun together, and made love with wild abandon for four more days. Then the male drifted away from Marthas Basin and Chocolate Legs wandered over Surprise Pass. And the next time they met, something was missing from their old magic.

Shortly after mid-June, Chocolate Legs pushed over the Continental Divide for her first 1987 visit to the east. She traveled through Dawson Pass, traversing down to Bighorn Basin, passing a gaggle of hiker tents at the upper end of No Name Lake during the height of a full moon. She then wandered around Pumpelly Pillar to the north shore of Upper Two Medicine Lake before morning.

This time glacier lilies were in their prime and she took her place among three bears already working the hillside for bulbs. And when the sun beat upon the lake and the first hiker emerged from the nearest tent, the field of yellow lilies above her camp was devoid of ursids of any stripe.

Later she mentioned to her two hiking companions how much she'd hoped to see a grizzly bear: "I don't care what you girls say, I don't think there's any bears in Glacier Park."

The older lady of the group chuckled. "Oh, Anna, look up on the mountain and tell me what you see."

Anna poured coffee and sat back on her haunches, lower lip protruding. "I see a mountainside full of yellow flowers, that's what I see. I wanted to see grizzly bears and all I get is flowers."

"And what other colors do you see?"

"A green carpet. Browns and reds in the cliffs above."

"And do you see any colors amid the green?"

Anna studied the field of glacier lilies and replied, "Yellow. All yellow and green. Perhaps a few patches of brown where ground squirrels or marmots have pushed up dirt."

The older lady stood with hands on her hips. "Look more closely, girl. Look at those mounds of brown. Are those marmot digs or bear excavations? Is it possible bears have been digging for lily bulbs during the night? Or do you have blinders on your eyes and will not see?"

Anna stood and shaded her eyes. At last she whispered, "Are you joking?"

"No, lady, I'm not joking."

That evening, Anna and the older lady and their third companion sat up by their dead campfire passing a pair of powerful field glasses from hand to hand. "Oh my word!" Anna murmured, more to herself than the others. "That ... that golden bear! Isn't she beautiful!"

Indeed, Chocolate Legs was beautiful by most human standards. By late June, she'd shed out the last remnants of her winter coat and was clad in a sleek summer model. Her legs, already dark via natural coloring, were even more brown than ever as a result of prodigious moist-hillside excavations for lily bulbs. In addition, the blond bruin was just entering her prime of life as a mature adult.

And don't forget, she'd just been bred. Somewhere inside, an egg had been fertilized by the dark male's sperm and had begun to develop into a tiny embryo.

It's a curious thing about bears, though. Almost immediately after fertilization, development of a grizzly sow's embryos are arrested and they remain free-floating, thus not attaching themselves to the uterine wall and continuing to develop, as in most mammals. As a result, bear embryos remain dormant for months, in a state of suspended animation—a marvel of evolutionary adaptation. Here's why, taken from the book, *Learning to Talk Bear*, pages 183-184:

> *Spring is ideal for mating; the weather is usually good, food will soon become abundant, and the bears are wandering around looking for it—a perfect time to find a mate. But summer through early or even mid-autumn is not a good time for a female bear to be developing and nourishing one, two, or possibly three embryos. Instead, she needs all the nourishment for her own body, to build up fat reserves for winter. Her problem is solved by delayed implantation, which takes the problem out of summer pregnancy.*
>
> *In late fall, if she has fed well and is in good condition, the tiny, undeveloped embryos drift to the uterine wall and become attached to it—implanted. Development can then resume, and it does—very quickly. That way, their birth is timed for midwinter, in the warmth and concealment of the den. And by then, the dozing mother has begun producing plenty of rich milk for them. They suckle and sleep and grow (and their growth is prodigious) until the time comes to emerge from the den....*
>
> *The cubs, when born, weighed only a few ounces each—no larger than juice glasses. That they quickly find their way from their mother's birth channel to her mammary glands is both mystery and fact. By mid-April, when they emerge from the den alongside their mother, they're usually as large as footballs. In two months, they'll match the weight of a cocker spaniel and have the disposition of a pit bull.*

Actually, with grizzlies in the Northern Rockies, more female bears than not will give birth to just a single cub during their first pregnancy. Perhaps limiting the size of her first litter is nature's cautionary way of providing new mothers with on-the-job-training without overburdening her with responsibility.

Chocolate Legs tired of glacier lily bulbs after a couple of

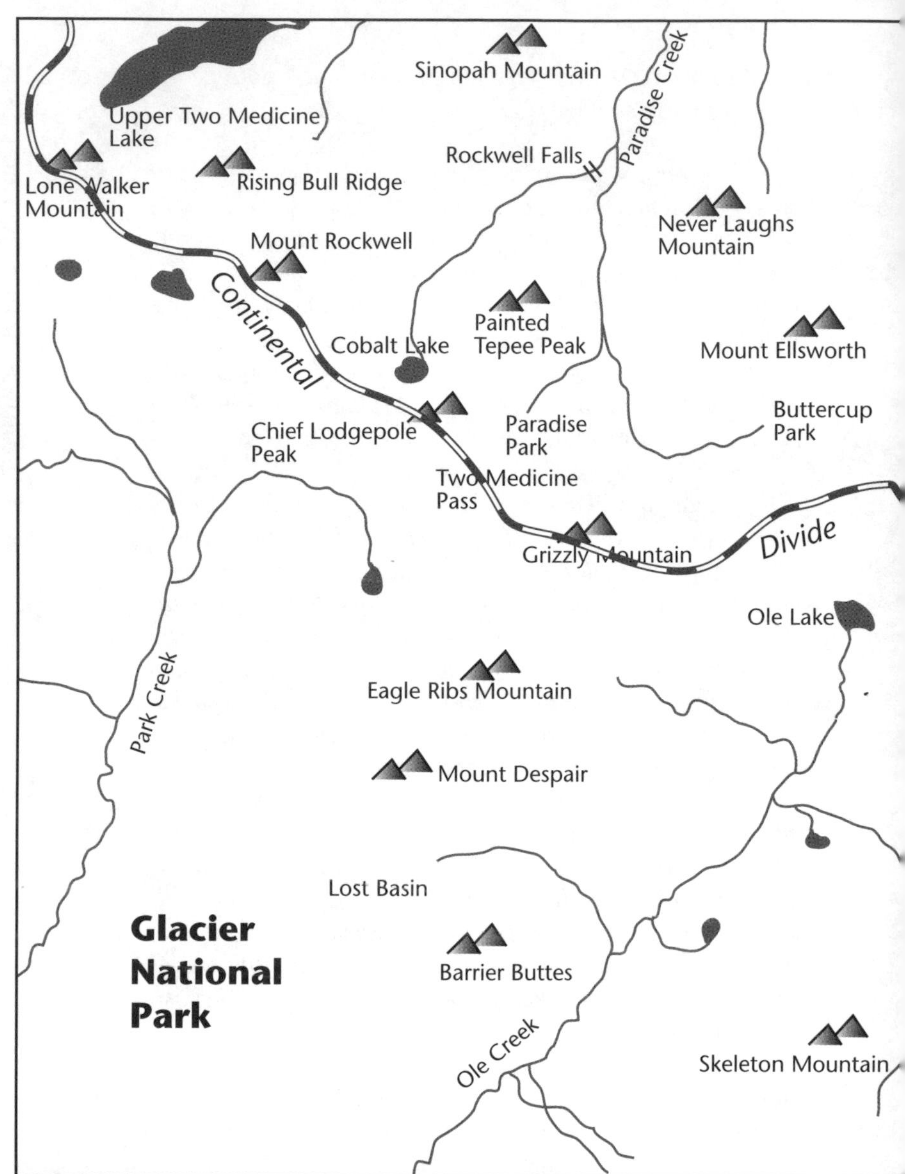

Talk about two faces of Eve! One side of the Divide sees relatively few visitor the other side, well, there's more. On both sides, though, are stunning mou tains, delightful lakes, tooth-aching coldwater streams and alpine beauty f which Swiss natives yearn. It's the kind of country that makes yodelers yodel.

**This map and others within these pages were produced in part through a DeLorme (Yarmouth, M. system that, in turn, used U.S.G.S. quads as their base. Detail–1:50,000* days and wound up drifting down the Two Medicine Valley for the first time. It turned out to be a food-rich bottom, lush in all sorts of root plants and forbs during a seasonal time before berries began to ripen elsewhere. But as far as the golden bear was concerned the valley contained one fatal flaw—it was so food-rich that other bears frequented it. Too many other bears.

And there were too many people, too.

Always before, during her Two Medicine forays, Chocolate Legs had merely skirted the heart of the valley: using the mountain ridges and alpine passes, and feeding in the high cirques. Even during her dash out to the foothills of the plains in '85 she'd generally followed the divide between Cut Bank Creek and the Two Medicine Valley. Yes, there'd been both bears and people during previous forays. But never so many as she discovered in the bottom between Upper Two Medicine Lake and the big lake below. Trails and more trails, people and more people, rich food and bears. It was a combination that made the young creature nervous.

Finally, Chocolate Legs found she could escape most of the bears and all of the people by retreating into the dense forest and brush tangle on the slopes of Sinopah Mountain. And so it was that she followed her nose around Sinopah Mountain to Cobalt Lake, then ambled the trail beyond to finally cross the Continental Crest south of Mount Rockwell in mid-July.

The land the blond bear entered after crossing the divide was new to her, but the headwaters of Park Creek proved to be food-rich, and with only occasional hikers. Neither were the basin's bears overly cantankerous.

The upper Park Creek region was high, however—its bottom higher, even, than her Nyack Creek homeland. And so she pointed her nose north, crossing through a series of high, broken, and barren ridges lying to the west of Lone Walker Mountain. She did swing out of her way long enough during the journey to call on a campsite at Isabel Lake. In the end, it was unfortunate that she did because campers had hung leftover pancakes from the limbs of stunted trees for pine squirrels and robber jays. The pancakes whetted her appetite for more and since no humans appeared to be in the immediate vicinity, Chocolate Legs began sniffing around. She located the rest of the campers' food cache in moments—in their tent. One slice, then two, and the bear was able to drag a pack through the opening. A few more drags with her sharpened three-inch claws and she liberated a candy bar stash, a tin of canned bacon, and a package of corn meal.

She'd been gone two hours when the two fishermen returned to camp to discover the results of their carelessness. By then the golden bear with legs of chocolate brown was passing through the saddle between Caper Peak and Lone Walker Mountain. In another hour the bear drank from the springs forming the headwaters of Nyack Creek. And by nightfall, the young bruin ate huckleberries from bushes downstream from Nyack Lakes.

18

Miracle of Motherhood

The year 1987 played out for Chocolate Legs more or less like her previous years in the country spreading across the Continental Divide, in Glacier National Park. She ranged on two other occasions into the Two Medicine country. Her last, in early October, the bear passed Upper Two Medicine Lake to circumnavigate the larger lake down the valley.

She'd been intrigued by a macadam road at the lower end, and the huge campground located there. The weather soured while she poked around empty campsites for scraps left on fire grates. Once, when she approached a tended camp too closely, a man rushed from the tent banging two pans together and the blond bear fled across a bridge and never stopped running until she'd climbed to the 5,800-foot level on Rising Wolf Mountain.

Forage was scarce on Rising Wolf late in the year, so the future mother returned to the rich bottomland between lakes, then wandered up Paradise Creek to sedge meadows along the stream.

Finally she crossed the Continental Divide at Two Medicine Pass and once again descended to Isabel Lake. On the 26th of October, during a snowstorm, she began digging her den at the 6,600-foot level on the north slope of Lone Walker Mountain. She entered it for the winter on the 7th of November.

The berry crop had not been an especially good one in '87, but proved adequate for the young bear to supply the fat reserves needed for a maturing mother. As a result, the fertilized embryos that had floated free in her uterus for five months attached to the uterine wall and began to develop.

Of this, Chocolate Legs knew nothing.

Her single cub, a female, was born sometime around mid-January. Chocolate Legs dozed throughout the birth process.

The tiny cub, no larger than a chipmunk, was born toothless and hairless, and was, as with most new-born mammals, blind. Not that the blindness had any real importance at that point in the cub's life since her mother's den, covered now by four feet of snow—and building—was as black as midnight in an auto trunk.

Somehow, though, one of the great works of nature prevailed and the oversized titmouse of a waif found its own way from birth canal to her mother's teat. Perched there, snuggled amid her mother's sheltering hair, the tiny cub nestled for three more months, suckling and sleeping and slipping in and out of consciousness.

Yet another mystery of nature was at work in that same den—the wonder of how a grizzly bear mother, without eating or taking on fluid for upwards of six months could provide mother's milk for a growing cub without dehydrating herself. But she did. And she did it without more than subconscious waking, with but slight shifting, with only an occasional half-hearted, satisfied sniff at the miracle at her mammaries.

Gradually that miracle's tiny belly distended. The waif became covered by downy blond hair. Tiny razor-sharp teeth poked through her gums and her eyes blinked open to the darkness.

And when chinook winds from the Pacific began to gentle the gales of more violent bent from the Arctic North, the waif's weight neared that of a fox terrier dog.

Finally came a day in April when Chocolate Legs plodded down from the shoulder of Lone Walker Mountain to Nyack Lakes. The furry little football trailed so closely that she kept bumping into the mother's dark-colored legs.

For her part, Chocolate Legs was still a bit overwhelmed by the wonder of motherhood. Instinct, of course, kicked in and confounded though she might be, she paused often and nuzzled long. Two feet of snow still covered this high country region of Glacier and each time the waif flagged or whined in distress, the mother stopped her slow, measured descent to sprawl on her back and let her cub scramble to her breast. Had there been anyone to see, and had they been discerning about facial features of grizzly bears, they might have noted wistful smiles flashing often between both.

The mother's food was, however, in short supply. Snowfields still covered the sedge at Nyack Lakes. But days were warm and skies blue. The snow melted rapidly and water gushed everywhere—which presented yet another problem to a fretting mother.

Chocolate Legs twice carried her tiny cub over freshets when the tyke first whined, then sat down and bawled in fright at the rushing water. But when mother and cub arrived at an ankle deep rivulet that was little more than a yard wide and the diminutive waif refused to cross on her own, mom whirled, splashed across, and smacked her babe end over end with a mighty forepaw, through the stream and beyond. And by the end of the week, when the two bears reached the roaring Pacific Creek crossing, the little cub had learned to plunge into lesser streams and swim for her life in order not to anger the monster who supplied her milk.

Nevertheless, Chocolate Legs blocked her young offspring's access to Pacific Creek, lifted the cub in her teeth and waded across the torrent, swimming strongly the last few yards. Then the two bears trudged on to the Nyack Patrol Cabin where, because the weather had soured and rain fell in sheets, they bedded down under an overhang for the day.

The weather turned colder at the end of the two-day deluge, but two inches of rain, added to the already flood-stage snow melt, sent every water course through Glacier National Park rampaging from its banks. When she was alone there was no feeder stream to Nyack Creek, no matter how high and swift the run-off, that would've stopped Chocolate Legs. But even she whined when she heard the roar of Thompson Creek. And when she came to banks of glacial till and saw them crumbling to the coppery flood, the blond sow sat on her rump like a puppy and swept the cub close.

Chocolate Legs returned upstream to a series of brush-filled bottoms on Nyack Creek and eked out a bare subsistence while foraging amid soft snow and rising flood. The lack of nourishment gaunted the once roly-poly golden mother and her milk began to subside. The cub lost some of its roundness and spent much of its time wandering near her mother and whining. At last, the Thompson Creek flood subsided enough so Chocolate Legs gathered her cub into her teeth and leaped in, exiting the swollen water two hundred yards downstream. By two o'clock the following morning, mother and cub arrived at the raging Flathead's Middle Fork.

The marsh where the cattails grew was flooded by the torrent. So was each sedge grass meadow the young mother remembered. But skunk cabbage was beginning to poke from the ground, and spring beauties and glacier lilies were bursting forth on the south- and west-facing slopes. The problem was that other bears had beat her to the scene and seemed scattered throughout the valley.

This was a new Chocolate Legs, however. A hungry Chocolate Legs. A Chocolate Legs with a starving cub. As a result, she was in no mood to argue borders or titles or territories or interests or ownerships. When the pugnacious female waded into the marsh rich with yellowing blossoms of pungent cabbage, she displaced two other bears of equal size. And when she began to dig, she ignored dominance displays from a much larger male—so readily that he gave up the effort as a waste of time.

The golden mother fed so voraciously—twenty hours per day—that she again began producing adequate milk for her flat-sided cub and the little tyke began to balloon. When the river subsided, Chocolate Legs moved to the marshes where cattails and swamp grass were quickly reviving.

Most bears followed the herds of migrating ungulates, but mother and daughter remained, gradually regaining vigor. And it was because they stayed during the migration that Chocolate Legs had the opportunity to ambush a whitetail doe. She'd spotted the deer swimming the still swollen river. The doe emerged unwittingly into the waiting teeth and claws of a female grizzly very much in need of life-sustaining meat.

Finally, at the end of May, a fully restored Chocolate Legs and her roly-poly daughter began to follow the earlier migration up into Glacier's high country. It took them a month to crest the Continental Divide. Along the way, the golden bear had been stalked by two different males: a magnificent silvertip, above Thompson Creek Falls and an ancient worn-gray veteran near the headwall of Pacific Creek, on the approach to Triple Divide Peak.

In both cases, an outweighed and outgunned, but outraged and out-of-bounds Chocolate Legs proved not only capable, but zealous in driving away what she perceived as threats to her cub. The silvertip on Thompson Creek was at least discreet enough to flee from her determined charge; but the bewildered old-timer took several good licks and lost a couple mouthfuls of wrinkled hide and shaggy hair when he wasn't sufficiently nimble to flee her rush.

After each altercation, the blond sow took her by now spaniel-size cub underfoot, guiding the little tyke on to the ridgetop north and east of Razoredge Mountain, where the sow knew ground squirrels and marmots and voles lay beneath the soil in abundance.

They were on the ridge on the 30th day of June when the thunderstorm broke about them. One moment Chocolate Legs pushed head and shoulders into one of her marmot excavations while the cub mimicked her mother a few feet away. The next moment lightning forked down from a roiling black cloud, striking the mountaintop less than forty yards distant.

Chocolate Legs was momentarily stunned. When at last she pushed dizzily from the piled-up dirt, her cub was nowhere to be seen. The smell of burnt cordite permeated the area and it took a few minutes before the mother was able to even locate where her cub had stood just a short time before.

It took two days more before she found the broken-bodied remains of her offspring at the bottom of a 500 foot cliff that had dropped into nothingness only five feet to the side of where the cub had last been seen.

19

Back from Bereavement

Chocolate Legs lay by the shattered body of her daughter for twenty-two hours and remained in the proximate vicinity for two weeks. Then she made a last meal of her cub's slowly rotting remains and dropped to Medicine Grizzly Lake for a swim—God knows, the wistful sow needed something therapeutic. She found it on a mountain east of the lake.

The way Chocolate Legs discovered the cutworm cornucopia was that after her swim in Medicine Grizzly, she, like so often with this bear, took a hike. Her intent was to check the bush-covered slopes for berries, but the golden bruin soon determined she was much too early in the season for berries at this elevation. What she did discover, however, was the scent of another grizzly bear beelining up one particular mountain. Soon she struck the scent of another. Then a black bear. Curious, she followed.

The summit of the mountain peak she chose to climb is nearly 4,000 vertical feet above the valley floor and is, as well, over a mile away—a very steep climb. It's a bit of a stroll, even for an animal with the dynamic metabolism of a grizzly bear. And so three hours had elapsed and night was falling before Chocolate Legs crossed the mountain summit and began traversing around, into the basin off its northeast corner, still following the trail of other bears.

Grizzly odors were strong as the blond bear with the distinctively dark legs paused on the basin's lip. In addition to the smell of other bears, Chocolate Legs' ears told her some of the bears were moving about. Thus prudence became the better part of valor and she paused in a thicket of alpine firs to wait out the night.

The basin that unfolded in the morning's growing light was

a relatively small cirque by Glacier Park standards. It contained twin snow-fed lakes of approximately fifteen acres each. Ice still floated on one of them. A mountain wall rose above the lakes to the mountain's summit. Talus fans spread from the foot of that wall to the lakes. Wildflowers were abundant.

In fact, wildflowers grew everywhere in these mountains in mid-July; down at Medicine Grizzly Lake, up the slopes of this mountain, atop its ridges, in each of the alpine basins; everywhere one looked wildflowers blossomed. And each night, army cutworm moths flew from the talus slopes on the mountain to harvest flower nectar.

With daylight, as the basin and talus slopes began to come alive with grizzly bears, Chocolate Legs studied the action through a screen of alpine firs. Within an hour of sun-up, seven grizzlies and two black bears took their place on the slopes above the lake twins and began turning over rocks and digging into the rocky soil.

A mere fifty yards from where Chocolate Legs lay, a small, silvertip female worked industriously, digging and licking, digging and licking. After a few minutes, the silvertip would move a few steps and sniff, a few more steps and sniff. Then she'd tear furiously at rocks and the gravelly soil, and again lick.

Beyond the small silvertip, a huge brown male worked halfheartedly. Beyond him, perhaps a hundred yards, a tan-colored female with two cubs busied themselves. Two subadult males worked at the top of the talus fan. And off to the edge, the blacks were tolerated by the grizzlies, but not exactly welcomed. All across the talus, brown mounds where bears had previously dug stood out like grease stains on a tablecloth.

At last, curiosity got the better of her and Chocolate Legs pushed through the screen of low-spreading alpine firs into the open.

Startled, the young silvertip galloped from her digging, only to stop a hundred yards away and rise on her hind legs to peer at the newcomer. The big male glanced up when the blond bruin first popped out, then ignored her. The sow and her cubs and the two subadults both paused in their digging to study Chocolate Legs, saw no threat to the order of things, and returned to dig and lick, dig and lick. Across the talus, the two black bears continued to warily watch the grizzlies.

Chocolate Legs moved cautiously out to the silvertip's fresh digging and thrust her nose into the hole. She was met by an odor she'd whiffed before. It'd never been this overpowering. The blond bear began digging and after a time was rewarded by licking out a tiny remnant cluster of the migratory cutworm moths.

So she moved to a nearby rock and turned it over, then began excavating for another remnant cluster. The silvertip edged back and began working, eventually moving to within thirty feet of Chocolate Legs before the blond bear made any overt note of the other's presence.

The big male could care less.

As noted earlier, moth forages for nectar are entirely nocturnal. During daylight they seek shelter under rocks, in cracks, under the soil. They tend to nest in clusters. Some clusters are large, some small. Bears search for those clusters.

Temperature affects the moths' ability to escape when they're exposed during excavations, as was shown by observation at moth sites near Yellowstone National Park:

> *"Moths exposed near the rock surface," according to a report: Grizzly Bear Use of Army Cutworm Moths in the Yellowstone Ecosystem, "had to flap their wings several seconds before flying away, but those exposed farther down where it was cooler had to spend more time warming up before flight, and as a consequence, usually fled by crawling deeper into the rock interstices. This mode of escape concentrated moths at the bottom of the excavations when they were prevented from going down farther by rock or ice."*

One of the blacks—the one with a dinner plate-sized white spot on his chest—broke off a wary watch of the grizzly bears and returned to moth pursuit. The other black continued to stare.

As the minutes clicked by, the land began to warm to the sun's embrace. The tan sow and her two cubs seemed absorbed in one place in the talus, attracting attention from the indolent male. He wandered their way only to have his path blocked by an ears-back, jaw popping female who hopped up and down before her cubs. So the big boar turned around and headed for Chocolate Legs and the silvertip female. The silvertip fled from the big animal's path, but Chocolate Legs held her ground, giving no sign she even noticed the male's approach. At fifteen feet, the boar stopped and began sniffing and digging.

His presence was too close for comfort, however, and the blond bear used the next half-hour to search for cutworm clusters farther and farther from the brown male. And by mid-day, the silvertip female and Chocolate Legs were again within a few feet of one another.

It was while the sun was still at its zenith when the two subadult grizzlies trotted downslope directly at the black bears. The blacks moved out of the talus and into the trees and the subadults, cuffing and wrestling on the way, trotted after.

The boar wandered to one of the lakes for a drink, then sprawled on the grass at water's edge. The sow and her cubs left the talus for a nearby rocky knoll and Chocolate Legs watched the mother scrape out a daybed.

Soon only the blond and the silvertip worked the talus. Then there was one. At last Chocolate Legs was stuffed. Unlike the others, Chocolate Legs was content to sprawl where she'd already fluffed up a mound of dirt while digging for moths.

Soon the brown male pushed to his feet and climbed the talus until he was within twenty feet of the golden bear. Then he scooped out a shallow depression, eased his bulk into it and promptly fell asleep. Chocolate Legs ignored him. Her mother's milk had dried up since the demise of her offspring, but her body's functions had not yet sufficiently altered from motherhood to bring her into estrus.

One of the blacks returned in mid-afternoon to turn over rocks at the talus edge. He was joined moments later by the other. Then the subadults were romping together at the lakes.

Chocolate Legs yawned and pushed to her feet. This time she didn't bother to move away from where the male sprawled, but immediately began searching for moths. The male raised his head to look, then again dropped chin to forepaws and slumbered. When he finally made the effort to re-enter the company of grizzlies, the blond bombshell was feeding halfway across the talus fan and all other bears were likewise on the slope.

The young silvertip female wandered to within twenty feet of Chocolate Legs and began nosing the talus. The tan sow and cubs drifted cross-slope, but the sow sensed some underlying distress in the blond newcomer and peeled away at thirty yards. And later in the afternoon, when the silvertip and the blond inadvertently came near, the tan sow became agitated and bounced stiff-legged and ears back, before the other females.

When night fell, Chocolate Legs was as stuffed as she could be. One by one, bears had winked out on the talus slope where so many had toiled by day. The blond bear with distinctively brown legs scooped out a day bed just off the promontory dividing the lakes. After she'd settled in, the brown male drifted to a point twenty feet away and scooped out his bed.

One of the black bears failed to reappear the following morning and the subadults wandered away from the basin at midday. But they were replaced by a second blond grizzly—a hesitant female with a tiny cub of the year. And just before dark fell on Chocolate Legs' second day at the moth banquet, a gaunt old male grizzly limped out onto the talus.

During the week Chocolate Legs spent working the moth slope, bears came and bears went: other lone females, a sow trailing three cubs, a cinnamon black, another grizzled old-timer—this one a female. At no time during the days spent on the slope was there any overt intolerance displayed by one bruin toward another. Sows with cubs fed near sows without cubs. All types of females intermingled with boars. Subadults came and subadults went.

Chocolate Legs left before the banquet ended. The moths were rich food, perhaps so rich she hungered for a change in diet. Therefore she went searching. She found cow parsnips in the Cut Bank Creek bottoms and foothill huckleberries along Nyack Creek. There was sedge at Nyack Lakes and marmots and ground squirrels and voles on the slopes of Tinkham Mountain.

Gradually, though, the forests and ridges and mountains and valleys of Glacier National Park turned dry during that summer of '88. Lightning forked from dark and angry clouds and fires were ignited. Hundreds of fires.

Up in Canada, three great blazes roared out of control in British Columbia and one in Alberta. Converging fires in Yellowstone threatened the entire Park and beyond. Two great infernos raged to the south of Chocolate Legs' home, in the Bob Marshall Wilderness. And over on Glacier Park's western border, a fire raced from national forest land to jump the Flathead's North Fork, burn a bridge, threaten a ranger station, and torch dozens of private dwellings.

But when September rolled around, there were bull trout in Coal Creek and buffalo berries and mountain ash berries clinging to bushes and trees growing on the mountainside below Flinsch Peak.

Eventually the blond bear with dark legs waxed fat and at seven years of age weighed two hundred and seventy pounds. She'd reached full maturity.

Chocolate Legs ventured but once into the Two Medicine country throughout her summer of discontent—the year she lost her first born. Hers was again an October foray and she was delighted to find fewer humans mingling with the ever-present bears. She was delighted, too, that berries still clung to bushes growing in the forested bottoms along Paradise Creek and the Two Medicine River.

She dug lomatium roots on the slopes of Rising Wolf Mountain, raided squirrels' cone caches on Aster creek, and ran afoul of patrolling rangers at the auto campground at the lower end of Two Medicine Lake.

"God, she's a pretty bear," one ranger muttered to another just before he lobbed the "cracker shell" near where the blond bear with distinctively colored legs nosed a camper's tent.

The explosion scared the hell out of Chocolate Legs and she didn't stop running until she was halfway up the trail to Scenic Point! Not that she hadn't heard or experienced a cracker shell before—they'd twice fired ones at her during her Many Glacier adolescence. But five long years had passed since the last time she'd been fired upon and her recall of those long-gone years of youth was dim.

However, the golden bear learned more from the impromptu adventure than just to avoid rangers carrying shotguns stuffed with cracker shells. She learned lomatiums also grew on hillsides along the way to Scenic Point. And she learned Appistoki Basin might be a future point for her reference.

Chocolate Legs' 1988-89 den opened to a front porch view of Lake Isabel. It was excavated off the main avalanche path from Vigil Peak. The site was not as well chosen as it could have been; twice during that winter the bear's slumber was momentarily disturbed by her hillside shaking to the roar of slab avalanches cascading down from above.

20

Corn Spill Cornucopia

The territory Chocolate Legs moved through when she emerged from her den in the spring of 1989 was new to her. It'd been the second severe winter in succession, and three feet of crusted snow lay beneath her feet. She hardly paused at the upper Park Creek Patrol Cabin, no more than to briefly check that all doors and shutters were properly secured, then she was on her way.

The first snow-free sidehills began showing up a couple of miles below the cabin.They were mostly steep, south- and west-facing mountainsides in excess of 65-degree slopes that had been periodically swept of powder by slab avalanches roaring down from Statuary Mountain.

Chocolate Legs, remembering how some avalanches acted as serving trays to hungry blond bears, found the long string of avalanche paths fascinating. She was disappointed that such a series of alpine conveyors still had so far to melt before releasing whatever mysteries they contained. She did find, however, that greening bunchgrass shoots were pushing from the ground at the 4,400-foot level, and that spring beauties and buttercups were mixed with them.

When she struck the Boundary Trail, Chocolate Legs paused as something clicked deep inside. The bruin gazed about, stared out over the extensive bottom, lifted snout to the gentle upstream breeze, and recollected that another cabin squatted a short distance upstream. She couldn't access this cabin either, so the golden bear returned to the Boundary Trail and began climbing the mountainside to the south. She'd followed this route once before and the trail led to another valley, then to yet another mountainside thick with elk and rich with succulent glacier lily and spring beauty bulbs.

Within hours, the golden bear with dark legs was once again rototilling succulent bulbs from the steep Elk Mountain foreslope she'd visited years before. Far below, trucks and automobiles buzzed up and down the busy highway, while between bear and highway, trains bearing containers with the names "Hanjin," "Sonjin" "Hyundai," "Cosco," or "NOL" plied the double set of Burlington Northern mainline tracks from St. Paul and Chicago and points East to Seattle and Portland and myriad other places across the sea.

"You suppose that's her?" a ranger asked, waving his companion to a spotting scope clamped to the window glass of his sage-green pickup truck.

"Where's her cubs?" the companion asked.

Both men waited while an 18-wheel tanker truck rumbled by, then the ranger said, "Hell, she killed the guy two years ago. She would've kicked those cubs out last year."

"And been re-bred. She should have cubs of the year with her now."

The ranger took a position behind the scope and ducked his head to again stare at the mountain through the eyepiece. "I helped pick up the pieces, you know."

"She still should have cubs of the year with her."

Again the ranger stepped aside. "Maybe she didn't take."

The companion sighed. "You saw the photos. Did the sow in those photos have legs so dark?"

"Come on, this bear is digging in muddy ground, you know that."

"And you don't think the one that killed the photographer in April had been digging?"

The ranger watched a motor coach roll by. At last he said, "I just asked what you thought."

His slighter companion, long brown hair flecked with gray and creeping over his jacket collar, shrugged, peering at the other man. There was no glint of humor in the thoughtful brown eyes. "Let's get on up to the grain spills, what do you say?"

The ranger unscrewed the instrument's window bracket and folded it against the scope barrel. "Still think bears are coming after the spilled corn, huh? Can you document it? What'll you do if they are and you can prove it?"

The slighter man's smile was frosty. "Which question do you want answered first?"

During the winter of 1988-89, three separate train derailments took place on Burlington Northern Railroad's mainline track, only a few miles west of Marias Pass. Several tons of corn was spilled along the railroad right-of-way and beyond, most of it occurring along a two-mile stretch. Though most of the corn was cleaned up, much that was considered unusable, or corn that was thought difficult to access or remove, was buried with topsoil.

The problem with the method of burial instead of removal was that the buried corn, thoroughly wetted with the melting of winter snows and spring rains took on a life of its own, providing an irresistible attractant to bears.

As a result, bears died.

As before, lots of bears moved through the low pass to the southwest of Elk Mountain. Two invaded Chocolate Legs' glacier lily sidehill, but neither remained longer than a few hours. Most bears ignored the promise of protein-rich bulbs to simply pad along to other places. Chocolate Legs began making repeated forays down her mountain to sniff along the trail.

There came a change in weather patterns and spring rains fell. Chocolate Legs sought a diet change and took the trail downhill to cross the busy rail tracks and wind up in the wet grassy bottoms near the Bear Creek Guest Ranch. There, skunk cabbage bloomed and there the blond bear lounged, feeding periodically, sharing the marsh with other passing bears, surrounded by the buzz from a busy highway to the south and east and a bustling railroad to the west and north. At last, Chocolate Legs followed a silvertip sow trailed by two yearling cubs.

The night was dark, gloomy with heavy overcast. Had the sky been clear, only the sliver of a moon would have hung on the western horizon. Trailing the bear family by scent alone, Chocolate legs followed up the slope to the railroad embankment. A grain train rumbled past down-track, heading for Columbia River ports and points in the Far East.

Immediately Chocolate Legs picked up the scent of several bears, both blacks and grizzlies. She crept closer. A large dark-colored boar dug vigorously between the railroad embankment and a small pothole pond. Farther along the right-of-way, below a signal switch, the sow and her cubs sniffed a cleared space at the forest edge. The golden bear with dark legs plumped her ample rump down below the tracks to watch.

Ten minutes later, the sow began digging. Meanwhile the boar began eating. Once he raised his head to peer at Chocolate Legs then returned to eat. A sweet, odd aroma wafted from his hole. He dug some more, then ate again.

An ebony black drifted past on top of the embankment and the boar waddled away to a promontory of land thrusting up near the pond's far end. The eastern sky was beginning to lighten and Chocolate Legs saw the boar settle into a bed he'd obviously used before.

She waited, peering up the tracks at where the sow and cubs busied themselves. Almost imperceptibly the ground beneath her began to tremble, then turned more noticeable. And, as minutes ticked by, to an animal as sensitive as a bear, it began to vibrate. At last, she heard the far-off chung-chung-chung of another freight train climbing toward Marias Pass.

Trains in the distance she'd become accustomed to. But the blond bear still remembered her frightening first experience when the coasting engines almost ran her down. And when the chung-chung-chung engines leading this giant mechanical caterpillar first hove into view, heading directly for Chocolate Legs, the blond bear galloped into the trees. She circled behind where the dark-colored boar snoozed, with head stretched onto forepaws.

"Hey, that's an eye-catching bear," the engineer said and the brakeman moved from his seat to cross the cab and watch Chocolate Legs streak into the forest.

"Where's 'gumbo'?" the brakeman asked. "Oh! There he is layin' in bed."

The engineer's eyes swept expertly across a medley of gauges. He again peered out the open window. The sudden wind gust took his cap into the dawn's early light. He clutched at it, swore, then said, "Hello, what's up the track? Got a new sow and cub, Ring?"

The silvertip sow and her two cubs, surprisingly, hadn't

deigned to notice the train, continuing their digging and eating for the full seven minutes that the loaded freight lumbered past.

"Naw," Ring replied, staring almost directly down at the bears as he passed. "that's Sunshine, sure 'nough. Cubs, too."

The engine radio crackled and both men paused to listen to an exchange between the foreman of a track crew working the Lubec section who was having trouble getting it through his headquarters chief's head what supply components were missing in order to finish their job. When the brakeman looked back at the feeding bears, the middle of the caterpillar-like train was crawling past the animals.

"You reckon there's anything to the talk that corn is fermenting under the ground?"

The engineer shrugged. "Don't know. But one thing is certain—it's attracting bears of all stripes. And if these are all bears who live around these parts, there's one hell of a lot more bears than anybody knows about."

"Did you hear that Augustine got one the other day; sliced the bear right in half from end to end."

"Yeah. I talked to him. Told me the damn fool was weaving on the tracks. Said he laid his ears back and was swinging his head back and forth just before the engine smacked him. Augustine told me they got Fish & Game up here to investigate. He heard they're going to monitor what happens between bears and trains."

The brakeman cackled. "I can tell 'em what happens. Them damned grizzlies lose ever' time." He fell silent, then asked, "Supposin' their study shows there's a problem? Supposin' they can prove it? What they goin' to do?"

The engineer peered over a pair of rimless glasses he'd perched on his nose. "Which question you want answered first?"

Chocolate Legs continued to study the situation as the tail-end of the train passed. Just then, four "helper" engines coasted downhill on the second set of tracks, toward their Whitefish Division point where they would soon be used to help push another train over the Rocky Mountains.

As soon as the helpers passed, a cinnamon-colored subadult black bear crossed the tracks to sniff around where the dark-colored boar had already excavated. Chocolate Legs waited until the young bears hind-end pointed skyward from the hole, then pushed to her feet and ambled to see what was the attraction. The subadult bolted at her approach. With a glance back at the promontory where the rightful owner of whatever lay at the bottom of this excavation sprawled, the blond bear thrust her nose into the hole.

Corn! Rich, tasty, aromatic corn! The boar had hit the mother lode! She threw good table manners to the winds!

Three hours later, when the boar left his lofty perch to reclaim his treasure, Chocolate Legs moved off to the side and watched. Then she began a series of test holes of her own. She was not long in uncovering her own lode.

Downtrack the young cinnamon black was working his own plot. Beyond him was the ebony black. And between the ebony and the track's bend two other grizzly bears worked.

Several trains passed going both directions. Chocolate Legs, taking a cue from other bears, held her ground. At first she quailed like a jackrabbit trapped at high noon in a supermarket parking lot. But by the end of the first couple of hours she paid no more attention to the passing freight cars than she would to a rock rolling down a mountain.

Once, an engine passed and the brakeman jerked open a door and shouted "Boo!" and Chocolate Legs lifted her head and stared curiously up at the man until the engine rounded the bend.

The sow and her cubs headed away from the tracks to the marsh. It was late afternoon when the dark boar topped off his tank and wandered to Chocolate Legs' hole. She abandoned it and moved up the track to the forsaken digging of the sow and two cubs. The boar followed, but she circled and returned to mine his old diggings. He wandered into the forest.

That evening the blond bear took the boar's old promontory daybed and slept half the night. When she awakened, rain again pelted down. A different sow and cubs had appropriated the boar's lode-hole of fermented corn, but they were all black bears. Chocolate Legs thought about preempting the claim, but decided whatever satisfaction she might get simply wasn't worth the effort. She returned to enlarge her own hole.

Later during the day, a pickup truck pulling a flatbed trailer up a service road arrived at the bend and a tractor with bucket and backhoe was off-loaded. Within minutes, the driver guided his tractor to the bears' diggings and began pushing dirt and gravel over the exposed grain while his partner sat in the pickup

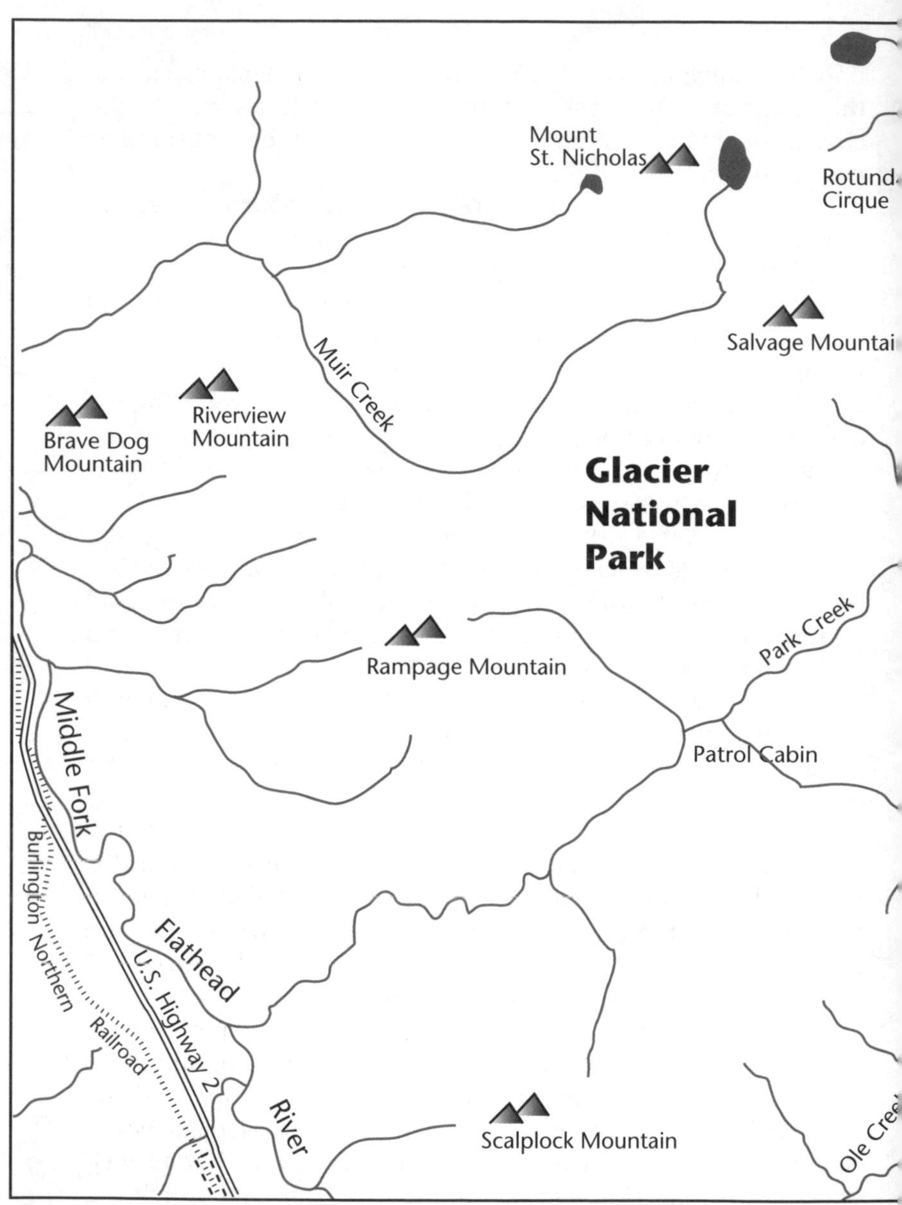

It seems an anomoly that this southwestern-most section of the Park is so seldo visited by humans seeking solitude. After all, this country is its birthplace.

**This map and others within these pages were produced in part through a DeLorme (Yarmouth, M system that, in turn, used U.S.G.S. quads as their base. Detail–1:50,000*

truck and listened to country western music from KSEN radio in Shelby.

With arrival of the backhoe, the bears had faded into the forest. Chocolate Legs, one of the scene's newcomers, re-occupied the boar's daybed and watched for a few minutes before falling asleep.

Soon a dump truck loaded with gravel arrived and loosed its load at two strategic points between the dozen-odd bear diggings. Shortly thereafter, a Ford pickup with a Montana Fish, Wildlife & Parks decal picturing the head of a grizzly bear arrived at the site, followed soon after by a dark green crew-cab truck with BN painted on the door. Men climbed from the truck cabs and were joined by the country/western listener. All three watched the backhoe operator at work.

Each of the grizzly diggings were filled, gravel spread, backhoe loaded, and workmen gone before the dinner hour. The slender biologist wearing the Montana Department of Fish, Wildlife & Parks arm patch sat in his truck until dark, watching the area of buried grain. He was aware of a blond female grizzly lying atop a promontory of land only 150 yards away, but could see no other bears. He finally drove away at seven p.m. An hour after nightfall nine bears were strung out alongside a mile of track. All were industriously moving topsoil from their open-pit corn mines.

Chocolate Legs relished the fermenting corn. She liked its taste, the ease of its acquisition, and its after-effects. She appreciated the social tolerance afforded by the corn banquet, how the abundant food supply led to proximate interaction with other bears: big males intermingling with sows and cubs, frisky subadults on their good behavior alongside barren sows and cranky boars. Even blacks occasionally intermingled with their greater cousins while the corn's fermented glow plied its peacemaking powers.

Meanwhile, trains chugged up-track heading east or whizzed down-track heading west.

Night or day made little difference to the ursids of both species. Chocolate Legs mined corn when she was hungry, slept on her promontory when she felt like it. On day six of her discovery of the corn spill, the dark male returned, stalked directly to her food vein and preempted it. Four hours later he reclaimed his daybed on the promontory. And for the next three days made her life so miserable by following her that she finally decided to decamp for old familiar places.

The decision was easy enough. She was well fed, with a greater spring weight than she'd ever before sported. Besides, with bears, a steady diet of any one thing grows tedious. Other bears left the banquet. Some returned, some did not. Some, like the dark boar, returned for other reasons than because fermenting corn was engraved on their palates.

Social tolerance was quite acceptable to the open female; social obligation was not. Though her physiology dictated that she would soon come into estrus and her superb early spring condition meant that she might be especially receptive to male advances, the date was only mid-May. The dark boar was not only a week or two early, he was also too pushy in his insistence. Therefore Chocolate Legs left for Mount Phillips and Nyack Lakes. And perhaps the Two Medicine country that contained so many possibilities.

From time to time, the blond sow checked her backtrail for the dark boar. And the truth was he pondered following. But he'd not received sufficient encouragement and by remaining where he was in this Central Park of ursid meeting places, his odds were much better for playing the field. Meanwhile, Chocolate Legs braced spring run-off and softening, melting high country snowpacks. She found the rigors of crosscountry travel not nearly so desperate for a fully matured bear as it was when she first tackled it as a skinny subadult. And finally, when the first day of June rolled around, the golden bruin found herself in Marthas Basin.

She also found Marthas Basin a lonely place.

21

Shorter Fuse, Longer Tantrums

Chocolate Legs mated on the 3rd day of June, 1989. The tryst took place on a flat bench southwest of Caper Peak, almost in sight of Lake Isabel. Her suitor was little more than a rambunctious teenager who found himself in the right place at the right time. The teenager was also blond and had it not been for the sow's strikingly dark legs, one would, at a distance, have trouble discerning which was which.

The young male mounted the compliant female repeatedly, but his dream-come-true ended abruptly when a silvertip that seemed the size of a Percheron stallion followed his nose to the boudoir. The Percheron ousted the teenager with little more than a swagger. And Chocolate Legs accepted the suitor-switch without even waving good-by to her wistful has-been.

The mighty silvertip and his golden-haired beauty were companions for two weeks. During that time, the female led the male up and over Two Medicine Pass, out the long ridge north of Chief Lodgepole Peak, and finally down into Paradise Park.

Aside from hibernation, mating season is the only period in a grizzly bear's cycle when the search for food becomes second priority. Paradise Park, as it turns out, is a nice secluded place for a couple of zealous lovers to practice amour. But amid the northern Rockies in June—especially in a north-facing basin at 6,500 feet—when it comes time to order up food, room service at Paradise Park doesn't have much of a selection. That's why the two lovers went foraging down to the boggy meadows in the Paradise Creek bottom. Those meadows are a thousand feet lower than Paradise Park and situated to catch a spring sun. It's a place that's attractive to other bruins in June, however, which is why the Percheron got in a shoving match over the good-looking blond with a grizzly the color of a Clydesdale.

The blond was bored by it all, though; so, when the two outsized males began their dominance dance, she wandered downstream to the main Two Medicine Valley, and to the big auto campground where people congregate.

The people were the reason neither winner nor loser, Percheron nor Clydesdale, followed her.

"Don't that look like the same bear you 'crackered' out of here last fall," the campground attendant asked.

The ranger nodded. "I believe it."

The two men warily watched Chocolate Legs stroll boldly along the campground road, past pop-up tents and travel trailers and $100,000 motor homes. The buzz of the bear's trek preceded her and campers and cameras peeked from locked automobiles and motor homes. One camping group boldly stood by the side of their tent drinking coffee, watching the golden bruin while she ignored them, observing good bear etiquette, padding past as if they were invisible.

A motoring family rounded a bend, met the bear, and stopped. The driver rolled down a window and offered a candy bar. Then he saw the Park Ranger coming up behind the bruin and quickly withdrew his hand, rolled up the van window and sat red-faced until both bear and ranger passed. The ranger carried a canister of a relatively new innovation—pepper spray.

The capsaicin pepper delivery system had undergone considerable research, development, and testing during the decade previous and was just now becoming available for experimental field trials in national parks. Positive results relative to the pepper spray's effectiveness were already flowing in; enough so the manufacturer's plan was to go public with the spray soon—as soon as production facilities and necessary financing could be secured.

All sorts of aromas wafted to Chocolate Legs as she strolled deliberately through the campground. She felt a certain measure of tenseness among those humans she did meet or pass, or, like the one stalking her. So she padded on to road's end and crossed the bridge, leaving the campground behind.

The golden bear with distinctively brown legs spent the next week grazing on the open slopes of Rising Wolf Mountain, much to the delight of watchers from the Two Medicine Campground and tourists riding the motor launch, "Sinopah." At last, she grazed west, dropping into Bighorn Basin, then climbing through Dawson Pass and winding up at her old Nyack Lakes haunts during the first week of July.

Mount Phillips and Mount Pinchot, Cloudcroft Peaks and Wolftail Mountain, Triple Divide and Flinsch Peaks, Razoredge and Tinkham Mountains. Chocolate Legs had developed into fighting trim when she consulted her date book and realized she'd already lost important feeding days in the moth cycle. She headed across the Divide for her mountain. She never made it until much later.

On her way through Cut Bank Pass and down past Pitamakin Lake and Morning Star Lake, the golden bear took a detour up yet another mountain-scratching peak and found a second cutworm moth banquet table.

Chocolate Legs certainly wasn't the first grizzly bear to discover the feast nor, during the eleven days she spent working the second mountain's talus slopes, was she the last. Twice she left the exposed, burning-hot mountain to swim in the lakes below. Twice she returned. Though the blond bear was a sow without cubs, nearly half the time she spent on the mountain, Chocolate Legs was the dominant bear, moving wherever she wanted, whenever she wished.

On two occasions other grizzlies joined the scene: one a cranky sow with a subadult cub she should've kicked from her nest earlier and the second, the same bumbling boar that had pursued Chocolate Legs on the previous year's moth mountain. In both cases, the well-fed blond bear yielded some of her space to the newcomers. But when the cranky sow wanted to displace the blond bear's dignity, too, there was resistance. The result was a stand-off with both sows slobbering and clacking their teeth, but eventually giving ground.

When the brown boar arrived, he deigned to so much as notice agitated displays by either of the sows, taking up a patch of talus between. In minutes he'd sprawled to sleep, and within an hour he was nosing the abandoned test plots of both females.

Just for the hell of it, Chocolate Legs sallied to her first moth site, fed among bears working its talus for three days, then left for an afternoon swim in Medicine Grizzly Lake. As darkness fell on the evening of August 2, Chocolate Legs rummaged around the boulder field at the foot of the cliff where she'd lost her firstborn. The boulder field's marmots were tasty, plentiful, and dumb. Still, something was missing, though she couldn't say what.

Chocolate Legs denned at the 6,800-foot level, off the north slope of a ridge thrusting west from Mount Saint Nicholas. The overstuffed sow entered the den on October 24 and emerged April 28. When she pushed through the still enveloping snow, two tiny balls bounced in her wake.

One, a roly-poly male, was of the same hue as his mother's legs. The second, a female, was cut from the same blond cloth as mom. Chocolate Legs had nuzzled each of the cubs in the blackness of their den, licking them clean even while she was groggy with sleep.

The expanse of snow, at den level, was still soft. Though the two light-as-fluff cubs could walk or trot on top, their mother broke through with every step. It made no difference that she floundered, however, for the mother bruin knew exactly where she wanted to go. Around and down the mountain the family traveled, with Chocolate Legs moving more cautiously and far more slowly than if she'd been alone.

As the little cavalcade descended from the heights, she discovered lower-slope cycles of freezing and thawing had been more dramatic and the crust thicker. Soon even the mother could walk atop the snowy expanse. By the time the family reached the Boundary Trail on Muir Creek, bare ground was beginning to peek through the white blanket. And by the time Chocolate Legs led her two footballs-with-legs over the low divide and dropped into Park Creek, snow lay only in patches.

Mom carried her cubs across stream after stream, with one wailing plaintively on one shore and one on the other as Chocolate Legs plied the waters between. She helped them over logs and broke through snowbanks that proved intractable to her babies. Progress was excruciatingly slow because a mother's love and concern was shamelessly exploited by the siblings.

Throughout their journey, Chocolate Legs supplied the cubs with nourishment as well as love and care, but she was on scant rations: a little sedge from the Park Creek bottoms, a little skunk cabbage from a brief detour down Ole Creek. She didn't care, however, because it was only her cubs that she worried about and cared for. And God help the creature that tried to come between them—like the grizzled male *Ursus arctos horribilis* in Ole Creek who soon learned he wasn't nearly so horrible when he inadvertently blundered into a meadow where a blond female lay on her back nursing her babies.

One minute the boar stood hesitantly in the sunshine, the next, cubs went flying and squealing as an enraged sow exploded from the short grass and bore down upon him, head swinging, teeth clacking, mouth slobbering. The bewildered male had no chance. He'd already spun about when Chocolate Legs barreled into him at express speed, rolling the grizzled newcomer and taking great bites of fur from his flanks and rear.

Not once did the much larger boar defend himself. His only thought was flight—dignity be damned! So he scrambled while the devil of a blond female rolled atop him, snarling and biting and clawing as dust and grass and twigs flew. Then he was free, streaking for the woods. The blond devil let him go, returning to the patch of grass where her cubs trembled and whined in tandem, frightened witless by a fury they'd never seen, nor understood.

She licked them each from head to toe, then sprawled so the youngsters could scramble up her furry side to reach her teats. Then the sow leaned her head against an anthill and closed her eyes to the sweet ecstasy of their nursing.

By the wee morning hours of May 4, Chocolate Legs jumped the claim of a black bear sow who mined fermenting corn alongside Burlington Northern's mainline tracks. One moment peace reigned between the two blacks and two grizzlies working the corn spill. Then the newcomer strode into the scene, trailed by her cubs, upsetting the trackside harmony.

Chocolate Legs didn't intentionally upset the corn spill's ursid order. But she was hungry. She was also tired. And most of all, she was crankily protective of the most precious things in life; the ones bobbing along in her wake. When she emerged from the forest and stalked along the tracks with head swinging low and eyes locking first on one bear, then another, each of the grizzlies, both younger, paused and looked away, exposing their throats. The blacks simply poised to flee. She chose the black sow's claim because a richer aroma seemed to emanate from it.

The two cubs, growing quickly in both size and curiosity, pushed into their mother's hole, nosing the sweet-smelling, swollen kernels of corn. They licked at the grain; the male, taking a page from his mother's book, even tried to eat some, tiny baby teeth worrying at a kernel, growling fiercely. At last the cubs sat off to one side and whimpered.

Their mother busied tanking up on the first decent meal she'd had since the previous October, paying the cubs no mind.

Then the ground began to vibrate and the two cubs' whimpers turned even more plaintive. Both cubs crowded trembling beneath their mother's belly, but Chocolate Legs never glanced up as the engine approached, its single searching eye switching relentlessly side to side in the darkness.

In time, the train passed and the cubs crept from their mother's fold. She continued to eat.

By daylight, Chocolate Legs was beginning to fill. She'd also became testy with her cubs and positively belligerent toward other bears working along the railroad grade. It was another sow, this one trailed by a year-old cub, that brought Chocolate Legs' belligerence to bay.

The blond bear had at last filled her stomach and taken leave for a daybed barely into the forest fringe. She exploded once from her bed to put the run on a passing cinnamon black and stood ready to do so again when a dark grizzly with silver hump and shoulders and trailed by a look-alike year-old cub innocently emerged along the uphill track and ambled toward Chocolate Legs' feeding station.

Once again, the blond bear burst from her daybed and caromed into the railroad right-of-way in an angered charge. But the other sow, an older, larger beast, spun in an instant and launched her own charge. The two bears collided amid snarling and slobbering and gnashing of teeth. Hide and fur flew as they rolled together. Then the dark sow's year-old cub spotted Chocolate Legs' two offspring standing fearfully at the forest edge and galloped toward them. Chocolate Legs tore away from her own life-and-death struggle to streak after the young bear she thought threatened her offspring. It took the dark sow only a moment to careen after.

The yearling cub saw blond death hurtling toward him and galloped, circling away. With the death of her cubs averted, Chocolate Legs wheeled to defend against the oncoming sow.

That mother, however, who'd begun pursuit in order to protect her offspring, cut across the circle the yearling was making, then turned to take a defensive position against another unwarranted attack from the temperamental blond beast with chocolate-colored legs.

With both females halted, poised to re-engage, the yearling cub stopped in mid-flight and squatted on his haunches to observe. Meanwhile, Chocolate Legs' two cubs continued to perch like curious kittens at the forest edge, fascinated by the most exciting few minutes they'd yet been privileged to observe.

Chocolate Legs, bleeding from an ear and her snout, lowered her head toward the other sow and began slobbering, pawing at the ground. The other sow flattened her ears and hopped up and down, all the while clacking her teeth. Then the dark sow ceased hopping and popping, raised her ears, gathered up her yearling cub and limped off downtrack, directly passing over Chocolate Legs' mining claim—just as she had been doing when the blond bear's unprovoked attack occurred.

For her part, Chocolate Legs turned her head as the other sow and her cub passed, observing more appropriate "thou shalt not see" manners.

And two hours later, when an ebony male of the *Ursus americanus* persuasion passed innocently through Chocolate Legs' corn claim, the golden bear merely yawned and returned her massive head to dark paws.

The only real casualty during the grizzlies' brief clash was a plastic tag ripped from the blond bear's ear. The tag was stamped "251" and identified the wearer as the bear Chocolate Legs, a "problem" bruin originally relocated seven years before as a subadult from Many Glacier to the headwaters of Pinchot Creek.

The only other result of the sow's battle was that a Fish, Wildlife & Parks biologist who'd been monitoring bear activities at the grain spill from a far-off mountain, swallowed his snoose and was still excited when he returned home at midnight. Switching on the bedside lamp, he shook his wife gently and said, "This won't wait for morning."

When her eyes widened in alarm, the bearded man grinned. "It's nothing bad, honey, so don't worry. But you'll never guess what I saw today...."

22

Accessing Nutritional Needs

It was during a full moon, in the middle of June, amid what was setting up to be another hot, dry summer. A dark brown grizzly cub of the year bounded around a Nyack Creek Trail bend, followed by a blond female sibling. The male darted behind a three-foot spruce, then pounced out as his sister passed. Chocolate Legs hoved into view as the two wrestled. She paused, eyeing the whirling cubs, then sprawled on her side and gave a low moan.

The cubs galloped back, shoved their way into the hair on her breast, found themselves a nipple each, and began suckling like there would be no tomorrow. Chocolate Legs licked each of her offspring from stem to stern, then lay back and savored the ecstasy of the moment.

Later, when the cubs had topped off their tank, the family moved away, this time with mom in the lead and cubs dutifully trailing behind. Within minutes, the three bears strode past the patrol cabin near the juncture of Pacific and Nyack creeks. The male cub wandered away to explore the cabin and Chocolate Legs called him back with a low murmur. The cub paused, glanced back, then trotted on toward the cabin.

In an instant, Chocolate Legs spun toward him, bowling over the female cub in the process. The dark cub squealed in terror, then bawled in pain when she slapped a mighty blow to his rump, sending him sprawling.

Inside the cabin, an exhausted member of a Park Service trail crew, a freshman college student from Boston, sat up suddenly in her sleeping bag and gasped into the moonlight streaming in from the window, "What was that?"

"Huh? Is that you, Julie?" called a voice from a bunk across the darkened cabin.

"That scream! I definitely heard a scream from outside the cabin."

"Oh for God's sake," groaned a lanky crew member from where his bag was rolled out on the floor.

"I heard something, too," came the muffled voice of another girl who'd scrambled down inside her bag upon the cub's terrified scream."

Silence fell. Snores, beginning softly, then escalating came from the lanky floor-sprawling crew member.

"Bill," the first voice called, "aren't you going to do something?"

"Aye," called the deep voice from across the room. "I'm going to sleep."

"I mean about the scream?"

"Go to sleep, Julie."

"How can I?"

"Then let the rest of us go to sleep."

While the exchange took place in the cabin, the dark cub returned squirming on his belly to his mother's feet, where he lay fawning with all four paws waving in the air, begging forgiveness.

Chocolate Legs had, of course, known of the trail crew, sensing their presence in the cabin long before she'd entered its clearing. Though she herself had no particular fear of humans, she thought it wise to instill a modicum of caution in her cubs about approaching the unpredictable two-legged creatures.

"Paul ..." a tremulous voice began.

The snoring stopped abruptly. "Go look for yourself," the lanky man on the floor said. The snoring started again.

Meanwhile, Chocolate Legs led her little troop into the forest. By dawn they were feeding on sedge at Nyack Lakes. And by the time the first trail crew member stumbled from the patrol cabin into the morning sun, having held off on his bladder as long as possible, the bears were lying among lodgepole pines, two hundred yards from the upper lake.

"Grizzly tracks outside," Paul said as he ducked his head to enter the cabin. "Female with a cub. Looks to me like they were right up to the door."

"I want to see," Julie cried, pushing the man back through the door. The second girl crowded behind, followed by the trail boss wiping his hands on a towel.

Both girls oohed and awed at sight of the dusty tracks for a moment, then raced each other for the outhouse, across the trail from the cabin.

There is no plant as widespread and prevalent in all the Northern Rockies as beargrass. Beargrass is also called basket-grass in some locales, squawgrass in others. All are misnomers for the plant is *not* a grass, but a member of the lily family.

There are several oddities about beargrass, the principal being that individual plants only bloom once every half-dozen years. This constitutes no real genetic problem for the plant because its distribution is so widespread that even in down-cycle flowering years there's enough blossoms to spread seeds for regeneration. But occasionally—about once every six years—every beargrass plant on a mountainside seems to blossom at the same time.

Once, hiking partner Doug Chestnut stood on a trail to Huckleberry Lookout and surveyed entire mountainsides white with flowering beargrass. He pulled off his cap and said reverently, "It ... it makes you want to stand up and applaud!"

I nodded, knowing how he felt.

"But to whom?" he added.

When beargrass blooms, what appears to be one large conical-shaped flower are actually racemes of tiny individual blossoms at the end of tall slender stems. I've counted up to 350 individual blossoms clustered into one beargrass flower. Each blossom matures into a seed the size of an unpopped popcorn kernel. In the fall, chipmunks—and pine squirrels to some degree—spend a great deal of time harvesting those seed pods.

It's amusing to round a trail bend and spot a beargrass stalk waving in the distance as a chipmunk clambers atop it, stuffing cheeks with seeds—almost like a pole vaulter waving in uncertainty at the top of his leap. By autumn, the three-foot-tall stalks are dried into buckskin tan, and are so brittle they can be broken with little more than a snap of a finger.

At the base of the stalk is a spreading tussock of long grass-appearing leaves that are tough and sharp enough to cut the finger of one trying to pull it. The flowers and immature seed pods are often nipped from the stalk by elk and moose and sometimes deer, and they are a preferred food for mountain goats. Despite the plant's popular name, bears utilize it but very little, with the exception that they sometimes graze on the white succulent leaf base in the spring.

The third week of June is still spring at some levels and on some slopes in the Northern Rockies. And feasting on white, just-sprouting leaves of beargrass tussocks was precisely what Chocolate Legs was doing on the steep slope west of Oldman Lake. To bears, however, beargrass offers more bulk than taste. The blond sow soon led her two cubs out of the Oldman Basin, down Dry Fork Creek to the Park entrance highway to Two Medicine Lake and the facilities located there. Several times, the protective mother led her cubs off the trail when they were approached by hikers.

The cubs, now the size of cocker spaniels and twice as pugnacious, took their cue, hiding behind their mother's legs while she peered through tree branches or willow brush at the passing, bell-tinkling humans.

It was three o'clock in the morning when Chocolate Legs and her cubs struck the macadam road. There was virtually no traffic, so she led her charges up the highway to the Scenic Point Trail. There the golden bear hesitated, weighing the country she'd discovered during her precipitous cracker-shelled flight of eighteen months before against the slumbering campground below. She turned toward Appistoki Falls and the giant, open, U-shaped basin beyond.

The family spent a week digging lomatium roots in Appistoki Basin and a second week tilling the sidehill to Scenic Point for marmots and ground squirrels.

The trail to Scenic Point is one of the more popular ones leading from the Two Medicine country. In addition, the area was swept by intense wildfire decades ago and is largely devoid of forest and underbrush, especially at its upper reaches. As a result, the blond sow and her two cubs, though never feeding near the trail, were usually within easy view of hikers equipped with binoculars or spotting scopes. They turned into show stoppers.

Chocolate Legs knew of the people, of course. She knew when the two photographers approached. She knew when the Park Ranger ran toward them waving and shouting. She knew when their argument ensued. And she welcomed the photographer's and ranger's retreat. But, though she constantly fretted over her cubs, the blond bruin never felt them threatened and so, gradually became more and more accustomed to people.

Other bears were something else, however, as her cubs—especially the dark-colored male—began wandering farther and farther from his mother's side. Instinctively, Chocolate Legs knew older male grizzlies were short tempered and could be inclined to make short work of a bear cub who might inadvertently ignite that fuse.

The troubled mother also remembered how she'd battled with another grizzly sow anxious for her own cub and how the tiny waifs, but days out of the den, had almost wound up in the middle of that altercation. That's why, when another grizzly appeared in Appistoki Basin or on Bison Mountain or the trail to Scenic Point, Chocolate Legs led her cubs away from the ursid visitor even if the animal appeared to be merely passing through the countryside. Though the entire Two Medicine Basin is top-notch grizzly bear habitat and the Scenic Point-Appistoki area, in particular, is important spring range, most bruins were, by the second week of July, merely passing through on their way to mountain peaks where army cutworm moths congregate during the insects' summer pursuit of wildflower nectar. Still, bears are bears, and around them Chocolate Legs harbored many fears for her helpless cubs. It was for that reason why she failed to visit the moth-bearing talus on either of her two known moth mountains until after the first of August. Hunger finally drove her to do so.

Chocolate Legs' milk was good and on it, her cubs sprouted like grain-fed hogs. But supplying the hyper cubs with all the milk they could drink drained the mother of energy and weight. Because of her tiny waifs, the blond sow was slow to reach the corn spills. True, she'd received a big boost when she did, but left too soon because of her concern for the welfare of her offspring amid the incessant intermingling with other bears. And as a consequence, her forays down Coal Creek, along the foot of Mount Phillips, and in Nyack Creek had not provided her sufficient sustenance to replenish her depleted body fat.

There's nothing unusual in Chocolate Legs' spring foraging regime—except for the corn. Other bears exit winter dens and continue to lose weight for two to three months until nature sets its table with a bounty of berries and grasses, cones and roots, pods and fruit. Maybe the grain spills were anathema to Burlington Northern, their shippers, and their insurers. But to bears, the spills were a godsend that provided key nourishment at a critical time of year. No wonder bears of all stripes, many from tens of miles away, are known to have visited the spills.

The cornucopias found at mountaintop moth sites, though coming at a different time of year, are equally critical. True, it's not a matter of *immediate* survival for ursids to have access to the enormously enriching moth clusters (as may have been the case with the corn). But the moths appear at a time—beginning in early July and continuing throughout much of August and into September—when the bruins need to begin putting on weight in preparation for the coming hibernation. The feeding frenzy that begins in mid-July is called hyperphagia and is nature's own metabolic process for bears to accumulate body fat. An abundant huckleberry crop can accomplish the same hyperphagic end, as can a summer and autumn filled with less natural ursid pursuits such as cattle rustling and dumpster diving.

As one might suspect, research has verified the importance of cutworm moth bonanzas as particularly important to female grizzlies with cubs. Again quoting from the "Yellowstone Ecosystem Report" by French, French, and Knight:

> *"They [moths] also appear especially important to adult females since each moth-feeding area contained from 1 to 3 distinctive family groups throughout each moth feeding season during this study...."*

O'Brien and Lindzey, in a similar study in the Absaroka Mountains of Wyoming, echoes French and Knight's work by writing that females with cubs "have higher nutritional needs."

Chocolate Legs held out against her need to begin laying on fat throughout the entire month of July and into August. Then she legged it to first one, then the second, moth mountains where the little family group fit right into talus slopes filled with foraging bruins of both *"arctos"* and *"americanus"* persuasion.

23

Railway Disaster

Chocolate Legs' two offspring were the size of Brittany spaniels and as fat as Bhuddas when they entered the den with their mother in late October. In addition, their mother had pretty much recovered her fat reserves, thanks to the restorative properties of thousands of cutworm moths consumed atop two mountains, supplemented by huckleberry banquets along the Two Medicine and in the Nyack and Coal Creek Valleys, and topped off with buffalo berries and mountain ash clusters along the mountainsides leading to the Continental Divide.

Since all three bears immediately fell into a deep slumber, the cubs no longer suckled and thus, were no longer a drain on their mother's reserves. So when spring arrived in 1991 and the bear family pushed through Mount Phillips' still-frozen wastes to reach sunlight, each of the threesome began their new season in top condition.

It was a good thing they did because there was nothing easy about the route Chocolate Legs traveled to reach the corn spills along the Burlington Northern right-of-way: thirty miles across the top of Glacier Park's world while winter still gripped the land. Up Nyack Creek and over the divide to Park Creek; around the upper basin on Park Creek and over a shoulder of Eagle Ribs Mountain to drop into Ole Creek; then down Ole Creek to the Ole Creek-Fielding Trail.

The cubs traveled well as yearlings, however, and unlike Chocolate Legs, were never without the nourishment she carried for them in her mother's breasts. Compared to the arduous journey of the previous spring, when her progeny were but tiny cubs-of-the-year, the family's 1991 odyssey was rapid, considering the route traveled and time of year —four days from den site to corn dig. All in all, the three ursids crossed through two 7,400-

foot passes, dropped into 4,000-foot valleys, plodded open storm-swept ridges, traversed avalanche-prone mountain slopes, forded ice-filled streams, and otherwise ignored any distractions while en route to their spring banquet.

The group arrived on April 27, without having first taken time to chase elk, or graze on greening shoots, or excavate for bulbs and roots on Elk Mountain.

The cubs had, of course, begun experimental foraging the year before, by licking occasional moths on a mountain and by nibbling huckleberries in the Nyack bottoms. And now, by the beginning of their second season, they were entirely ready for supplements to their mother's milk. It was a good thing, too, for, as the cubs mushroomed in size, their demands increased commensurately. And though Chocolate Legs emerged from the den in better condition during the cubs second season, the decline of her own fat reserves became more precipitous as a result of the cubs' increased intake.

As in other years, bears of all stripes and colors came and went from the corn spills. Chocolate Legs filed claim on a likely site abandoned by a black bear family upon the grizzlies' approach. The site contained a plentiful corn lode and Chocolate Legs and her hungry offsprings set immediately to work expanding it. They stayed for a week before the tractor again appeared to spread soil and rocks over the exposed holes—most of which were re-opened within hours of the backhoe's fading into the sunset.

Meanwhile, trains came and trains went. Early each morning a short, fast Amtrak passenger service sped up the grade, heading east. The same rapid transit express whistled west, heading down-track, usually around sundown. In between, huge freights lumbered both directions, their speed usually affected by direction, train length, and extent of loads carried. Occasionally, helper engines were deadheaded back to Whitefish where they would, as needed, be tacked on to loaded freights needing a boost over the summit of the Rockies. All in all, their rumble became routine.

Of the two cubs, the male was the feisty, venturesome one. He was also considerably larger than his sister, topping her by two inches and ten pounds. He began the family's 1991 corn sojourn by pausing in his foraging to eye other bears traveling to-and-fro. Several times he ventured out to greet newcomers only to be warned back by his mother's throaty growl. Twice, she had to intervene when other bruins resented approaches by the mahogany cub sufficiently to put the run on him. Several times, she soundly thrashed her wayward cub—enough so to bring him whimpering and squirming on his belly in remorse.

Weeks passed. Two. Three. It was a clear evening with a sky full of stars and the hint of a rising moon just glistening over the eastern horizon—the kind of night that makes man and beast feel they live less on the land than in the sky. A gentle breeze had turned to humming a lonesome note.

Chocolate Legs led her charges to their claim, ousting a poacher—an old, scraggly coated female silvertip nearing the end of a long life. The single bruin watched the family approach, then stalked off across the tracks, deciding it was time to get on with her life.

Chocolate Legs and her look-alike daughter began digging and feeding immediately, but the mahogany cub stood as a statue, peering after the shaggy old bear. Then he trotted across the steel and stood on the embankment on the far side, again staring after. At last he trotted down the embankment and into the forest, following a game trail the old sow had taken.

He heard his mother's angry cry and hesitated, then turned and galloped back. Only then did he take note of the unwinking, searching, side-to-side eye of the oncoming helpers speeding on their way back to Whitefish. Only then did he take note of the roadbed vibration and the low murmur of the coasting engines. Only then did he comprehend his mother's urgency and the danger posed.

Comprehension came too late. One minute the mahogany cub trotted curiously after the unknown sow, the next he was mangled bits of bloody pulp, ripped-up hide and dirty fur lying between the tracks.

Upon the death of the male cub, mother and daughter, already close, became inseparable—so much so it seemed as if invisible strands held one within only a few feet of the other. With milk consumption reduced by half, Chocolate Legs lavished her surviving cub with twice her previous allotment until the daughter waddled when she walked. When an especially tasty pocket of lily bulbs was uncovered mom invited the offspring to take the first serving. When she located a squirrel's pine nut cache, mother stood off to the side while daughter cleaned out the pocket. It wasn't even uncommon for the daughter to take a still-squirming marmot from her mother's teeth.

They fished together, slept together, swam together, and stalked up mountainsides together. They crossed the continental spine in early July and foraged on glacier lily bulbs in the high country and cow parsnips in the low country.

Other bears were there in the Two Medicine country, of course. And people. Gradually Chocolate Legs learned to use one against the other. If she foraged in an area where a more dominant bruin also fed, she discovered she and her cub could move more readily from one rich food site to another without attracting the larger bear's attention if humans chanced to be passing on trails in the vicinity. Conversely, if an intimidatingly large party of humans happened to approach her and her cub's location, security could be had by finagling her movements until other bears foraged or bedded between her and her cub and the advancing group of people. It was easy, once the inevitable mutual discovery between bears and people was made, for Chocolate Legs to slip away through the forest to a more isolated place.

More than once, amid the ensuing tumult, Chocolate Legs and her cub found themselves alone by simply remaining in placc.

And there was always their Sinopah Mountain sanctuary; the retreat where the two blond bruins with distinctively colored legs could find tranquil solitude.

Chocolate Legs made important discoveries during 1991. The first was the most important moth site on the east side of Glacier National Park—and it had been right under her nose all the time.

Rising Wolf Mountain dominates the valley of the Two Medicine. The mountain—well—*rises* nearly 4,500 feet immediately north of Two Medicine Lake. In excess of 9,500 feet in elevation, it's the highest peak in the southeastern section of Glacier and always rears in photogenic readiness for every camper, Sunday driver, and tour boat passenger in the valley.

Montane forest covers the lower one-quarter of Rising Wolf, fading to scrub, grassland, and finally alpine. Mostly, though, from a distance the mountain gives the illusion of barren rock.

First impression is indeed that the mountain's texture is red; and why not, the top half of Rising Wolf is composed of a very ancient, pinkish-colored, sedimentary stone. The mountain actually lies athwart the Lewis Overthrust—America's best known mountain-building thrust fault. In a nutshell, the earth fractured as a result of tectonic plate collision and the western crust slid over the eastern crust. Thus, a portion of younger rock was overlain with the western slab. Then, over the course of millions of years, the younger rock on the overlaying slab wore away, exposing the ancient layers of pinkish-colored stratums over the top of much younger light-textured limestone.

Rising Wolf is a dominant mountain in more ways than height—its breadth, too, is substantial, with additional summits, one of more than 9,000 feet and two well over 8,000.

Chocolate Legs had been on the lower slopes of Rising Wolf several times, usually foraging for bulbs or forbs in the montane, or working along mid-level benches grazing and looking to pick up an occasional ground squirrel or find the carcass of a deer or bighorn or mountain goat killed either accidentally or on purpose.

The golden bear with the distinctive brown legs had even circumnavigated Rising Wolf Mountain, journeying down the Dry Fork from Pitamakan Pass, then following the highway back to roads-end, at the campground. She'd also worked the basins of Old Man and Young Man Lakes. And she was almost on a first-name basis with Bighorn Basin. Oddly, however, she'd never foraged on Rising Wolf in mid-summer.

But during 1991, she led her surviving offspring from Appistoki Basin through the auto campground at the foot of Two Medicine Lake, across the footbridge, and along the lakeshore. It was the end of the third week of July and Chocolate Legs' immediate interest was focused on moth sites of other mountains. But she was pleasantly surprised to find the Two Medicine bottoms generally devoid of other bears. On a whim, she decided to climb the slopes of Rising Wolf Mountain. It was a blisteringly sunny day.

Up, up the bears climbed. They climbed through montane and shrub and onto grassy slopes, up to the ledges and beyond, working their way around cliffs and cols and aretes. Flowers bloomed everywhere: parsley and penstemon, paintbrush and primrose, wild rose and cinquefoil, kinnikinnick and mariposa, larkspur and lupine—perhaps fifty different varieties. Or a hundred. In vast fields of purple or yellow, white or blue.

When Chocolate Legs and her cub reached moth bearing talus atop the mountain, eleven other grizzlies toiled there. Or slept there. Or lounged there. The talus was so rich in moths that merely stepping on a flat stone might send hordes of the winged creatures fluttering from beneath.

The harvest was so rich, Chocolate Legs spent the better part of a week on Rising Wolf, then dropped into the Dry Fork for a little greenery. They worked both directions in the Dry Fork bottoms until Chocolate Legs led her charge to Boy Lake, then back up the ridge to Rising Wolf Mountain and the moth fiesta it contained.

"Some sight, don't you think?" the National Park Service management biologist said as he laid a pair of binoculars alongside his daypack and leaned back against a rock outcrop that sheltered the man and his companion from the keening wind.

The lady biologist-trainee peered through her own binoculars and said, "That blond bear with the dark legs and her cub are certainly beautiful. The wind is rippling her hair. Don't you think she's beautiful?"

"Oh indeed." The man reached for his glasses. "It looks as though she's pretty much in the prime of life. Should have another cub or two with her. But the one she has looks good."

The biologists sat on a high ridge above a talus slope that seemed filled with bears. The scientist and his student assistant had spent all the previous day hiking up the mountain, establishing a dry camp on a bench 700 feet below the summit. This was their first day unobtrusively observing the big gathering of feeding bears. Thus far they'd counted fourteen different animals, including a single rangy-appearing black bear, and had recorded that each animal spent an average of 4.7 hours per day digging for and feeding on the moths. The feeding times for the dominant adults were morning and evening, about equally divided at two hours each. Less dominant bears—subadults or adult sows without cubs—were more likely to be found on the rockslide during any particular daylight hour when larger bear were absent. Still, the biologist glanced at the tablet on his lap, the subadults averaged less than five feeding hours per day themselves. It all added up to a tremendous abundance of the bears' highest quality food.

"Don't you wish we could stay here until the bears all leave?" the trainee murmured.

"Washington calls," the management biologist said, again lifting his glasses.

"Still ..." the trainee began.

"If they didn't, West Glacier would. And if West Glacier didn't, Saint Mary—hey! Isn't that a new one?"

The trainee glanced to see where the biologist focused. It looked like a big male, almost too dark for a grizzly. The biologist snatched up his radio receiver and twisted the dials. He was rewarded by a steady, high-octave pulse. "Where you been, guy?" the biologist murmured. "I thought we'd lost you."

"Who is it?" the trainee whispered.

"Two-eleven. He's been out of contact all spring. I was afraid he was lost. Or else his collar was lost where we couldn't pick up the pulse."

"Look at the other bears scatter!"

"He's hungry. Look at how gaunt he is. What in God's name has he been up to?"

The newcomer upset the established regimen and considerable social tolerance previously common to the cutworms' talus slope. To begin with, the big dark-chocolate male worked all parts of the rockslide eight, ten, even twelve hours per day. And woe betide the innocent who intruded anywhere within fifty yards of the big bear.

Warnings were usually sufficient—flattened ears and a lowered head. If the intruder persisted in digging within what the big boar considered his domain, the beast clacked his jaws and began swinging his head and slobbering. If the intruder still failed to heed the warning, the big boar invariably launched into a full-fledged charge.

Not once, however, did the cantankerous animal catch the offender. Nor did he ever establish a territory near two other large boars who, while more placid, might also prove more resentful.

Several bears, already well-fed from their weeks on the slope, wandered away to seek less stressful pastures. And gradually, as the big dark grizzly stilled his hunger and began adding much-needed fat for the coming winter, the lines of his personal territory shrunk. Eventually, harmony again reigned on Rising Wolf and many of the departed bears returned to the feast.

Chocolate Legs and her growing cub stuck it out for eleven days on their second foray to Rising Wolf Mountain's moth talus, until it seemed they could hold not one more moth. Then they wandered back to the Two Medicine bottoms for salad and berries.

It was the taste of berries that sent the two blond bruins back over the Continental Divide, into Nyack and Coal creeks. Those western berries took the bears into September. September took them to the spawning bull trout at the Coal Creek log jam. And the superb taste of bull trout led them back to closer scrutiny of Nyack Creek and the fabulous discovery that the larger creek harbored an even larger spawning run below the giant falls.

After developing an insatiable taste and running amuck through Coal Creek's and Nyack Creek's bull trout redds, the two golden ursids again moved across the Continental Crest and wound up on Scenic Point shortly into October.

It was in the foothills southeast of Scenic Point when Chocolate Legs made her second monumental acquaintance of the summer of 1991—*Canis lupus*, the gray wolf....

24

End of an Era—Cornucopic Disaster

Both were, after all, wild animals.

Strike that. These were the *wildest* of wild animals.

The wolf simply stood as a glacier-borne boulder might perch—in a lush, naturally sub-irrigated meadow just inside Glacier National Park's eastern boundary. The meadow was but eight miles from East Glacier, and the mammoth lodge and golf course located there. Volunteer timothy, originally introduced through the droppings of concessionaire saddlehorses straddled by dudes from Minneapolis, Mobile, Manchester, and Munich, grew in the meadow. The lush timothy stood nearly three feet high, with ripened heads waving in a gentle down-slope breeze.

To a casual observer, only the wolf's ears thrust above the meadow grass. But it was the eyes—if one knew precisely where to look—that were most unforgettable. Not a muscle moved as the animal stared fixedly up the hill to the meadow's edge. Within the forest fringe, there'd been the suggestion of movement. Then a golden grizzly and her look-alike yearling ambled into the open, only fifty yards from the wolf.

Just then, as sometimes happens in the mountains at break of day, the breeze shifted. The larger bear in the lead stopped abruptly, as if she'd run into a glass wall. She lifted her snout to the wind, then reared on hind legs to peer in the direction from whence the unidentified odor had come. From the vantage of added height, Chocolate Legs spotted the ears immediately (bears are not nearly so blind as humans sometimes credit them) and stood for several minutes peering at the wolf's grass-shadowed outline. Then her cub whined from behind and the sow dropped back to all fours, continuing to peer in the wolf's direction as a rising sun gradually poured light over mountain peaks, then mountain ridges, then foothills, finally creeping onto the aspens at the grizzlies' rear and, at last, the bears themselves. The wolf was still rooted in shadow.

Shadow suited him (it was a "him"). He was dark, this wolf, though not as dark as an ebony black bear—more like sooty black; as if someone had knocked over a clogged stovepipe as he trotted past; a sort of dusty black-all-over, from perked-up ears to long, furry, half-mast tail.

Except for the eyes.

The wolf's eyes might best be described as burning, yellow half-moons, staring unblinking from out of the shadowed timothy.

The dark wolf's white mate pushed to its feet at the far forest edge and began scratching, throwing dirt and twigs and grass clumps beneath its belly. Even then, Chocolate Legs continued to study the black wolf and weigh options.

True, she'd never before smelled a wolf. But she'd seen dogs. True, they'd always been on a leash and these ran free. True, the leashed dogs had tried to hide upon her approach and these creatures seemed to harbor no particular fear of the grizzlies.

But, then, neither did she fear the newcomers. Still, there was something unsettling about those unblinking yellow eyes.

Forty-five minutes passed and the sun continued its inexorable rise and the shadow's edge retreated until the black wolf stood exposed in sunlight. Then the white wolf trotted into the trees.

Chocolate Legs swung her head to glance back at her daughter, then returned beady black orbs to peer into the shining half-moons of the wolf. The leathery black nose at the end of her snout, guidance system to one of nature's wrecking machines, continued to wrinkle and pulse. Beneath the nose, a rose-pink tongue hovered within the bear's half-opened mouth. At last, the sow made a decision and she lumbered on into the meadow. Her cub followed.

The black wolf had not moved since the incident began over an hour before and he continued to hold his ground even as the sow advanced. When she reached twenty feet, however, he suddenly spun and trotted away, following the white wolf into the aspen forest.

Chocolate Legs never paused where the wolf had been, lumbering straight through the place and through the meadow as if the other animal never existed. She stopped, however, before reaching the aspens and began grazing. Ten minutes later, she'd grazed back to where the wolf had stood. There she spent several minutes sniffing, filling her nose with the unusual scent. For some unknown reason, a vague unease stole over her.

It's not surprising that Chocolate Legs had no experience with gray wolves prior to reaching maturity. *Canis lupus* only began repopulating the western fringe of Glacier Park in the early 1970s, immigrating down from Canada. Eventually, thanks to protection afforded by the Endangered Species Act, the animals prospered, finally splitting into three different packs that worked the Flathead's North Fork River valley.

Dispersal of individual animals also continued and by the late 1980s a pack was reported along the eastern boundary of Glacier Park. By 1991, ranchers on the Blackfeet Reservation were losing cattle to wolves and members of the pack were reported as far south as East Glacier. It was *Canis lupus* from this band that faced off with Chocolate Legs in the timothy meadow south of Lower Two Medicine Lake.

Chocolate Legs and her surviving cub visited the corn spills the following spring. The daughter was, at age two, only a few inches shorter than her mother, and weighed but a hundred pounds less. Throughout their 1992 spring tour, neither of the golden bruins spent more time near the steel rails than was needed to cross where the male cub had died the previous spring.

Days ticked past. The bears wandered from the corn spill into the mountain fastness to the north. Not only were days ticking by, but so was their biological clocks. One day a blocky male bear of the color of rusty nails strode purposely from the forest surrounding Nyack Lakes and took Chocolate Legs under advisement.

As the two bears wandered away, Chocolate Legs' daughter tried to follow, only to have her mother, for no apparent reason, turn savagely upon her, sending her running away in bewilderment.

The following spring, Chocolate Legs emerged from her den with one blond and two rust-colored cubs.

The new cubs were all females. All three were of shy temperament. But it turned out that the tiny blond wasn't sufficiently robust to survive in a grizzly world and thus expired on the family's odyssey from den to grain spills. Chocolate Legs loitered nearby for a day, then left her dead baby to resume the journey.

It was a ravenous mother with two bewildered little tagalongs that strode confidently out onto Burlington Northern's mainline right-of-way on Friday afternoon, April 23, 1993. The smorgasbord was a beehive of activity—and none of the bees were grizzly bears!

"In the winter of 1988 and 1989," according to a report prepared for Burlington Northern Railroad by KRW Consulting, Inc. of Lakewood, Colorado, "three separate train derailments occurred on Burlington Northern (BN) tracks located along the southern boundary of Glacier National Park in northwest Montana ... These derailments spilled loose corn along BN's railroad right-of-way. Salvage and clean-up efforts performed during the Spring and Summer of 1989 removed the majority of the spilled corn; however, unusable corn or corn that was difficult to access or remove was buried with soil."

The report stated that smaller spills occurred in this same area prior to 1988. But what wasn't clear at the outset of the *PROJECT SUMMARY REPORT - Corn Spill Clean-Up Activities South of Glacier National Park Near Essex, Montana* was just how extensive the spills were. Careful scrutiny of the report disclosed that the spills scattered corn over a total of four miles of track and were concentrated within two. Along those four miles, buried, fermenting corn was discovered in ten sites covering a total surface area of just over five acres.

"During the Summer of 1992," the report continues, "it became apparent to BN and State and Federal officials that this buried corn provided an ongoing food source for Black Bears and Grizzly Bears in this area. In the Fall of 1992, a decision was made by Burlington Northern Railroad to excavate and remove the buried corn from the various spill site areas and thus remove the bear attractant or food source from the area."

Not entirely clear within the report was the fact grizzly bears were dying; so many in fact that some biologists were quoted claiming Burlington Northern Railway trains as the greatest "single source of grizzly mortality in the Bob Marshall-Glacier Park area." The corn spill cleanup was the result of an agreement (which, in turn, was due to biologist Shawn Riley's research work) between Montana's Department of Fish, Wildlife & Parks and Burlington Northern Railroad to clean up the transportation company's act.

Another point not mentioned in the report was that Burlington Northern may have been influenced by their commitment to corn removal by the fact that two environmental groups—the National Wildlife Federation and the Great Bear Foundation—filed litigation in U.S. District Court, under provisions of the Endangered Species Act. The environmental groups sought to force Burlington Northern Railroad to alter its train operations along the southern boundary of Glacier National Park to keep from killing more grizzly bears.

Once a decision was made to remove the buried corn, mobilization took place immediately. Each of the ten problem corn sites was identified, surveyed, staked, and mapped. Then the first pieces of heavy equipment was brought in as early as October, 1992.

Winter weather soon brought a halt to excavation and corn removal throughout the winter; but activity commenced in earnest in early April, 1993. Heavy equipment included two Caterpillar 977 track loaders, one Caterpillar 325 track excavator, one Caterpillar D-6 dozer, one Caterpillar 936 rubber-tired loader, one hydro-mulch truck, one water truck, two three-inch trash pumps, several ten-wheel tandem dumps trucks "with or without 'pups'," and several belly dumps.

Work continued throughout daylight hours. The excavated material (corn mixed with gravel and soil) was trucked 100 miles east to the Shelby landfill, well away from occupied bear habitats. Upon removal of contaminated soil, replacement gravel, ballast, and topsoil was hauled in, dumped, graded into place, then seeded to bring the area back as near as possible to its original state.

There can be little doubt the effort was monumental. To provide a better picture of the work performed during corn spills cleanup, consider these numbers:

There were 21,506 cubic yards of corn/soil material removed from the spill areas in just two months time in the spring of 1993. In real terms, that volume translates into one thousand eight hundred and seventy-eight belly dump truckloads weighing 75,000 pounds each, transported a hundred miles to a distant landfill.

Chocolate Legs and her two tiny cubs wandered into the middle of this activity late on the afternoon of April 23, 1993.

The bulk of the excavation work being conducted was near the end of the marshy willow flat, at the place where the golden sow usually did her corn mining. Rain mixed with snow pelted down and men cursed and machines groaned through mud. Chocolate Legs watched from forest cover for a while, then led her babies farther from the tracks and into a willows marsh where she dug cattail roots and monitored the activity on the railroad grade to the north. Finally, after darkness descended and the equipment stopped roaring and the workmen drifted away, the blond sow and two brown cubs ascended to the tracks and began nosing about.

It quickly became apparent that there was no grain at locations where it had previously been plentiful. But where it was plentiful was in the big mounds of corn and debris heaped into huge "staging" piles for loading onto dump trucks the following Monday. Three other bears were already at the staging piles and others were on their way. A wary, jumpy Chocolate Legs joined them.

Had the golden bear with distinctively brown legs not been so drained by her newborn cubs, she might have left the corn and the clanging, raucous, bustle for quieter valleys farther north. But the need for nourishment trumped any inner disquiet at the human activity surrounding her. Besides, the nightly piles of excavated corn ready for next-day loading took away any need for a bear to have to find and dig on her own. But because daylight hours belonged to humans, Chocolate Legs—as did all other grain spill bears—became totally nocturnal in her cereal-driven spring feeding.

At last, Chocolate Legs and her tiny entourage wandered away. Two weeks after she left, the bulldozer took a final swipe

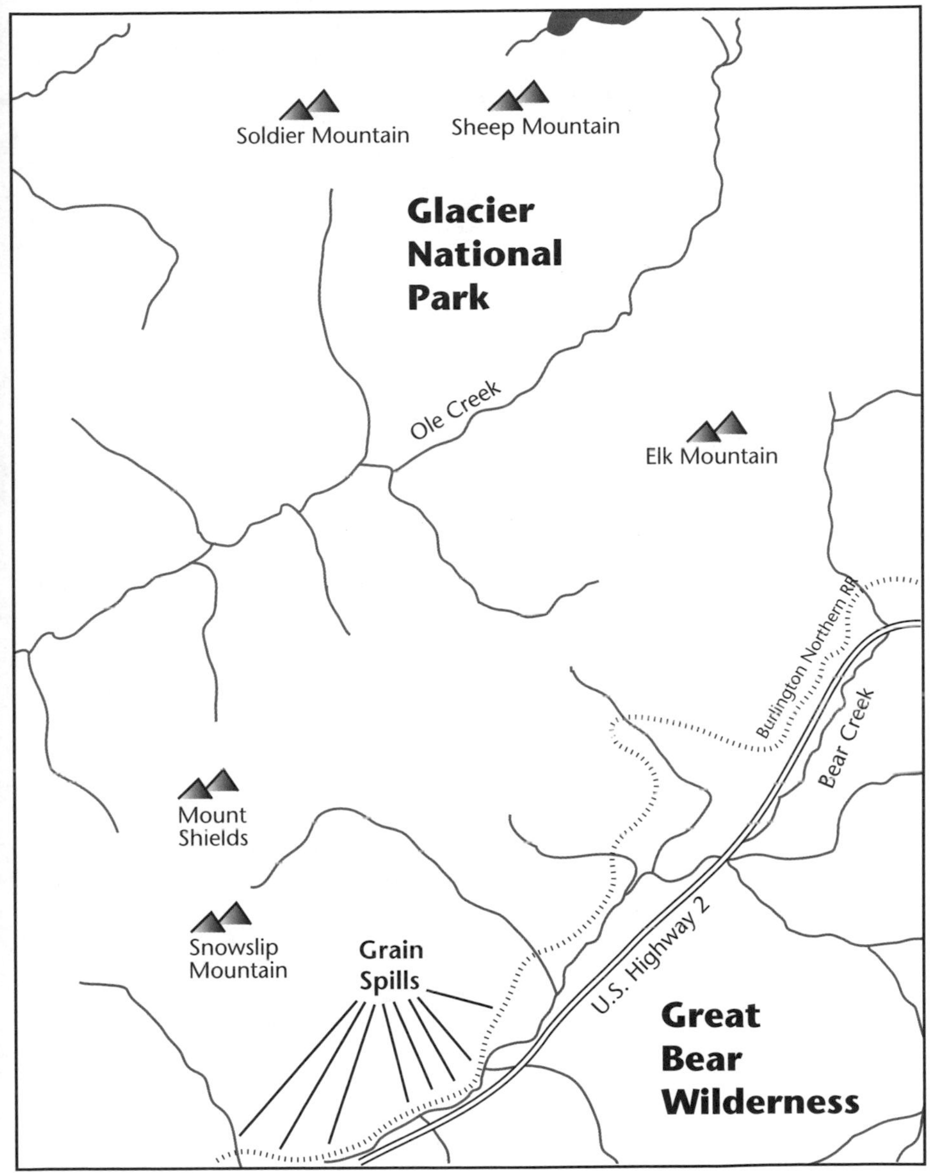

It's a hell of a way to run a railroad—feeding grizzly bears instead of starving multitudes in far off countries. But what cannot be doubted is that, when Burlington Northern committed to cleaning up their mess, they pursued it with evangelical zeal. All in all, BN hauled out 1,878 belly dump truckloads of corn-soil mix, weighing 75,000 pounds each!

**This map and others within these pages were produced in part through a DeLorme (Yarmouth, ME) system that, in turn, used U.S.G.S. quads as their base. Detail–1:50,000*

and the reseeding crew blew the last of their seeds and the last of their mulch into place.

The cycles continued for the bears, however: carrion from avalanche paths on Park Creek and Ole Creek, marmots and ground squirrels along the high country near Dawson Pass and Cut Bank Pass, glacier lilies at Upper Two Medicine. There was sedge grass at Nyack Lakes and cow parsnips at Isabel Lake. The cubs, growing like weeds by now, found the rattle of cutworm moths beneath the talus stones of Rising Wolf Mountain fascinating. And when they turned a stone over, the insects fluttered away, tickling the cubs' tiny noses.

It was at the campground at No Name Lake, in Bighorn Basin, when Chocolate Legs again ransacked a human camp. The target was too easy: food odors wafting from inside the closed tent, no humans in sight. She cased the campground carefully from a patch of nearby brush, deducing that humans had not been in the vicinity for some hours. So, with the assurance of a top-of-the-food-chain creature, she strode directly to the Eureka Timberline and collapsed it by leaning on one of the aluminum struts. It was quick work to open the tent and rifle the food carelessly scattered inside.

Hikers from the camp observed the robbery from atop Pumpelly Pillar. But from that distance they were helpless to do anything to prevent the vandalism. The incident even went unreported by the chastened hiking party since they knew they'd have some explaining to do for not properly hanging their food while absent from camp.

From Bighorn Basin, Chocolate Legs and her two rust-colored offspring moved to the food-rich bottom between Upper Two Medicine and Two Medicine Lakes.

The Two Medicine River is born in Glacier National Park's southeastern corner, then flows through the Blackfeet Indian Reservation to join Birch Creek and Cut Bank Creek to form the Marias River (named by Meriwether Lewis for his cousin, Maria Wood).

The name "Two Medicine" apparently was coined by the Blackfeet to indicate a headwaters region of religious significance (great medicine). It's a name that, along with its basins and cirques and glaciers and mountains and lakes and meadows, captures the imagination of subsequent visitors of most races, creeds, or colors—truly a region of great medicine.

There are anomalies about the Two Medicine headwaters, however, not the least is in the glitter of its central gems. Let's see, the trickle begins at its uppermost with Upper Two Medicine Lake, then flows down valley to Two Medicine Lake.

So far so good, but here the confusion begins.

From Two Medicine Lake, one travels downstream to Lower Two Medicine Lake. Obviously there could and should be a Lower Two Medicine Lake and an Upper Two Medicine Lake, but where does Two Medicine Lake come in? Shouldn't there be an Upper and Lower and Lowerest? Or a Lower and Upper and Uppermost? Or how about an Upper, Middle, and Lower Two Medicines?

To compound the problem, the valley contains yet another lake that is tagged No Name Lake, which may say a lot about the valley's first blue-eyed place-namers.

Across the ridge to the north there's another valley with other place names: Oldman, Pitamakan, Morning Star, and Medicine Grizzly Lakes; Bad Marriage, Kupunkamint, and Eagle Plume Mountains; and Triple Divide Pass. Obviously place names in the Cut Bank Creek drainage never originated from infertile brains of European extract.

Chocolate Legs and her little family made a last end-of-summer foray after Rising Wolf moths. It was mid-September and although individual insects still pursued nectar from the last wildflowers, only a few remnant clusters remained.

Few grizzly bears remained either, so Chocolate Legs felt a higher comfort level about hanging around the mountaintop—and did so for a week. Then the weather soured; wet, heavy snow fell across the land.

The little family fled from the mountain during the storm, picking their way past Sky Lake, down into the drainage of the Dry Fork of the Two Medicine, to a level the snow had not yet reached. From there, Chocolate Legs turned west along the bottom, grazing on sedge and buffalo berries. It was just good daylight when the family ambled out into the middle of a large meadow. The meadow was already occupied....

25

Canis Survival

Circumstances were much the same as before—a wolf immobile amid shoulder-high grass, ears pricked and yellow half-moon eyes glistening. Beyond him, however, two others hovered. Each were silver hued. Each might have been statues.

Chocolate Legs swung her head and saw a cream-colored wolf creeping toward her from the creek. She raised her snout and sniffed. The scent of several of the animals were intermingled on the fitful currents. She reared upon hind feet and spotted two others trotting from a grove of aspens up ahead.

Not even bothering to look behind, Chocolate Legs gave a "huff" and broke toward the cream-colored wolf on her left. Her cubs, well along to spaniel-size bounced after.

The sow saw with a quick glance that wolves were all streaming toward her family—all except the cream-colored *Canis* who crouched across her path, awaiting the rush. Just at the last moment, the cream-colored wolf leaped aside, then back to snap at a cub.

Chocolate Legs spun as the wolf lunged, throwing up great clods of grass and mud. Her pause diverted the wolf and it fled. Meanwhile, the pack was fast closing and she spun once more to gallop for the creek.

Bears are, of course, far more nimble on their feet than is often thought, but they were no match for the wolves. Just as a black wolf neared her trailing cub, an enraged Chocolate Legs whirled to do battle, jaws popping, saliva flinging, ears flat against her skull.

The black wolf leaped back and Chocolate Legs used the moment's respite to gather her cubs beneath her. Then one of the silver wolves closed from the rear and Chocolate Legs whirled. Another wolf grabbed her in the flank and was flung off, taking a mouthful of fur with him.

Around and around the battle raged, wolves darting, Chocolate Legs whirling, her hair and blood flying. Both wolves and bear were snarling and roaring and grunting and yipping. The cubs were rolling underfoot, trampled by the whirling melee above. Then she got in one solid blow, knocking one of her tormentors rolling, while great red welts squirted blood from its side.

The lucky shot brought a second's respite and Chocolate Legs burst through the circle of wolves like a Peterbilt through a picket fence. Somehow her cubs rushed through in her wake, continuing on at their mother's command when she made a feint at their tormenters, causing the onrushing wolves to hesitate, giving the cubs another few yards.

At last, the fleeing family reached a fallen cottonwood and at Chocolate Legs' bawled command, the cubs cowered under the trunk's curve, while she backed against it, facing out at these terrible enemies. There was a momentary lull in the action, then a wolf reached over the log to take a nip from Chocolate Legs' shoulder. She spun and two darted in from the front. A wolf leaped atop the log and she reached for him. Another took a mouthful of fur and hide from her rear. Whirling back, she pinned that one against the log long enough to slash him with her teeth.

A silver wolf began to dig beneath the log and Chocolate Legs made a lunge across the whitened old tree. When she did, one of the other silver wolves darted in and nearly succeeded in dragging a cub from his lair. The mother leaped back and the wolves leaped in and out, and dug furiously, and taunted her.

At her command, the family fought their way down the log to a new position and the wolves finally halted their attacks to reconnoiter, sitting on their haunches, tongues lolling. The two injured wolves lay off to the side licking their wounds. At last, the canids circled the bears and again began creeping forward.

A lunge, a bellow, a snap, a roar. On and on the battle raged. Again the canids dug beneath the log; again Chocolate Legs moved her charges and defended her forefront with unflagging savagery. Again the wolves took great tufts of hair and bits of hide from her exposed back, but was unable to affect any real damage.

The wolves paused to reconnoiter for a second time. After

doing so, the entire pack simply trotted off down the valley in single file.

It was the cubs, of course, who was the real focus of the wolves attention. The chances of even a large wolf pack tackling and killing a full-grown grizzly are virtually nil. In fact, adult grizzly bears—especially males—have been known to take a fresh-killed elk or moose from a wolf pack by the simple expedient of wading in and preempting the carcass. But it's not unknown for wolves, especially a large pack, to isolate a cub long enough to kill it by diverting the mother. And had not Chocolate Legs acted swiftly and courageously, that's precisely what would've happened in this instance.

But it was a bloody and battered mother who, upon the wolves' departure, lay panting near the log that had provided protection for her cubs. Finally a little black-nosed waif crept out, followed by the second. Both cubs were also scarred and bleeding—their flight through the wolf pack and their own ragged defense beneath the log had not been without price. Chocolate Legs licked them both clean before rolling over and inviting them to her nipples.

Later, as she slept, the cubs licked their mother's own wounds until at last her blood stopped seeping. Then they curled against her and slept.

Chocolate Legs wasn't certain the wolves had really departed, or whether they merely waited out of sight until the grizzly family chose to leave the security of their cottonwood fortress. Finally, some eighteen hours after the attack, the blond and blooded mother led her little family from the fallen log to the stream. Upon arrival and upon their mother's instructions, the cubs climbed a standing cottonwood snag while Chocolate Legs bathed in a pool and rolled in a soothing wallow.

Autumn came and autumn went. Snow descended over the northern Rockies. And when spring at last returned, Chocolate Legs and her yearling cubs discovered that their annual Burlington Northern corn banquet was no more.

The lesson might have been especially difficult for Chocolate Legs had she and the cubs, on their return to the Park's

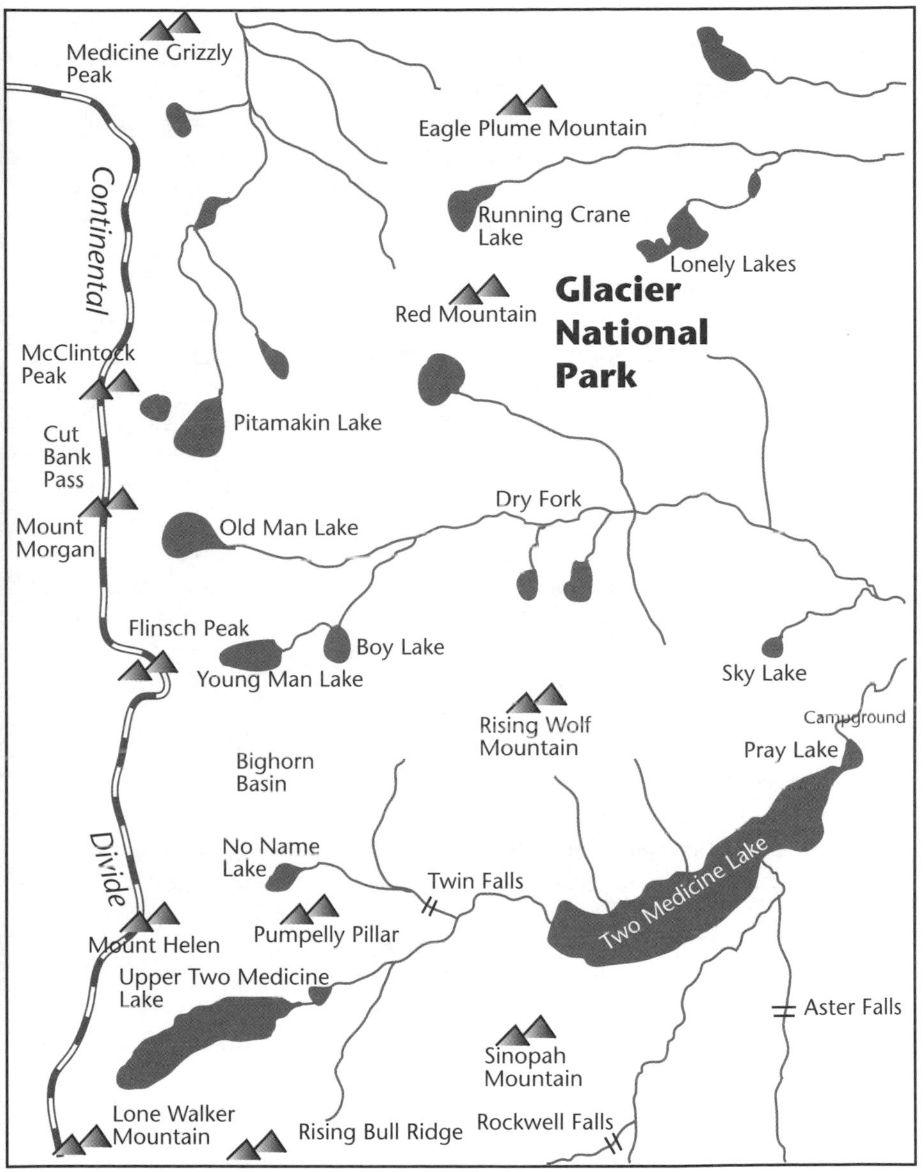

Their names have mesmerizing rings. Pitamakin! Medicine Grizzly! Rising Wolf! Eagle Plume! Running Crane! Bighorn Basin! Makes you want to hike off into the sunset, leaving factories to workaholics and Monday night football to the couch set. Yep, it's a land—a common ground for most gods and a few commoners.

**This map and others within these pages were produced in part through a DeLorme (Yarmouth, ME) system that, in turn, used U.S.G.S. quads as their base. Detail–1:50,000*

interior, not chanced across an Ole Creek avalanche fan just beginning to regurgitate the carcasses of three elk. The elk had been overwhelmed and killed in a huge late-winter snowslide triggered by a collapsing cornice.

A year went by. Then another. The rust-colored cubs were booted from the nest and Chocolate Legs mated with a handsome light-colored boar with a placid disposition and a superb knowledge of food-gathering techniques.

Her fourth litter of cubs, born during January, 1996, were also mother look-alikes, a male and female. By now the blond bear with the distinctively colored legs was solidly into middle age; successful by any bear measure. Her territory lapped over the Continental Divide and included the valley of the Two Medicine to the east and the headwaters of Nyack, Coal, Park, and Ole creeks to the west.

Within this vast territory, few food sources were unknown to the golden bear, few retreats unlocated. But with disappearance of the spring corn she'd once depended on, emerging from hibernation was an unfailing period of high stress. So for the first time, Chocolate Legs led her two tiny rat-sized offspring directly into the Two Medicine country. She was no longer the fussbudget mother of earlier litters. The now veteran mother helped these newest cubs only where and when they needed help, sternly disciplining them when they needed correction.

And, as she backed into ursine middle age, the blond bear with dark legs became more and more pushy around people....

"They were off the trail," the man said, "no more than fifty feet ..."

"Less than that!" the buxom lady with the pageboy cut broke in.

"... So we stopped and I began talking to them."

Her laugh was a nervous cackle, still governed by the event they'd experienced three hours earlier. "You did not! You ran back the way we came."

"You were running, too."

"I never said I wasn't. It's you that said you talked to them!"

"Bears," the ranger prompted "there were more than one?"

"Three," the man said and the woman agreed.

"Color?"

"Blond," they both said simultaneously.

"All three," the woman added.

"And they threatened you?"

"Isn't that what you'd call it?" the man said, squaring his shoulders. "They charged us."

"And what did you do," the ranger asked, scribbling in his notebook.

"Well, let me tell you what he didn't do," the woman said, pointing at her companion. "He didn't talk to them. He passed me and I was running."

"But there was no contact?"

"He didn't *hit* me, if that's what you mean. But I would've sure clobbered him if I could've got my hands on him right then."

The ranger raised an eyebrow at the man, who said, "If you mean did the bears actually come into contact with us," the man said, "no. They stopped at our packs, we think."

"I beg your pardon?"

"Our packs are still up there," the woman said. "We left them where we dropped them and there's no way I'm going back."

Later that afternoon, four hikers stopped at the Two Medicine Ranger Station to report finding two ripped packs near the Dawson Pass/No Name Lake trail junction.

"Wasn't much left inside either pack," the bushy-bearded oldster said. "Few candy wrappers laying around. An empty donut box. A waxed wrapper that looked like it might've had meat in it. We cleaned it up as best we could. Stuffed the sleeping bags into what was left of the backpacks and hung 'em in a tree just to the east of the junction."

"We don't have any idea what happened to the people," one of the suntanned younger men said. "Bear tracks around. Big and little ones. No blood though. I'm guessing somebody abandoned their packs when they spotted a bear. Any report on that?"

The ranger nodded. "We have a report."

Later, a blond bear with two cubs of the year were reported digging for glacier lilies in the campground at Cobalt Lake. The incident occurred in late June.

"I got a little nervous," the ponytailed youth reported to a passing NPS trail crew. "She came right up to my tent and started digging like she owned the place. I wasn't about to tell her any different."

"What did you do then?"

The camper squinted at the trail foreman. "What do you think? What am I supposed to do? I thought about throwing a few rocks and yelling, but then I had another thought and decided not to cause her to notice I was in that tree over yonder."

The trail foreman marked the tree with a glance, then asked, "Did she get into your tent?"

"Yeah, sure. Look at the rip in the side."

"Any food?"

"No way. I had it hung on the pole."

"So she got no food?"

"None," the camper replied.

"How about the cubs? Blond, too, you said?"

"How about them?"

"They didn't get into your food either?"

"You think they can fly? Of course they didn't get into my food. No mama si', no baby si'.

The third rumble of a family of blond bears approaching humans too closely occurred near Twin Falls, only a short distance above Two Medicine Lake. It was a large group of hikers—teenagers from a Presbyterian Church in Great Falls—out for the day. They were a noisy lot broken into small clusters, with girls chattering about boys and boys chattering about girls. Then the decibel level from one cluster elevated enough to attract attention from the others.

Chocolate Legs ignored the screaming clusters as she pushed through a patch of broad-leafed cow parsnip onto the path. Then, followed by her two blond cubs of the year, the golden bruin with brown legs disappeared into the five-foot-tall parsnip across the trail, paying the humans no heed at all.

The advent of cutworm moths may have broken the 1996 cycle of Chocolate Legs' growing indifference toward people. Mountaintops hosted only an occasional person, whereas the valleys were crowded with them. Too, mountaintop humans, taken as a whole, seemed to emit an aura of competence to the mother bear not always exhibited by valley people. Overall, Chocolate Legs found the strange bipeds of all stripes of some interest, but it was with erratic valley people where she sometimes went to find human food.

And it was atop Rising Wolf Mountain where she and her offspring went to find the delicious moths.

Rising Wolf was the Blackfeet name given Hugh Monroe, an early mountain man and trader with the tribe. Monroe homesteaded and ranched near Marias Pass, only a few miles south of the Two Medicine area. The man's knowledge of the rugged land that later became Glacier National Park was unsurpassed by men of European extract.

By 1996, fifteen years into life, Chocolate Legs was solidly middle age. Though not overly large as far as grizzlies go, there was little to be found in nature to intimidate the golden sow. Totally driven by the need for food, by a need to take on, in just six months, sufficient nourishment to sustain her body for twelve; motivated by evolutionary instinct and sharpened with animal senses; guided by experience and tempered by expedience; Chocolate Legs had developed into a nearly perfect ursine machine at the food chain's very pinnacle. With cubs in tow, not even grumpy grizzly boars intimidated her. Thus she moved onto the cutworm-bearing talus of Rising Wolf Mountain without so much as a second glance at other nearby bears.

She'd arrived at last.

26

Devil Incarnate Capture by Carney

The saga of Chocolate Legs now enters the final stage as she once again blips our radar. It's coincidental that the countdown to the end may have begun, and certainly finished, on the same mountain.

Sinopah Mountain rears 8,271 feet to the southwest of Two Medicine Lake and separates the drainages of Paradise Creek and Two Medicine River. Sinopah is Blackfeet for the kit fox. Kit Fox was the name of Hugh Monroe's Blackfeet wife.

Sinopah (or Kit Fox) Mountain, thus stands across Two Medicine Lake from Rising Wolf Mountain, or the mountain named for Hugh Monroe. Dense forests of spruce and pine surround Sinopah on three sides; the open, rocky, windswept Continental Divide butts up against the mountain's western connecting ridge. There is no well-traveled trail to its summit, nor, in fact, no easy route for hikers or climbers. The view from the top, however, once reached, is as good as it gets.

It was reports of the nature of this view that may have attracted Matthew Truszkowski....

Chocolate Legs reappeared on our screen when she and her two yearling look-alikes boldly strode through Red Eagle Campground. The official report, later released, is brief:

> *5/29/97 Female and 1 of 2 yearling cubs were trapped by tribal biologists in a culvert trap at Red Eagle Campground, a private campground 1.5 miles east of the*

park boundary on the Blackfeet Indian Reservation. Bears had been approaching people in the area, licking a barbecue grate, and trying to get into dumpsters, but apparently did not get a food reward. The bears were released on site and hazed from the area. The female was ear-tagged with number 235.

Let's try to bring the picture into sharper focus: The Red Eagle Campground sprawls across a picturesque meadow-and-aspen flat at the outlet end of Lower Two Medicine Lake. Circuitous graveled roads wind through the area and a central playground is fenced with rustic red-painted rails. The campground runs the gamut of diversity from primitive sites without amenities, to numbered individual spaces with barbecue grills and picnic tables, to group locations circling a central gathering place. There are showers and restrooms and garbage dumpsters. Outhouses are scattered through the campground for more immediate comfort. A shaded creek burbles merrily along one side, the Two Medicine River on the other.

It was through this campground that Chocolate Legs and her two yearling cubs wandered on the afternoon of May 28, a Thursday.

Grizzly bears and black bears are not *that* rare to the Red Eagle Campground—after all, it snuggles against the eastern boundary to Glacier National Park, located in some of the best spring and fall bear habitats along the Rocky Mountain Front, where the central plains collide with the main continental spine. But always before, the bears were midnight dumpster divers, or late-movers surprised by the advent of another sunrise.

The blond bear with the distinctively dark legs and her look-alike offspring were different. They ignored shouts and pans banging and horns blaring. They ignored campers hurriedly jerking meals from picnic tables and parents gathering toddlers from their path. They explored empty spaces, nosed around occupied places, licked barbecue grills and ambled on their way.

An hour later they were back, unhurried, unfrightened, *unnatural*. Tribal wardens were called and Dan Carney, Blackfeet biologist, was alerted. Carney hazed the animals from the campground using cracker shells and rubber bullets.

The bears returned.

Carney wheeled in two culvert traps and baited them with

his most fetid road-killed deer. That evening he got strikes in both traps—Chocolate Legs in one and her male cub in the other. When he returned to the campground, the biologist found the female cub hanging in the vicinity. Both Chocolate Legs and her incarcerated cub raged in their cages, exploding upon human approach. Carney prepared his injections with drug dosage based on estimates of each bear's weight. Then using syringes on the end of a long stick, the biologist maneuvered until he could jab first one, then the other in the rump.

Within minutes, the bears were unconscious. Working swiftly, the biologist, keeping a constant eye on the yearling female cub who paced nearby, estimated age and weighed Chocolate Legs (14 yrs. 220 lbs.), fitted her with a radio transmitter collar (freq. 4.535) and placed tags in each ear (right 235, left 236). The male cub weighed half as much as his mother (110 lbs.) and was fitted with ear tags numbering 238 and 239.

Carney, realizing that new techniques in DNA testing might someday be important in identifying individual animals, had routinely been taking hair samples from each grizzly bear he handled. Thus samples were pulled from Chocolate Legs and her male cub to provide hair follicle roots for analysis.

Not wishing to break up the family group, Carney decided to release the bears on-site. He swiftly finished his work, then, while the recumbent bears sprawled just north of the campground, waited for the Telazol to wear off.

Within minutes the wobbly cub pushed to his feet. Chocolate Legs lifted her head, then flopped back to the ground. Another minute. Two. Suddenly she popped to her feet and the entire family streamed up the road, across the meadow, and into the aspens.

And she never returned to Red Eagle Campground.

Dan Carney also trapped a second blond grizzly with two yearling cubs that spring of 1997. Unlike Chocolate Legs, the second grizzly family had little known interest in campgrounds. But the mother seemed to be taking an unhealthy aptitude for the same mountain pastures where Herefords and angus grazed, along the Park's eastern border. The capture took place just twelve days after—and five miles from—where Chocolate Legs was released. This second blond sow was also drugged, weighed, aged, ear-tagged (240 and 241), fitted with a radio collar, and released on site. As did Chocolate Legs and her cubs, Number 240 and her offspring fled the abysmal treatment accorded them by the Blackfeet biologist.

The result of Chocolate Legs' capture was the middle-aged mother was now fitted with a location monitoring device—a device soon to come in handy.

The ranger who squatted miserably under a tree, waiting out a rainstorm wasn't equipped with a transceiver, however. His tree was along the Paradise Point Trail. It was 7:30 pm on the last day of May. Suddenly he spied a blond cub bounding toward him. Alarmed, he shouted. A blond sow loomed from the brush, approached and, according to the official report, "barked" before leaving.

Another park service employee observed a blond adult and two blond yearling grizzlies during the same evening and in the same vicinity. The bears were at the Scenic Point Trailhead at 9:30 pm.

Chocolate Legs and her cubs were still in the vicinity three days later, radio-tracked to a point between Paradise Creek and Aster Creek. The Glacier Park report states, "...bears were trying to cross road into picnic/campground area."

Apparently they made it because the next day, according to the report:

> *Bears (tracked by telemetry) skirted Two Medicine Campground and tried to cross stream near footbridge; Karelian bear dogs used to encourage bears to move out of campground at 8:00 am. At 11:30 am, NPS employee used cracker shells to chase bears from campground across footbridge; bears went up Rising Wolf Mtn. Bears near Sky Lake, chasing goats, in afternoon.*

So they came back. They were chased by dogs, and still returned. Before noon! The cracker shells, fired from a shotgun, did it, though. Cracker shelled at noon, chasing goats at Sky Lake in the afternoon. (For those unfamiliar with the area, the elevation of Sky Lake is over 7,000 feet; the surface elevation of Two

Medicine Lake is 2,000 feet lower.) They got the message.

But isn't there an undercurrent here? Chocolate Legs once seemed, *indifferent* toward humans. But one wonders if that indifference has been ratcheted up a notch to disdain?

> *6/6/97 Bears were observed resting & foraging in an avalanche chute above the North Shore Trail, on the south slope of Rising Wolf Mtn. from about 11:00 am to 12:30 pm, when they were seen moving down slope toward trail. Hiker on North Shore Trail near western end of Two Medicine Lake moved off trail to let bears (adult and 2 yearlings, all blond) pass on trail, within approximately 100 feet, at 2:30 pm.*

This new level of human relations might easily be misinterpreted by novices to bear behavior:

> *6/10/97 Glacier National Park trail crew of 3 encountered collared female on South Shore Trail at 30-35 yards at 10:00 am. They started chain saw, but she did not move off immediately. She eventually moved off on her own. Family group was observed near camp store at 3:00 pm, within 100 feet of 4 people, and was observed on Scenic Point Trail near trailhead at 4:00 pm—many people encountered bears, reported them as "friendly"; they did not approach or move away from people; within 100 feet of people.*

Chocolate Legs and her two yearling cubs continued to push the envelope. On June 12, they were "radio-tracked at base of Rising Wolf Mtn. just north of Two Medicine Campground, across creek to north." On June 13: "Radio-tracked at base of Rising Wolf Mtn. just across creek from Two Medicine Campground at 8:00 am. Bears were observed on the North Shore Trail by NPS employee from boat dock area at 6:45 pm."

> *6/15/97 Bears feeding close to trail on avalanche chute on Sinopah.*

> *6/20/97 Observed by concessions employees on North Shore Trail, from boathouse area. On trail in avalanche*

chute on Rising Wolf.

6/21/97 Bears were seen feeding in avalanche chute east of Twin Falls Trail junction at 10:45 am; bears were within approximately 100 ft of hikers who made noise, and bears ran to cover. Hikers walked around bears feeding near the North Shore Trail junction—east of Twin Falls junction, at 1:00 pm. Bears would not move off; bears within approximately 100 feet.

6/25/97 Bears were radio-tracked by tribal bear management personnel near South Shore Trail & Two Medicine Pass Trail junction; observed in avalanche chute on Sinopah Mtn.—moved into cover.

6/26/97 Bears were observed along north shore of Upper Two Medicine Lake by people fishing across the lake from the bears; bears moved upslope and westward; no interaction with people.

6/30/97 Bears observed from boat near trail at about 4:00 pm (no other details).

7/4/97 Bears were radio-tracked near the south shore of Upper Two Medicine Lake, off-trail, at 10:30 am. Bears were never observed; location based on radio signal only.

7/5/97 Two hikers observed female with 2 yearlings, all blond, on Twin Falls Trail, at head of Two Medicine Lake at 5:00 pm; hikers moved away; distance approximately 300 feet between bears and hikers.

The evening of July 5 is when Matthew Truszkowski was supposed to meet friends at Two Medicine Lake. The 25-year-old Glacier Park Lodge employee said that he planned to make a solo climb of Sinopah Mountain. When he failed to meet them at the scheduled time, authorities were notified.

According to a news release issued by the National Park Service on July 7,

… A ground and aerial search was conducted by

park personnel on Sunday, July 6 following the standard trail and climbing route up Sinopah Mountain. Search personnel encountered a female grizzly bear with two cubs on the south slopes of Sinopah, but after a brief wait the bears moved on and they continued searching without incidence.

The Park Service's *Summary of Activities of Grizzly Bear Family in Two Medicine Drainage, 1997* (But issued in 1998) put a little different spin on the searchers' encounter with Chocolate Legs and her offspring:

7/6/97 Bears (blond female with 1 lt. brown yearling) acting "strange" and erratic, darting about; during search; over 1/4 mile away (10:00 am) on Sinopah Mtn. (Remains of goat carcass found here during search in 1998). Later in day (12 noon) female with two young ran toward hikers between Rockwell Falls and Cobalt Lake; observers made noise and bears stopped about 40 yards away; searchers may have spooked bears.

Searchers found no sign or evidence of Matthew Truszkowski on either the South Shore Two Medicine Lake Trail or on Sinopah Mountain. More personnel were brought in, helicopter support was added, and a team of search dogs transported to the Two Medicine area.

The young Michigan native was described as having sandy blond hair, standing 5-feet 8-inches tall, and weighing 145 pounds. He was thought to have been unprepared for an overnight stay—wearing only Docker-type trousers, a light shirt, and sneakers.

High Tech entered the search with addition of an airborne infrared heat sensor. By Wednesday, searchers were losing heart. And on Thursday, severe thunderstorms moved into the Two Medicine country, bringing hail, rain, and high winds.

Finally, the search for Matthew Truszkowski was suspended.

But a year later—almost to the day—searchers, armed with information gleaned from subsequent events, again hit the slopes of Sinopah Mountain, this time in company with "cadaver dogs" trained to search for human remains. It was during the 1998 search in the vicinity where the grizzly family had exhibited "strange and erratic behavior" that the goat skeleton was found.

The 1998 effort was reported as "... the last official hunt for Matthew Truszkowski in the [Glacier] Park."

Matthew Truszkowski has never been seen again.

27

Over the Line? Indifference to Humans

Matthew Truszkowski's disappearance and the possibility of the bear Chocolate Legs playing a part in it gained considerable credence amid the glare of subsequent events. From hindsight of a year's lapse, events were recalled, memories triggered. The "strange and erratic" behavior of bears on Sinopah Mountain the day after the young man's disappearance took on sinister aspects. Emotions ran high with Monday morning second-guessing. Truth and closure were the objectives. But truth and closure might have been sought amid an atmosphere where multiple objectives can be mutually exclusive. Let's examine the written record:

According to the NPS press release issued a day after the event occurred—July 7, 1997—searchers did indeed encounter a female grizzly with *two* cubs on Sinopah Mountain. "But after a brief wait the bears moved on and they continued searching without incident."

So the press release contained no mention of "strange and erratic behavior." Instead, the charge of queer behavior first surfaced within the written record in the *Summary of Activities of Grizzly Bear Family in Two Medicine Drainage, 1997 (female #235, BIR)*, for 7/6/97. Also appearing in that summary was "...(blond female with 1 lt. brown yearling)" and "...(Remains of goat carcass found here during search in 1998)."

One oddity in the summary is that the first parenthesized section for 7/6/97 mentions only one cub, and it as "lt. brown," instead of blond. In addition, inclusion of the second parenthesized section mentioning the goat carcass found in 1998 means this summary was prepared in 1998, a year *after* the incident. As a result, it's difficult to reconcile the discrepancies between the press release, issued the *day after* the event occurred, and the summary of Chocolate Legs' activities that obviously was compiled (or at least revised) much later.

Did the bears spotted on Sinopah number two or three? Was there one brown cub or two blond ones? Were the ursids acting queerly or did the searchers simply wait a discreet period of time to allow the bears to exit gracefully? Or both?

It's difficult to understand how a press release issued *at the time* could've erred about two blond cubs if there was but one brown one. Yet it's understandable why the release omitted the bit on the bears acting strangely—it's not the purpose of such press releases to excite public imaginations. But again, why the mention of two blond cubs?

Going back once more to the summary of Chocolate Legs' activities in 1997, the report for the day Truszkowski disappeared is worth more careful evaluation:

> *7/5/97 Two hikers observed female with 2 yearlings, all blond, on Twin Falls Trail, at head of Two Medicine Lake at 5:00 pm; hikers moved away; distance approximately 300 feet between bears and hikers.*

The *summary* doesn't clearly state these bears were Chocolate Legs and her offspring, but it implies as much by listing them in a summary about Chocolate Legs' activities. Certainly the incident was consistent with their actions during the period. But assuming they were the bears in question, the report still makes it plain that Chocolate Legs was a mile from the base of Sinopah Mountain in late afternoon and two miles or more from Matthew Truszkowski's probable route up and down from the summit. These are not impossible distances for animals with the mobility of these bears, but it does imply, at the very least, that a certain coincidence occurred if Chocolate Legs and the solitary concessions employee did, in fact, meet.

Returning to the single light brown cub reported on Sinopah the following day—what about it? The mother was blond, the brush dense. One can easily surmise the circumstances of searchers blundering into grizzly bears on such terrain and surrounded by such vegetation, was sudden, tense, and turmoiled. It would be easy for the blur of a blond cub running pell-mell through shadow to be interpreted as light brown, especially one with dark-colored legs. It's also easy, under such conditions, to spot only one cub when two existed.

Yet no mention was made in the report of the blond sow wearing a collar—is that surprising? Perhaps not so much as one might think. Again, the action was swift and tense. Mere identification of a *grizzly* at close quarters would cause an adrenalin rush, not to mention kicking in survival-first instincts. A collar, almost camouflaged by the heavy neck hair (see the cover of this book), would be easy enough to miss.

The bears' strange and erratic behavior is also worth examining. Perhaps to truly understand bear behavior we must first get into their minds—or let them into ours. There's little doubt from the available information that Chocolate Legs was accustomed to lots of people treading the trails of Glacier. But one can assume that off-trail, especially in forests filled with dense vegetation, encountering people might be an ursid rarity. Might not a bear—any bear—suddenly surprised by a gaggle of searchers behave strangely, even erratically, at the moment of encounter? Especially if the humans themselves were also, in her experience, acting queerly?

But the discrepancies still haven't been explained. Why Chocolate Legs? From the available eyewitness evidence provided later, why does the press release issued a day after the event mention a blond bear and *two* cubs?

Easy. Because through signals from her radio collar, searchers *knew* Chocolate Legs and her cubs were on Sinopah Mountain. It would be reasonable enough, one assumes, for that piece of information to find its way into the press release. One assumes, too, that authorities must have known the blond bear family was near Twin Falls on the previous afternoon in order to have included the 5:00 p.m. visitor-sighting in their *Summary of Activities of Grizzly Bear Family in Two Medicine Drainage, 1997 (Female #235, BIR)*.

But knowing the bear is on a mountain and pinpointing her exact locations are two different matters altogether. Leaders of the search teams, responsible for sending their people into possible harm's way, felt individuals they had available for radio monitoring weren't as proficient as the guy who'd placed the collar and assigned the radio frequency in the first place. As a favor,

Dan Carney, Blackfeet Tribal Biologist was asked to join the search team. His sole assignment, after the man agreed, was to monitor Chocolate Legs and advise search teams of her exact location for their safety.

Here's Dan Carney's story, in an interview. First the setting:

The Two Medicine tour boat, coincidentally named Sinopah, dropped Carney off at the upper end of the lake. Equipped with his radio monitor and a hand-held two-way radio to stay in contact with search teams, the biologist immediately began receiving signals from the bear's location. Now Dan:

"It didn't sound as though she was up on Sinopah [Mountain], so I started hiking the South Shore Trail back toward the lake's lower end. My readings were coming in, but I still couldn't pin-point her exactly so I kept moving and collecting readings. Where the horse trail and hiker trail separates, the signals became stronger. I crossed the footbridge across Paradise Creek and continued down to the little meadow where the two trails join—you know, where there's a signpost marking the trail."

I nodded, having paused at that very signpost while doing research for this book.

"Well, the signal was really strong, so I knew the bears were close. I'd just passed the signpost and the trail fork when I spotted one of the cubs at the far [east] edge of the meadow. So I backed up to the trail fork and was sitting, leaning against the post when all of a sudden the mother bear walked out of the timber where her cub had been. She had her ears flattened and nose thrust in the air, sniffing. She'd picked up my scent during a wind shift! It was like she was looking for *me*!"

The biologist paused, then shook himself and said, "I felt that bear was zeroing in on *my* scent."

I was stunned! Throughout the brief tale, Carney had been leaning back in his chair, focusing on a spot over his desk, speaking in a dispassionate monotone that I had to strain to hear. He stopped and I stared at him, not realizing he'd quit until he swiveled his chair and turned toward me, one eyebrow raised. "That's ... that's ..." I trailed off.

"Hard to believe?" he prompted.

I exhaled the breath I'd been holding. "Why you?"

He shrugged. "I'd just trapped her a few days before, drugged her, handled her, put tags in her ears and a collar on her neck, took hair samples. I'd trapped and handled her cub. Earlier, I'd chased them from the campground with cracker shells and loud noises. Now, here was my scent again, somewhere near her cubs."

"And you thought she was remembering *you* as something or someone to hate?"

"I don't know. I only know what I saw. I only know that when she turned back into the brush and the radio said she was circling to get behind me, I got out of there and ran back the way I came as fast as I could. I only know she gave me the willies and raised the hair on the back of my neck. Let's just say it was in no way a normal bear encounter."

I studied the guy. Of all the men working with grizzly bears I know, I feel the Blackfeet biologist is least given to hyperbole or exaggeration. Neither is he a novice around grizzlies, having worked as a bear biologist for nearly twenty years, first trapping the ursids for a study conducted in the Mission Mountains, then working in Canada for the Border Grizzly Project. For the last thirteen years, Carney has worked for the Blackfeet.

"So this explains how Mark Derr's story in the *New York Times* mentions Chocolate Legs searching for you," I said, digging in my files for a copy of the Tuesday, August 18, 1998 feature story.

I read from a highlighted sentence: "`Later, the female came onto a trail sniffing the air and looking around, as if searching for Mr. Carney.'"

The biologist nodded.

"So you told him about this incident?"

"I told him nothing about it."

I frowned. "Well, how did the *Times* journalist get it?"

"I reported it on the radio when it happened, that's how. Every search team member with a radio on Sinopah Mountain heard it, that's how the story got around. I presume somebody hearing it that day told the *Times* guy."

The tribal biologist and I discussed the incident further. He was the one who mused it might've merely been that Chocolate Legs smelled a human scent near her cubs and was trying to pinpoint the location in order to practice avoidance.

But I'm the one pointing out this particular bear family was repeatedly near humans both before, and certainly after, her campground capture, exhibiting no previous interest in avoidance. As a consequence, I thought it unlikely that mere proximity to humans would upset the bear at this particular time, "unless," I said, "she was upset over something else."

Was that something else a biologist for the Blackfeet Nation named Carney?

28

Drift to Disdain

Two days after Dan Carney's 'close encounter of a bear kind,' according to the Park Service summary of Chocolate Legs activities during the summer of 1997:

> *7/9/97 NPS employee monitoring radio signal during search in area: bears in Bighorn Basin at 11:00 am, moving toward Twin Falls at 4:00 pm, near head of Two Medicine Lake at 6:20 pm, and seen moving east above North Shore Trail at head of TM Lake at 7:00-7:20 pm.*

Reports on the bears the very next day make it plain Chocolate Legs and her cubs were continuing to bounce around the Two Medicine valley. It also continues to portray the bears' cavalier regard for humans:

> *7/10/97 NPS employee monitored radio signal during search in area: observed bears well above the North Shore Trail at 9:10 am, signal near head of TM Lake at 1:50 pm, and observed on South Shore Trail in avalanche chute at head of TM Lake at 3:30 pm. At head of Two Medicine Lake at 3:00 pm, hikers came around corner and cubs saw them. Hikers retreated; female walked towards hikers and stopped; bears within approximately 300 feet. Hikers backed out, bears did not follow. At 7:00 pm on Oldman Lake Trail about 1/4-mile from trailhead at Two Medicine Entrance Station, 3 hikers saw 3 bears walking up trail 30 feet away. Hikers backed up and moved off trail as bears continued up trail. (2 sites 4-5 miles distant; female bear #235 or #240? Probably #240)*

Though hardly clear which bear family was which, this is the first mention of bear #240, the second *grizzly* sow trapped and radio collared by Blackfeet Tribal Biologist Dan Carney earlier in the spring. There were soon to be more, adding to the confusion about Chocolate Legs' activities—like the confusion rampant in reports of Jesse James robbing banks in Kansas and Kentucky on the same day.

> *7/15/97 Bears in open area 35 yards from hikers 100 yards from Two Medicine Campground at 8:00 am. Adult bear walked parallel to hiker for a while and then headed up hill away from hiker.*
>
> *7/16/97 Bears radio-tracked from airplane north of Upper Two Medicine Lake at 6:45 am, near middle of lake on lower slope of Mt. Helen.*
>
> *7/18/97 Female (probably #240, not #235) and 2 yearlings observed on the NW shore of Oldman Lake, foraging & playing at 7:00 am, and west of Oldman Lake at 2:50 pm, opposite observers; female had limp - left hind leg.*
>
> *7/21/97 Climbers saw bears near summit of Rising Wolf Mtn. at 6:30 pm, "indifferent" to climbers; female noticed climbers, but continued to "dig" and "play" in snow (sliding); bears within approximately 50 feet. Radio collar observed on female; she would not put any weight on right rear leg. This was probably #240, not #235.*

These reports indicate how unreliable eyewitness information might be. One indicated the mother bear limped on her left hind leg, the other said she limped on her *right* hind. Neither reported the bears' colors. Both were assumed by authorities to be bear #240, but enough doubt existed so each was listed in the summary of Chocolate Legs' activities for 1997.

If it was indeed bear #240, then she, too, was said to be indifferent toward humans, digging and playing in plain view of mountain climbers a mere fifty feet away. Think of it! Scrambling up a steep mountain, probably unable to run and no place to go if their life depended on it, watching wild bears who cared not a whit they were there! The mother and her cubs sliding down snowfields, then climbing to do it again! I only hope the observers gave the actors a round of applause when they scrambled on.

> *7/29/97 Radio-tracked on northeast side of Upper Two Medicine Lake at 6:45 am. Another collared grizzly bear (#240) with 2 yearlings radio-tracked near peak of Rising Wolf Mtn. at 7:00 am (medium brown adult with 1 medium brown young and 1 blond young).*

There's the color confusion again, this time by trained observers—#240 and one of her cubs is medium brown, while the other was reported as blond. Was one cub standing in sunshine while the cub's mother and sibling were in shadow?

One thing seems clear from the summary: As the season progresses and food becomes more readily available, Chocolate Legs appears less confrontational toward humans.

> *8/1/97 Radio-tracked near summit of Rising Wolf Mtn. (feeding on army cutworm moths?)*
>
> *8/4/97 Two visitor reports of an adult grizzly with 2 yearlings, all blond, near Twin Falls junction and Upper Two Medicine Lake, 1 of bears running up the north shore of Upper Two Medicine Lake at 12:30 pm.*
>
> *8/5/97 Radio-tracked just southeast of Upper Two Medicine Lake outlet.*
>
> *8/7/97 Radio-tracked about 1 mile south of Upper Two Medicine Lake.*
>
> *8/11/97 Radio-tracked at summit of Rising Wolf Mtn.*
>
> *8/13/97 Radio-tracked about 1/2-mile east of Upper Two Medicine Lake outlet, south of trail and creek.*
>
> *8/18/97 Radio-tracked at summit of Rising Wolf Mtn. at 7:30 am. Another radio-collared female (#240) with 2 young (medium brown female and 1 young and another blond young) also at summit of Rising Wolf Mtn. (9 bears*

at summit) Locations from airplane, by tribal biologists.

8/26/97 Radio-tracked at summit of Rising Wolf Mtn.

8/29/97 Radio-tracked at summit of Rising Wolf Mtn. at 7:30 am. Another radio-collared female with 2 young (also all blond) at summit of Rising Wolf (#240). (8 bears at summit)

There's the color confusion again. Was bear #240 medium brown, or blond? Did she have two blond cubs, or one medium brown one? Was she the bear acting "strange and erratic" on Sinopah Mountain on July 6, or was it Chocolate Legs? Or was it a different bear altogether?

9/2/97 Radio-tracked on south side of Pumpelly Pillar just north of Upper Two Medicine Lake outlet & female grizzly #240 radio-tracked to north side of ridge above Young Man lake at 7:30 am. First group was all blond; latter group had one light brown young, other 2 blond.

9/3/97 NPS employee saw family group of 3 bears on slopes above No Name Lake at 1:00 pm; bears were feed ing and exploring area (#235?). Same employee saw bears, probably #235, at 3:00 pm, on slopes below Pumpelly Pillar on Upper Two Medicine Lake side; bears were far away, walking & exploring. Bears did not look down when employee was pounding (tent stakes??) in Upper Two Medicine Lake Campground.

9/5/97 Radio-tracked about 1/2-mile east of Upper Two Medicine Lake outlet, north of trail. Visitor sighting of blond family (2 subadult young) grazing in avalanche chute on north shore of Upper Two Medicine Lake.

9/8/97 Radio-tracked southwest of Upper Two Medicine Lake & #240 southwest of Boy Lake; both groups were all blond.

More color confusion! A wag once said it's difficult to tell the players without a program. But in this case, it's hard to tell the players even *with* a program.

9/11/97 Radio-tracked about 1/4-mile north of trail about 1/2-mile east of Upper Two Medicine Lake outlet.

9/14/97 Visitor sighting of female with 2 young, all blond, on southeast face on Sinopah Mtn. above campground.

9/17/97 NPS employee sighting of female with young, all medium brown, on west side of Oldman Lake (probably #240).

9/19/97 Three grizzlies of unknown age, 1 blond, 2 medium brown, bluff-charged 2 hikers a couple of times 2 miles up the North Shore Trail, once within 25 feet. (report received at WG [Park Headquarters at West Glacier] on 12/1/97.

More questions, fewer answers. All raised two-and-one-half months after the incident. Were the bluff charges perpetrated by Chocolate Legs or by #240? *Or by another grizzly sow altogether?* After all, there's no mention of a radio collar and both Chocolate Legs and #240 were each wearing one. Twenty-five feet seems proximate enough to spot a collar, especially along an open trail, even amid the adrenaline rush of two false grizzly charges.

Also, one wishes for more information. How old were the cubs? What was the circumstances of the sudden meeting? Most bluff charges by sow grizzlies are initiated when she feels her cubs threatened, or the mother feeling herself threatened. Bluff charges usually conclude when the bear no longer feels threatened, either by her cubs escaping or when the perceived threat ends. Did the cubs flee? Climb a tree? Or did the hikers flee? Climb a tree?

Or was there yet another response to these questions?

9/23/97 Radio-tracked south of trail and creek about 1/4-mile east of Upper Two Medicine Lake outlet.

9/28/97 NPS employee sighting of female with 2 young, all medium brown, on west side of Oldman Lake (probably #240).

9/30/97 Radio-tracked about 1 mile south of Upper Two Medicine Lake.

10/6/97 Radio-tracked on south side of Pumpelly Pillar, about 1/4-mile above trail, about 1/2-mile east of Upper Two Medicine Lake outlet.

The *Summary of Activities of Grizzly Bear Family in Two Medicine Drainage, 1997 (Female #235, BIR)* ends with the 10/6/97 entry. There are simply no further reports on the bears' sightings, no conflicts between bears and humans. Nor is there information in the summary regarding Chocolate Legs' den site.

I found it interesting to note that with the possible exception of two bluff charges on September 19, there are no reports of Chocolate Legs approaching humans after mid-July, either in campgrounds or along trails.

Whether it was she who actually launched the bluff charge in September or not, one must accept the possibility—the incident happened well within her adopted home range. But what about the colors? One charge came within twenty-five feet along a cleared trail. By September at that elevation, much of the vegetation has lost its leaves. One could expect two hikers, in such circumstances, to get the bears' colors right. If so, the "1 blond, 2 medium brown" description appears to preclude Chocolate Legs and her cubs from being players in that game.

How about #240?

That seems problematic, too. Careful analysis of the Summary of Activities of Grizzly Bear Family in Two Medicine Drainage, 1997 (Female #235, BIR) discloses ten probable sightings and/or radio locations of #240 and her cubs throughout the spring and summer. Not one of those locations are *south of a line running due east from Young Man Lake over the summit of Rising Wolf Mountain.*

Yes, it's possible #240 and her family, seemingly chameleon-like in color, could've been down along the north shore of Two Medicine Lake on September 19. But the actual record discloses it would be inconsistent with what we've learned of her territorial limits. And yes, following that line of reasoning also precludes #240 from being on Sinopah Mountain on July 6, 1997.

Sinopah, on the other hand, was clearly within Chocolate Legs' adopted home range. In fact, the golden bruin's home range carved out the heart of the Two Medicine Valley's most heavily used human corridors: Upper Two Medicine and Two Medicine Lakes and the valley bottom between, Bighorn Basin, Paradise and Buttercup Parks, Aster and Paradise creeks, Scenic Point, Rising Wolf. If one computed the time Chocolate Legs spent in areas heavily used by humans as opposed to more remote regions, her adaptations to them might prove shocking.

A couple of things disclosed in the *Summary* are fascinating: One is how many times Chocolate Legs bounced back and forth between the summit of Rising Wolf Mountain and the Two Medicine Valley bottom. Up for a day or two, then back amid humans. Up for three more days, then back to wander the bottoms between Two Medicine and Upper Two Medicine. One wonders why? Number 240 trundled to the top of Rising Wolf and stayed, presumedly until she topped her reserve tank for the following winter.

On the other hand, #240 had a bum leg. Perhaps had she been equipped with sound appendages, she, too, might have bounced back and forth. Somehow, though, one doesn't believe it. Somehow one believes the bouncing, from mountaintop to valley bottom was more a Chocolate Legs' novelty than is normal for most female bears with young at their side. If so, why?

What was the attraction pulling a healthy, middle-aged mother from a mountaintop bonanza back to slum among humans? She, too, needed to feast in order to build fat for the coming winter. Was she finding sufficient food among humans to do just that? Enough so that it ran competition to the rich moth banquet atop Rising Wolf? Were candy bars and garbage tendered in sufficient quantities to toll the bears down from on high?

There's no doubt that Chocolate Legs was enterprising as well as pushy. She was also, in some cases, thought "friendly." Make that winsome. She was a beautiful bear, have no doubts about that. Her cubs were cute. It was an irresistible combination to novices to bear country hailing from Poughkeepsie or Kalamazoo. What harm could come from throwing the bears a few grapes or cookies or chocolates?

But—and there's usually a "but" somewhere—the record doesn't show Chocolate Legs working campgrounds during the last half of the 1997 season. Neither does the record disclose her spending much time on trails after mid-July. So the golden bear with dark-colored legs must have been finding food elsewhere—enough to assuage her needs. Berries, probably. Huckleberries. Rich, sweet, juicy, huckleberries. It's a diet humans might also prefer over sifting through mouthfuls of cutworm moths.

But there's a gap in the records after October 6, brought about by a series of high winds that cancelled subsequent flights until November 12, after she'd denned. And information is available on Chocolate Legs' and her offsprings' den location from sources other than the official Park Service Summary. During the winter of 1997-98, the den was located high on the south side of Rising Wolf Mountain. Apparently she was finally recorded as denning on the east side.

As a result, the bear family appeared to spend the entire spring and summer of 1997 on the east side of the Divide. Which raises the question about whether she denned on the east side during the previous winter? Or gone west, after having done so for so many years? Was her move to the east virtually complete by 1997? Did the disappearance of the corn spills have anything to do with a shift in her home range?

There was no pursuit of bull trout redds for the family in '97; mid-October is much too late for that. But mountain ash berries and russet buffalo berries should be in their prime by then, just waiting for an enterprising ursid family to cross the Divide for them. Did she make the journey?

In addition, where did the golden bear and her offspring den for the winter of '96-'97—East side? West side? Isn't it a pity official interest seemed focused on Chocolate Legs for management purposes, to the detriment of behavioral research?

Over all, hangs the specter of the bear Chocolate Legs' apparent change in temperament as the year progressed. Was it hunger—the most important motivation in every bear's life—that drove her to become more pushy after emerging from hibernation? Or might it have been the trapping and handling?

If it was the trapping and handling and Chocolate Legs developed a hatred for humans, why didn't she take it out on the first lone human she met? Instead, when the bears bumped into the NPS employee waiting out a rainstorm on May 31, near Paradise Point, the sow merely "barked" before leaving.

Yet the bears seemed to grow more pushy, more disrespectful around humans by the day, until mid-July. Why the belligerence if not for the need of food? Conversely, why the moderation from late-July on if not for the fact that need for food was being met?

Too many questions, not enough answers. Why, when we finally get a few clues to solving our most pressing concerns, do they raise even more questions? Including that most important mystery in a lot of folks' minds:

What *really* happened to Matthew Truszkowski?

29

Beyond No Return

So, in the late fall of 1997, Chocolate Legs and her two look-alike cubs denned on the south slope of one of the most scenic mountains in all of Glacier National Park. Her den site, was near the 7,200-foot level, overlooking a valley that is considered among the choicest of grandeur in the entire northern Rockies. She dug the den some time in late October and lined it with boughs stripped from nearby alpine firs, overlain with beargrass blades. She and her two burly half-grown cubs entered in a state of torpor sometime before November 12, amid a howling, gusting white-out down from the Canadian North.

It was the pattern she'd followed for each of her sixteen seasons; the pattern all others of her kind had been programmed to follow for millenniums.

She and her cubs curled together and fell immediately to sleep. Within minutes their entry hole drifted closed and for all intents and purposes, the three bears disappeared from the face of the earth. Later, when the Arctic storm blew itself out and temperatures plummeted, glistening northern lights shimmered across the night sky—great belts shivering in will-o'-the-wisps translucent blues, tinged in pink. Beyond, great stars glistened and twinkled jewel-like: rubies and topaz and diamonds. Windblown snow, crystallized into drifts and catching the shimmering light, reflecting it onto an empty, quiet, frigid land of shadow and mystery.

Throughout all of November and December, January and February and March, the giant beasts slumbered. And one fine sunshiny day in mid-April they awoke.

It was the male cub, larger now than a wolf and blockier than a Berkshire hog, who pushed through the drift blocking their den, seemingly wide awake and ready for quest. The cub's mother thrust her head above the snowy surface and gazed sleepily around. The already-emerged offspring trotted to his mother and washed her face with his tongue, diverted from time to time to lick the snow, then return to his mother's bath.

Behind, deep within the den, the second cub whined. Chocolate Legs pushed further through the opening, again pausing to rest. The male cub washed her face for a second time, taking a few licks at her neck and shoulder. Then a wind gust rattled through the tip of an alpine fir thrusting above the drift. The male, ready for action, attacked the audacious tree tip.

Chocolate Legs crawled groggily from the opening to lie fully upon the snow. The female cub thrust her head out the den's hole and again whined. The male washed his sibling's face, then returned to his mother to pursue another cleansing. Two minutes later he found a nipple and settled in for serious work. His sister joined him in seconds and the mother rolled to her back and sighed.

We can't know precisely when Chocolate Legs switched her spring range from west of the Continental Divide to the east, but one presumes it was sometime after the corn spills' were cleaned up in 1993. Why did she choose to do so in any event? The west side drainages were as much as a thousand feet lower than the Two Medicine country. As a result, its lower reaches bared off sooner in the spring, vegetation sprouted earlier. The Two Medicine Valley, on the other hand, was usually pummeled by repeated Arctic storms—at least more so than the mountain lands to the west.

Though wild and beautiful, her Two Medicine home harbored fewer ungulates than the Nyack/Coal/Park/Ole drainages to the west. But were there more grizzly bears on the west side? Even if there were higher densities of grizzly bears west of the Continental Divide, would it have made any difference? After all, Chocolate Legs preempted what humans think of as the best of the Two Medicine Valley for her home range, establishing at least some indication of her dominance as a leading female *Ursus* within southeastern Glacier, despite her something-less-than-dominating size. Had she wished, couldn't she have applied those same aggressive techniques over west?

Her choosing east over west might more readily be understood had she learned to range farther out into the foothills and the plains as does other Glacier Park grizzlies inhabiting mountain fastnesses east of the Divide. She could've turned to cattle killing and dumpster raiding on the Blackfeet Reservation. She could've raided bird feeders in East Glacier and sought out ranchers' "boneyards" where the stockmen disposed of winter-kill carcasses and dead spring calves.

But she didn't. The record shows Chocolate Legs visited outside the Park but twice. Neither time did the golden bear with dark legs do more than stalk through a campground and lick a few barbecue grates.

So, again, why?

It was the third day of May when Chocolate Legs and her two cubs ambled side by side down the valley of Paradise Creek, through meadow and marshlands still partially locked in winter. Eight inches of soft snow covered the meadow. The moon was bright and it should've been cold but wasn't. Off to the side, the creek was high and a little muddy, rushing swiftly in youthful exuberance to get to the Gulf of Mexico.

Suddenly the male cub darted to the creek and plunged in, only to emerge thirty yards downstream and gallop back to crash into his sister; they both rolled and tumbled in frolic. Around and around they whirled as their mother plodded on, seemingly indifferent to the dervishes around her. Then the cubs broke apart to gallop away in opposite directions, reversed course and careened back in wild abandon to crash into their plodding mother.

She cuffed the male, knocking him sprawling into the snow—to little effect. When he rolled to his feet the cubs galloped away together into a willow thicket where they rolled in play before charged back upon their mother. She began dancing about, galloping short distances with them. At one point the cubs charged upon her from opposite directions and she leaped into the air just before they collided, then charged away through willow brush like a runaway freight as the cubs careened after.

They walked logs across the creek. They walked logs partway across the creek, then plunged in to emerge fifty yards down, streaming water. The female cub crashed into her mother even as she shook water from her coat, then galloped away.

The play ceased and all three bears paced sedately, cubs on either side of their mother. Of a sudden, Chocolate Legs made a mighty leap and fled across the creek, splashing water onto driftwood and snowbanks, then ambushed the cubs as they galloped belatedly up looking for her.

Then it was the cubs' turn to gallop ahead and spring their own ambush. Once, while the cubs lay in wait, side by side, hindends twitching in anticipation, the mother quietly circled them and ambushed the ambushers. Afterward, all three rolled in one giant, spinning, snow-flinging tangle.

Snowplowing was still under way a couple of days later, when the family wandered into the complex at the outlet end of Two Medicine Lake, heading for the auto campground and picnic area along Pray Lake. Workmen busied themselves pulling plywood panels from windows at the general store and others worked on the boat dock. None of the workmen spotted the bears, however, as Chocolate Legs took considerable pains to lead her offspring behind snowbanks and tree clumps. And that evening, they bedded near Pray Lake.

They were on the move in the dark of the moon, however, their claws clicking on the newly bared road surface. First they checked the dock area and store front for bread crusts or cookie crumbs and found none. Then they headed for the Ranger Station. It was there that the male cub stood hidden in the darkness while a lady ranger followed her flashlight to the outhouse (flush toilets were not yet in service) only a few feet from the young grizzly. Chocolate Legs and her daughter watched as the male cub's ears flattened, then raised again as the outhouse door slammed.

Come morning, a few bare spots were peeking from the slopes of Rising Wolf Mountain, so the bears crossed the footbridge and climbed the slopes before humans began stirring below. Foraging was tough, however, and the bears, still unbeknownst to Two Medicine workmen toiling below, sought other diversions. This time it was the female cub who initiated the game.

The family had climbed a long, open, white-blanketed, fifty-degree slope to reach a rock outcrop bared by wind and sun. Such grass and forbs as might have grown on the outcrop had long since disappeared down the gullets of hungry mountain goats. While the male cub climbed even higher and his sister perched on the snowfield and whimpered, the mother half-heartedly turned over rocks, searching for insects that were yet a month from emergence from nest or pupae. Then the female cub began sliding.

It was a still very early spring in the mountains of the Two Medicine country. But though the wind was crisp, the sun proved warm and the snow surface slippery. The young bruin quickly accelerated in the upright, puppy dog slide down the white expanse. Though it may have appeared different had observers been watching from below, this was not the first time this bear (or these bears) had gone snow schussing—part of the art and games inherent to bears of all species. With wind from her passage rippling through a long winter coat, the young female cub found she could vary directions in her plummet down the mountain by leaning first one way, then the other. A hundred yards from where the vast snowfield plunged into a band of trees, the speeding young bruin rolled to her belly and thrust her claws into the icy snow and slid to a stop.

Even before his sister's exciting ride ended, the male cub rushed past his mother and leaped from the outcrop to belly flop onto the snow for his own precipitous ride. While he was but halfway down, his mother had also leaped from the rock ledge onto snow for her own rump-riding slide down the mountain.

Humans, like bears, also schuss. Usually it's called skiing or snowboarding. But occasionally it happens accidentally or, as with the female cub, inadvertently and a human hurtles down a mountain—without three-inch claws to arrest the plunge at will. Out-of-control humans die. Out-of-control humans are injured. Every year. In the dozens, hundreds, perhaps thousands.

Icy slopes can seem innocent and innocuous. I once angrily warned my wife from sliding at the top of a spring snowfield only to watch helplessly while her friend Marilyn lost her footing near the bottom of the "fan." The slope there was gentle, about twenty degrees. Yet the woman careened crazily for fifty feet before tumbling into a boulder-filled chasm.

Marilyn escaped with bruises instead of breaks. But her uncontrolled plunge into the chasm's icy water once again punctuated our lack of mastery over outdoors techniques many wild animals take for granted.

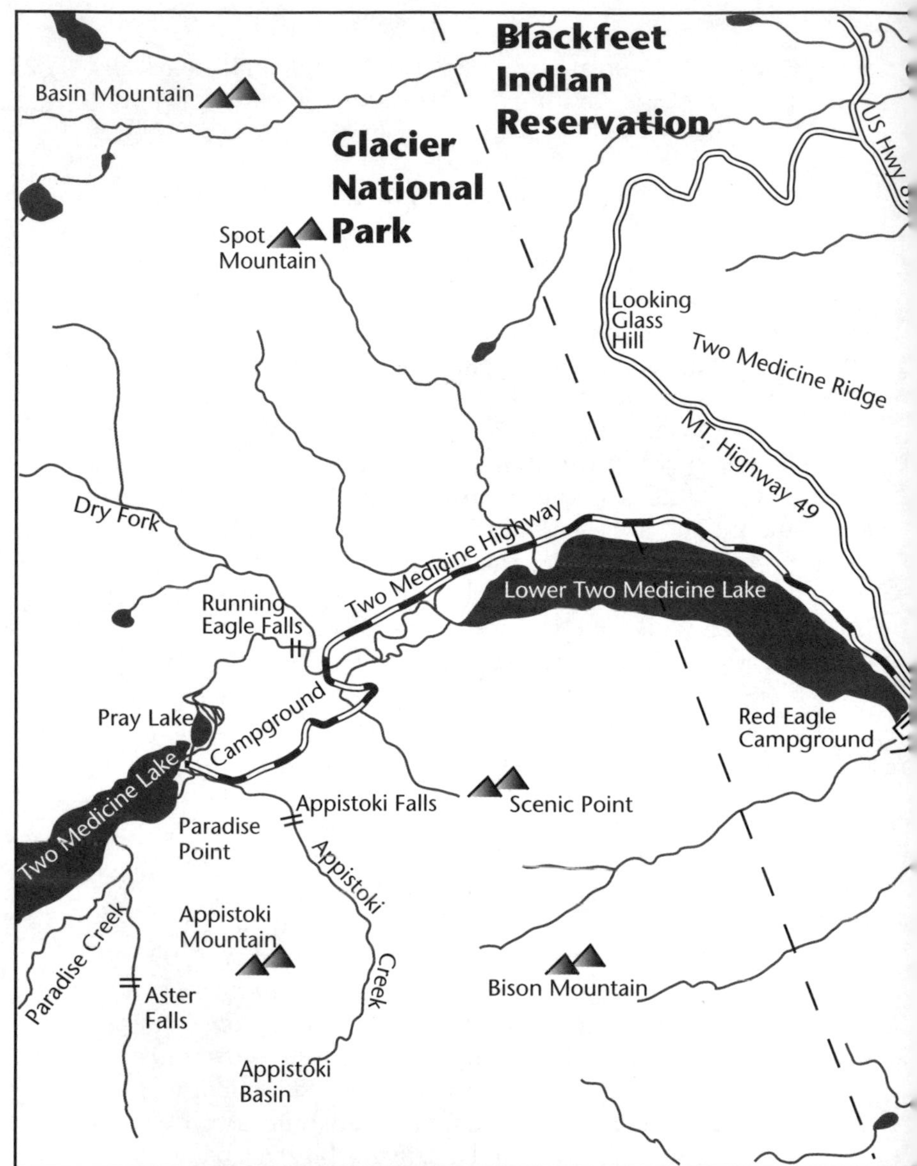

Ghosts of the past—and perhaps ghosts of the future—contribute to the legend of the Two Medicine country. It might have begun with the first men carryin Folsom spears looking for snowbound mammoths. But the legends are certainl alive among today's Blackfeet. And other legends are even now developing i tomorrow's histories of today's people.

**This map and others within these pages were produced in part through a DeLorme (Yarmouth, ME system that, in turn, used U.S.G.S. quads as their base. Detail–1:50,000*

After all three blond bears gathered together at the snowfield's bottom, they looked at each other, sniffed all over, and washed faces. Then Chocolate Legs led her two offspring back up the white slope, trudging over the furrows they'd just plunged down in such sheer ecstasy.

Fifteen minutes later, the three bruins had reached the exposed ledge and the mother stood on hind legs to peer over its lip. Then she whirled and flopped to her belly and shot off back downslope. Both cubs leaped after.

Twice more, the family trudged up the slope and hurtled down. And when mom and daughter broke off to enter the forest below, the male cub climbed the snowfield for a last hurrah, schussing down like a bobsled competitor, barely braking for the trees, then galloping into the sunset after the others.

Midnight found Chocolate Legs and her brood circling the Ranger Station, boat house, and General Store searching for morsels. Again, there were none.

Morning found them working the few snow-free openings on the slope east of Appistoki Creek, digging for the bulbs of spring beauties and the roots of lomatiums.

The following day they waded in the marsh and delta where Two Medicine River runs into Lower Two Medicine Lake. There the golden bears with distinctively dark legs spent several days eating marsh grass and cattails roots, waiting impatiently for winter to loosen its icy grip upon their chosen home range.

When the nearby highway opened for Park visitor use, all three bears wandered its edge, staring at each vehicle to pass. Once, the male bear took a stance in the middle of the road, but had the bad fortune to choose to accost a workman instead of a tourist. It might have been an ugly moment, but the cub was yet unsure and backed off just as the vehicle window slid down and the canister of pepper spray crept up. The incident, as sometimes happen with others, went unreported

Again the bear family scouted the campground. Again, they retreated to the Scenic Point Trail, drifting up Appistoki Creek.

Much had changed in the ten days they'd been gone. Only patches of snow lay in the bottom and after one emerged from the forest onto the open windswept slope above, the mountainside was moving well into spring. Buttercups and spring beauties colored the gravelly soil, the first greening shoots of bluebunch wheatgrass pushed upward. Ground squirrels peeped from every direction and marmots scurried over rock outcrops at the bears' approach.

Appistoki Basin was still shrouded in snow, as was each of the other surrounding mountains. But the trail to Scenic Point beckoned. The bears began to hunt, dig, climb.

Craig Joseph Dahl was a lean, fit outdoorsman with brown curly hair, brown eyes, and a ready smile. He stood six feet in his stockings and weighed 170 pounds. Dahl was raised in northern Minnesota, near the small community of Cromwell. Growing up in the country as he did, the lad gravitated to outdoors pursuits, boating, fishing, hunting. He canoed in Minnesota's Boundary Waters Wilderness Area and hiked and bicycled through much of the land of his youth. Upon graduation from high school, the young man enrolled in Bemidji State College, graduating with a degree in sports management.

The call of the wild never lessened, however, and Craig Dahl headed west, to Colorado, where he was employed at the Snow Mountain Ranch, leading youth groups on overnight backpacking trips. Most recently, Dahl had spent the winter skiing near Winter Park, Colorado.

He was a competent outdoorsman, "with a thorough knowledge of outdoor living and a love for the natural environment," his stepmother, Gail Dahl, was reported to have said in a subsequent newspaper interview.

Dahl's outdoors competence was echoed by one of his coleaders during the Colorado YMCA-sponsored backpacking expeditions. "When I was with him, I knew I had no worries," Gretchen Young, of Milwaukee, Wisconsin was reported to have said of the young man. "He was the most competent leader I ever knew."

Miss Young, as it turned out, was the last person to see Craig Dahl alive. Both were, by then, concessionaire employees of Glacier Park Incorporated, operators of hotels and other public services in and around Glacier National Park. On the evening of

May 16 they'd made plans to hike together in the Two Medicine Valley the following day. But the weather deteriorated and by the time Miss Young checked, Craig Dahl had gone on without her.

Being alone apparently posed no problem for the man. Gail Dahl told *Hungry Horse News* reporter Emmett Berg that her stepson "liked his privacy and was known as an independent person." She added, "It was not unusual for him to hike alone." She also thought Craig to be "in excellent shape and knew the dangers of the mountains."

Gretchen Young seconded that. "He was a smart man. The danger involved with grizzlies definitely sunk in on him." She told how Dahl had previously spotted a grizzly bear from the roadway and how they'd discussed the differences between these bears and the ones they'd known in Colorado.

Destiny brought Craig Dahl to East Glacier from a ski area in Winter Park, Colorado. Fate, it seems, turned the young man from his first job choice with a bike touring concern out of Puget Sound. Fate had Gretchen Young working for GPI for the summer and brought Craig, at loose ends after the Seattle job fell through, to visit her. Fate handed him a job driving one of GPI's "jammer" tour buses, the ancient, red-painted, open-air coaches of White Motor Company manufacture.

Fate also decreed that the young outdoorsman never lived to become really proficient at driving the "jammers."

30

Investigative Conclusion

Appistoki Creek begins in a giant, open, bowl carved by an ancient glacier. The bowl spills out to the northeast and is anchored on one side by 8,847-foot Mount Henry and on the other by 8,164-foot Appistoki Peak. Facing north and east as the bowl does, snow lingers there longer than other easily accessible high basins in the Two Medicine Valley and is a favorite for the late-spring skier and snowboarder set.

On Sunday, May 10, Craig Dahl had joined Martin Connelly and Deidre Heaton for an afternoon practicing telemark techniques in the Two Medicine Valley. The three youths had driven to the Scenic Point Trailhead, hiked to the first big switchback, then bushwhacked up the open east slope of the Appistoki drainage until finally donning skis and entering the bowl.

It was a week later when Craig Dahl again hiked the Scenic Point Trail, this time alone.

Craig Dahl wasn't the only single individual on the mountain that day. Birley Oats got an earlier start from the trailhead, carrying his snowboard and following the same general route Connelly, Heaton, and Dahl used the week previous. Oats had the basin all to himself and lost no time climbing up and zig-zagging down, climbing up and zig-zagging down. It was sometime around mid-afternoon, while Oats clambered up for yet another run, that the young man heard a voice shout. He paused to cock an ear, but nothing followed—only keening from the wind.

At that same time, two youths, also GPI employees from East Glacier, hiked the Scenic Point Trail. They'd begun later in the afternoon than either of the others, following the same route. They hiked steadily until they broke out into open country denuded by long ago wildfire. At one point, they, too, heard a male voice shouting, but Jeremy Peterson and his friend believed it came from the Appistoki Creek area. However, they, too, were unable to pinpoint the location.

With the wind and snow picking up, Birley Oats made his final snowboard descent of Appistoki Basin and Jeremy Peterson and his friend returned down the Scenic Point Trail. None of the three had an inkling, that a few yards above the trail, in the forested vicinity of Appistoki Falls, tragedy had occurred and that a hideous scene was unfolding....

Meanwhile, a wet snow settled across the land, whipped by gale winds from the northeast.

Shortly after noon of the following day, two hardy young men parked their vehicle at the trailhead where a tan-colored 1984 Buick with Colorado license plates was already parked. The Buick was covered with rapidly melting snow.

The young men hiked up-trail toward Scenic Point. At approximately 2:00 pm they reached the next-to the-last switchback, high up the mountain, and noticed what they thought was tracks in the old snow, largely obliterated by yesterday's new covering. The tracks appeared to be coming down from above. The men paused to discuss what they felt might have been tracks made by a person running downhill, possibly being chased by an animal. They described the tracks as "skinnier," with a three-feet-wide "disturbed" area over them, overlain with windblown snow and no single animal prints visible.

One of the men followed this track uphill for a distance, then moved to the side and paralleled them until they neared the northern point of the highest switchback. He could see the tracks continuing above this highest point. The man then returned to his companion. Near there, the men found a daypack about ten feet north of the tracks, lying in the snow. The pack contained three candy bars, a water bottle, and a jacket.

The two men could see the tracks continuing on down the mountainside below the lower switchback. They then returned on the trail to their vehicle, taking the daypack with them. At about 4:00 pm they hung the jacket on the signpost marking the trail, kept the daypack, and departed the area.

They, too, passed Appistoki Falls without the slightest hint of the grisly scene still unfolding a few hundred yards into the forest above.

This last report given by the two young men from St. Louis, Missouri, who found the daypack, did not reach Glacier Park rangers until May 28, after word of the tragedy occurring in the Two Medicine Valley made national news.

Meanwhile Craig Dahl's disappearance had not gone unnoticed. The man's co-workers were puzzled that he'd not reported for work on Monday morning, May 18. And after their work shift ended, Gretchen Young, Martin Connelly, Deidre Heaton and Jeremy Peterson drove to Two Medicine Lake to search for him. It was there, at the Scenic Point Trailhead, they found his automobile and became truly alarmed. At 9:00 o'clock in the evening of May 18, they reported the missing man.

Here are excerpts from Glacier National Park's Case Incident Report on the Dahl search:

> *On May 18, 1998 at approximately 2050 hours [8:50 pm], Ranger Taylor received a report of an overdue hiker. Glacier Park Incorporated (GPI) employees advised Ranger Taylor that Craig Dahl (new GPI employee) did not report to work this morning and that they had found his vehicle parked at the Scenic Point/Mt. Henry Trailhead....*
>
> *Planning began for an early morning hasty search. Six hasty search team members began searching 0700 hours [7:00 am], May 19, 1998. As the day progressed and no clues were found the search expanded. Main search efforts were completed by 1900 hours [7:00 pm] and planning began for the following day.*

Blackfeet Tribe's biologist Dan Carney was alerted by a friend that a search was going on for a missing Scenic Point hiker and he and his friend drove up to use his scanner to see if any collared bears were in the general area. Carney reported to Two Medicine Ranger Dona Taylor that bear 235—Chocolate Legs—was near Appistoki Falls. The report continues:

> *After the search team exited the backcountry on May 19, 1998 Blackfeet Tribal Biologist Dan Carney used radio telemetry to identify if any radio-collared bears were in the*

Two Medicine Valley. Dan Carney quickly determined that a collared female grizzly with two two-year-old cubs were in the Appistoki drainage (main focus of search efforts). With Dan Carney's assistance we began to monitor the grizzly family group.

Ranger Taylor asked the Blackfeet biologist if he would return the following day to continue monitoring Chocolate Legs. By the following morning, the suspect bear family was six miles away, near Cobalt Lake.

Meanwhile dog teams were assembled to join the search, including bloodhounds. Dahl's car gave up a few scent samples for the dogs to identify and pick out a trail. The samples proved insufficient for the dogs to "get" the scent. Searchers were in the process of selecting items of clothing from his East Glacier room when word came that his body had been found.

The body was discovered when Incident Commanders, equipped with the new telemetry information, dispatched their search teams with a more narrow focus. Little more than an hour after teams began on May 20, radios crackled over the Two Medicine Valley:

... At 0915 IC [Incident Commander] received a report that Craig Dahl's remains were found and that it appeared to have been a bear attack. All search teams were advised of the find and the potential bear danger. Teams were asked to exit the search area as safely as possible.

This was no ordinary bear attack, however—Craig Dahl's remains had been fed upon by bears. But which bears? The area was secured pending arrival of an investigative team that included Blackfeet Tribal Police, the Glacier County Sheriff's Department, and staff members from Glacier National Park.

From the report, "Results of Investigation" / Craig Dahl Search, Case/Incident Number 980106:

After discovery of the victim, an armed flight was made. The area around the successful search team (Volunteer Team 2) was closely examined with no sign of bear being observed. Although signs of bear activity and some of the victim's clothing were observed upon close observation from the air, it is unlikely that this site would have been discovered without a ground search. The [investigative] team was informed of the best route to the trail and escorted to that point.

Site investigation followed after search teams returned to TMRS [Two Medicine Ranger Station]. Rangers Kim Peach, Ron Goldhirsh, Reggie Altop, and Biologist Rick Yates were transported by helicopter to an area near the victim to provide security [to ensure the bears did not return]....

The site, a patch of krumholtz located below an easy cliff band, was secured and the investigation team was brought to the location.

Richard Mattson, a capable ranger with outdoor's experience, and accompanied by Peach and Yates, began following the three-day-old backtrail. By this time, the fresh snow of May 17-18 had pretty much melted, uncovering and freshening the scuff marks, drag marks, and faint tracks made by Dahl and the bears. From Mattson's report:

... A faint trail of disturbed rocks and patches of clear dried liquid (?) were followed upslope. Broken eyeglasses and pieces of cloth were discovered and their location flagged approximately 100 yards above the victim. No definite trail was observed in the cliffy area above this find. Above these cliffs, the terrain was mostly scree with small patches of krumholtz. This area was traversed upslope. Several sets of tracks which could have been made by humans or bears, were observed heading down hill in this area. Upon reaching the trail, approximately 540 vertical feet above the victim, tracks were observed heading down slope. These tracks were followed down for approximately 200 vertical feet, where a stocking hat was found under a small bit of krumholtz. The hat, later positively identified by the victim's girlfriend, was collected and the site flagged.

Obviously one of the chief concerns of the investigating teams was how did Craig Dahl die? Mattson's investigation narrowed the focus:

Note: The tracks leading down from the trail toward the site of the victim did not indicate a speedy descent. This area is probably used to "cut switchbacks". The small broken cliffs above the victim are easy to get through, even when wet. No evidence of a "fall off the cliffs" was observed.

During the investigation, several samples of bear scat were collected from near the victim. Three different hair samples were also collected and the entire package forwarded to a University of Idaho lab specializing in DNA analysis. Also sent for comparison purposes were hair samples of Chocolate Legs—identified by telemetry as the bear near Dahl's remains—and her male cub taken by Blackfeet biologist Carney the year before.

Even while the investigation continued into the circumstances leading to the grisly scene above Appistoki Falls, Glacier Park's staff moved from questions about Craig Dahl's whereabouts and what happened to him, to what to do about the bears?

It could not be doubted that #235 and her nearly grown offspring were prime suspects, implicated by their proximity to the horrifying scene in the Appistoki drainage. But in today's world, even managers of national parks—perhaps *especially managers of national parks*—hesitate to authorize destroying grizzly bears without something more than implication; especially females because they are desperately needed for recovery of the species.

But with a hungry media prowling the story's perimeters, growing impatient by the day, to do nothing seemed unthinkable. Still Park administrators hesitated.

The one thing they had going for them, however, was the Blackfeet Tribe's radio collar around Chocolate Legs' neck and the steady location pulse it provided. The one thing telemetry soon made clear was that the blond bears with such distinctively colored legs found the Appistoki hubbub too calamitous and vacated the drainage.

From a report titled Chronology, Case/Incident number 980106:

May 21, 1998 The female was located in the general location of Cobalt drainage. The trail from the junction up to Cobalt Lake was "CLOSED" due to known bear activity.

May 22, 1998 Telemetry signal for the female placed the bears in the Upper Two Medicine Lake area. During a patrol of the closed area, telemetry was used to locate the grizzly family group—it was located behind them on the trail. [emphasis mine]

The bears' rapid movement and the difficulty monitoring rangers had keeping track of her finally led to an administrative decision to close backcountry use of the entire valley. From a May 27 press release:

... A temporary area closure of the Two Medicine Valley backcountry is now in effect until further notice. Because of telemetry monitoring, this family group has a very large home range that includes the entire Two Medicine Valley. In addition to the backcountry area closure, due to the family group's presence in the Two Medicine Campground area Sunday evening, rangers are temporarily restricting camping at Two Medicine to hard-sided units until further notice.

Meanwhile decision-makers awaited pathology results from the autopsy of Craig Dahl's remains, as well as results from the DNA analysis from University of Idaho. The investigation continued.

Birley Oats, the snowboarder in Appistoki Basin on the day Craig Dahl died, read of the investigation and reported his recollection of hearing a shout, confirming Jeremy Peterson's report of hearing the same distant cry. On May 28, the two St. Louis hikers reported their finding Craig Dahl's daypack in the snow and said they were returning it for the investigation.

Meanwhile investigators had interviewed Barbara Hanson, Craig Dahl's mother, and already suspected there were some missing personal effects belonging to the victim, including a camera. Searchers were re-dispatched to go over the mountainside down which the victim was thought to have fled. A special investigator, supposedly better trained in clue recognition and identification, was called in by the Park Service. From the report on his May 24th investigation:

Details of Incident: The Mount Henry [Scenic Point] Trail was searched from the trail head to the top of the big switch-backs. We ended the search about 1/4-mile up from the last big switch-back (about 7,200 feet). The edges of the krumholtz and the areas adjacent to the trail in the treed area were also searched. We did not find Craig Dahl's backpack or his camera in the areas we searched.

The following was observed at the top of the last big switch-back and just East of the treed area. At the top of the switch-backs we found a skid mark, of unknown cause. The skid mark was about 20" long and 4" wide. Small rocks were scattered on top of the short vegetation just off the trail at the end of the skid mark. At the top of the last switch-backs we found what appears as one human track coming off the trail and going down hill. The human track stays 20 yards off the tree line going down hill. The human track also crossed the trail in three spots. This is where we lost the human track. We also observed what appears to be three different bear tracks coming down onto the trail from above the trail. The three tracks cross all the trails right along with the human track. The three tracks follow the human down below the trail where we lose all of the tracks. All four tracks were in scree and did not indicate a speedy decent.

The investigation was largely complete. Now it was a matter of biding their time until the autopsy and DNA analysis was in. A May 27 Glacier National Park press release brought up-to-date information on the autopsy report. The press release was especially interesting since it indicates Park officials still had a high level of interest in how Craig Dahl died:

Pathology results from an autopsy will not be available until next week; however, preliminary results indicate there was no evidence of head trauma or other injuries caused by a fall. Preliminarily, autopsy results indicate that Dahl's wounds were consistent with scavenging by wildlife.

The same press release also disclosed Glacier Park's interest in consulting with bear experts from other agencies and from universities regarding the incident and its concomitant circumstantial evidence before deciding on any future management action.

Meanwhile the news media worked every lead. Jack Potter, Glacier's Assistant Chief Ranger was quoted as saying in a May 27 Kalispell *Daily Inter Lake* story:

> *"The field investigation is complete and there were no witnesses or telltale clues to what transpired," Potter said.*
>
> *"Our biggest thing to go on is to determine if that sow and those cubs were there," he said.*
>
> *Rangers want to confirm the identity of the scavengers before taking any action.*
>
> *"Removal from the system is one of the options we are considering," Potter said.*
>
> *"That can mean sending the bears to a zoo, relocating them far from the area, or killing them."*

In the meantime, the bears are being treated as a threat to visitors. The entire Two Medicine backcountry is temporarily closed, and tent camping is forbidden at Two Medicine campground until further notice.

As the news story indicated, a search was initiated for approved facilities [zoos or research labs] who might take one or more of the bears should the decision ultimately be to place them in captivity. None were found.

Nearly two weeks had passed since Craig Dahl's death and Glacier Park's administrative lack of action toward any guilty bears was causing rumbles in the press. For lack of any direct information on the Dahl fatality, the ghost of Matthew Truszkowski was resurrected. As early as May 20, on the day Dahl's remains were found, the Daily Inter Lake wove Truszkowski's disappearance into their story:

> *... This week's search in Two Medicine Valley had ominous tones from the onset. It was eerily similar to a frustrating search in June 1997 in the same area.*
>
> *In that case, another 25-year-old GPI employee was hiking alone. He failed to report in, and searchers covered 17,000 acres in the following weeks. No sign of the Michigan man, Matthew Truszkowski has ever been found.*

31

Scattering the Targets

It seems ironic that, despite the painstaking nature of the examination into Craig Dahl's death and the equally laborious decision-making process on what to do about it, the investigative conclusion was buried in a single sentence of the final paragraph of a June 5 press release, after the decision was rendered on a course of action and the action largely complete. The sentence reads:

> *Investigators suggest the following scenario: Dahl, who was hiking alone, surprised a family group of grizzly bears; fled; was pursued, killed, and then consumed.*

Not very revelatory, that bit of information, coming after the cumulative effects of copious evidence. And it seems strange the Park Service waited so long to release their official conclusion—and in such an obscure fashion.

There was, after all, the state of Craig Dahl's remains. That scavenging took place was never in doubt, nor whether a bear or bears were involved. It was only whether predation occurred that was in question. And clearly, the evidence weighed heavily that it did. Dahl's broken eyeglasses, the bits of torn clothing, the stocking cap, his backpack (though its location wasn't confirmed until several days later), all seemingly discarded as if the man desperately tried to divert pursuit seems more than just circumstantial evidence that he was stalked or chased, then killed.

Indeed, it might be laudatory that the agency waited—however impatiently—for the results of the autopsy and for the DNA analysis before passing judgement on which bears were perpetrators. But evidence about *who* did it has no bearing on whether it was, in fact, done.

In addition, there's a phase about the investigation that also puzzles—the special investigator who climbed the mountain a week after Craig Dahl fled down it. Specifically, some individuals find it amazing that anyone, no matter how "special" the investigator might be, could find tracks in the pea gravel scree, let alone read evidence into it that a man was pursued by three bears and that none of them were engaged in "a speedy descent." Especially one might consider it amazing when weather records are examined and it's found that snow fell on the mountain during and after Dahl's flight, followed by two subsequent days of rain.

In addition, according to a June 5 Glacier Park press release, the young men who found Dahl's backpack testified they "saw tracks in a *snowfield*." [emphasis mine] And that "they observed human footprints that appeared to be running straight downhill directly above where Dahl's body was later found."

As a result, one might have trouble with the special investigator and his findings that appear to be questionable enough to have been designed. The most regrettable fact about the special investigator's muddying the waters with questionable findings was that the evidence already seemed sufficiently conclusive without his corroboration.

Despite any questions, the conclusion remains: "Dahl, who was hiking alone, surprised a family group of grizzly bears; fled; was pursued, killed, and then consumed."

With *whether* finally put to rest, administrators now turned fully on *who*?

Obviously, Chocolate Legs and her two offspring were prime suspects. No doubt suspicion focused on those three bears even before Craig Dahl's remains were located, probably from the moment the receiver began pulsing the blond sow's location from the forest above Appistoki Falls. But suspicion is one thing, proof another. And the font of knowledge bubbled oh! so slowly while Park officials waited for proof, one way or the other.

Meanwhile, Chocolate Legs and her cubs fled from an Appistoki drainage saturated with humans. To the bears it must have become speedily clear that they were confronted with circumstances they'd never before experienced. Paradise Creek and Cobalt Lake, Sinopah Mountain and Upper Two Medicine Lake, Bighorn Basin and Rising Wolf. Everywhere they went they found the land empty of people—except for armed and vigilant rangers working only in pairs. Each was equipped with two-way radios and without exception, all knew Chocolate Legs' location before the blond bruins even knew humans were in the vicinity.

To compound their problem, the last week of May and the first week of June is yet a period of short rations for grizzly bears. And if, indeed, these bears had begun to associate humans with supplemental rations during critical periods, they'd suddenly been dramatically cut off from all opportunity.

So they ceaselessly traveled, looking for something perhaps they couldn't identify. Their wide-ranging search for food first led them to the auto campground at the foot of Two Medicine Lake, the one place in all the valley where hard-sided camping was still permitted. From the *Chronology* report, Case/Incident number 980106:

> *May 23, 1998 Female grizzly and two cubs were seen above Pray Lake. At approximately 1300 hours [1:00 pm] the DNA Research Crew spotted the bears on the Northshore Trail, across from the picnic area. The bears were viewed walking down the trail toward the campground. For about ten minutes the bears were out of sight, until they were seen at the foot of the bridge that crosses Two Medicine Creek. The two cubs walked on to the bridge.*
>
> *At the time, Kim Peach, Joe Manley (both armed with a shotgun), and Blackfeet Tribal Wildlife Biologist Dan Carney approached the bears to within approximately 150 feet, yelled and drove the bears off the bridge. The bears stayed there after continued yelling.*
>
> *Kim Peach fired one cracker round [an explosive noisemaker for use in shotguns], the female ran, the cubs stayed put. One more cracker round was fired hitting one cub in the rump. Both cubs then ran off to join the female.*
>
> *The bears were later spotted up slope from the trail, and safely viewed by numerous visitors for more than two hours.*
>
> *Three visitors were cited for entering a "Closed" area.*

As late as May 27, Park Service press releases were still so circumspect no one could charge officials with premature decision-making:

> *Rangers hazed a radio-collared 13-year-old female grizzly bear with two, 2-year-old young from entering the Two Medicine Campground Saturday, May 23. Given there are no other known collared grizzly bears in that area, this collared female is suspected to be the same bear whose telemetry signal was detected in the Appistoki Valley above Scenic Point Tuesday night, May 19. That next day, the radio-collared bear was detected farther up the valley. Although this family of grizzly bears is suspected to have been involved in scavenging at the scene where Dahl was found, park officials are awaiting results from DNA tests to verify this assumption before determining a management direction or specific actions.*

As one can readily see, the case, though solved on the ground and nearing lab completion, was a many-headed hydra. With the decision rendered that bears had pursued (perhaps even stalked) and killed Dahl, and a decision nearing on the bears responsible, Park staffers next began consideration for the penalty phase. From a June 2 press release:

> *The adult female's recent history has been compiled and has been considered in the ongoing investigation. The female grizzly has had a history of habituation to people and frequenting trails and developed areas. She was trapped last year just outside the park on Blackfeet tribal lands after approaching people and licking barbecue grills in the area. At that time, the adult female and one cub were trapped and hair samples were collected, while the mother was fitted with a radio collar. Both bears were ear tagged, released on site, and hazed from the area.*

Strangely enough, it was only after the Tribal biologist captured a blond grizzly sow in the tribal campground and told research biologists at Park Headquarters of it that anyone wondered if the trouble-making blond Two Medicine bear with the brown legs could be Chocolate Legs? Carney said he'd noticed the sow he captured at the Red Eagle Campground in 1997 had at one time been tagged in her left ear, but that the tag no longer existed. The bear's age and the missing-tag matchup fit.

Further research disclosed that the bear known as Chocolate Legs, a two-year-old, was darted at Many Glacier in July, 1983, and transported to the head of Pinchot Creek. And that she'd had an ear tag punched into place on her left ear. This latest document connecting the Chocolate Legs of yore with the blond Two Medicine sow concluded with this analysis of her Many Glacier capture and relocation:

> *... it seems the main complaint was it [she] appeared to be habituated and overly familiar with humans on the Iceberg Lake Trail. I find no report of aggressive behavior.*

At last, the end of the circle approached its beginning—Chocolate Legs at Many Glacier and Chocolate Legs at Two Medicine. Authorities wondered then what to do with her, just as they wondered now.

She wasn't making it any easier, however, as the chronology of the family during that last week in May demonstrates:

> *May 24, 1998 Female and cubs last seen on the south side of Sinopah at 1218 hours.*

> *May 25, 1998 Telemetry could not locate bears and no visual of grizzly family group.*

> *May 26, 1998 Telemetry signal received on south side of Sinopah.*

> *May 27, 1998 Telemetry signal places female towards head of Two Medicine Lake, possibly in the upper drainage.*

> *May 28, 1998 Telemetry signal of female on the large ridge off Rising Wolf, on the north shore of Two Medicine Lake.*

> *May 29, 1998 Telemetry signal of female in Upper Two Medicine drainage.*

But it wasn't just the family's mobility that concerned Park officials. While they waited for DNA and autopsy results before deciding on a proper course of action, the bears themselves approached their own denouement. The cubs were, of course, teenagers in the ursid world. For all practical purposes, they were ready to go it alone.

With the cubs reaching for adulthood, the mother was ripe to cycle back into estrus. If she were to go into "season," it followed that at least one adult male bear would soon appear on the scene, rupturing the family. If the nuclear family flew apart, on-the-ground rangers responsible for accomplishing actions laid down by their bosses could be faced with finding three separate bears instead of one tight-knit group

Of this possibility, officials were aware. By the end of May, their worst fears were realized. With no other recourse, there was a modicum of wishful thinking. From a June 2 press release:

> *Rangers have been closely monitoring the family group of grizzly bears since [the remains of Craig] Dahl, 26, of Winter Park, Colo., was found near the Scenic Point Trail. In recent days, the female has been observed with a male grizzly bear. Her two young remain in the general area although not immediately with the female. Grizzly bears will typically separate from their mother on a gradual basis. They usually venture out and return to their mother numerous times before ultimately separating from her altogether.*

Now the fat was in the fire! The entire incident, from Craig Dahl's disappearance until the end—whatever it might be—represented a crisis (as it would in any national park) for Glacier's administration. They were, however, as the same June 2nd press release made clear, ready to move:

> *West Glacier, Mont - Officials at Glacier National Park announced this morning that efforts are underway to remove three grizzly bears believed to be involved in scavenging at the scene where Craig Dahl's body was found Wednesday, May 20.*
>
> *Park officials have been awaiting results of DNA tests to confirm identity of the bear (or bears) involved in scavenging on the body. Initial DNA test results indicate a match between hair samples previously collected from the adult female and DNA obtained from scat collected at the scene.*

They'd covered their bases pretty well:

> *According to Acting Superintendent Charles (Butch) Farabee, "Based on our investigation, on management criteria set forth in Glacier's Bear Management Plan, and on consultation with officials from the U.S. Fish and Wildlife Service, the Interagency Grizzly Bear Committee (IGBC) and international grizzly bear experts, rangers have initiated management actions to remove the three bears from the populations. Rangers will undertake the management actions necessary and consistent with existing guidelines, while using the safest methods available to remove the bears, including trapping, snaring, shooting, or other methods as necessary."*

The decision to remove the bears was based entirely (at that time) on the results of DNA analysis that Chocolate Legs and her cubs were the bears feeding on Craig Dahl's remains. But the decision to remove the bears was made without forensic evidence that they did, in fact, kill the young man. Not everyone agreed with the decision, posthumously including the victim, Craig Dahl, according to his girlfriend. In a June 4, 1998 *Hungry Horse News* story by Emmett Berg, Gretchen Young was reported as saying:

> *Of his untimely death, Young has few delusions. She says she knows it was a grizzly that killed him, and that he must have gotten himself into a situation that he couldn't handle by himself.*
>
> *She feels, however, that plans for the removal of the bears linked to the scene would be contrary to Dahl's wishes. If anything, she maintained, it was the humans who invaded upon the grizzlies' space, not the reverse.*
>
> *"Craig would never want an animal destroyed because of what happened to him," she said.*

Gretchen Young's views were echoed by others in mail, faxes, e-mails, and letters to the editor in newspapers around Glacier National Park. But, again, officials had done their homework.

One area newspaper reported the consulting panel of bear

experts from different agencies and universities, after evaluating the evidence at the scene, as well as the bears' previous bold behavior, were "nearly unanimous" in concluding that the bears should be destroyed.

The lone professional dissenter was Dr. Charles Jonkel, director of the Ursid Research Center at the University of Montana in Missoula and one of the most respected and experienced bear researchers in the world. Dr. Jonkel's dissent was directed mostly in defense of the young female cub, "and her value to the Park, to Montana, to the Blackfeet. From what I know, the evidence implicating her was `thin and circumstantial'; given proper aversive conditioning, I think that she could have stayed a successful grizzly bear."

His contention, of course, was that the female cub may have been guilty of nothing more than scavenging. And he still believes it might have been possible to change or alter her behavior toward humans through "aversive conditioning"—by teaching her that contact with humans can be unpleasant.

Dr. Jonkel was an early proponent of aversive conditioning as tools to change unacceptable bear behavior in the animals' relations with people. For instance in the early 1980s, graduate students working with Dr. Jonkel's Border Grizzly Research Project were instrumental in experimental development of an effective capsaicin pepper spray for bear defense.

It was in this cutting-edge work that Carrie Hunt got her start. From there, however, the attractive lady's professional career has gone to the dogs....

Closing the Ring

When most people think of biologists to the *Ursus arctos horribilis* clan, they probably think of hulking, black-bearded, bushy-haired, wild-eyed, social misfits who are human equivalents to the animals they trap and study. Carrie Hunt doesn't fit the mold. Instead of hulking, she's 5'1" and weighs in at 115 pounds. Instead of black-bearded, she's fair-haired and has no need for Burma Shave. Instead of wild-eyed, the lady has spent much of her life shrewdly analyzing ways we human animals can help bear animals survive into the 22nd Century.

Hunt's M.S. Thesis at the University of Montana was titled: *Behavioral Responses of Bears to Tests of Repellents, Deterrents and Aversive Conditioning*. In the course of research for her thesis project, she was first to seriously investigate and develop the use of capsaicin pepper spray on bears, actually conducting tests on captive and free-ranging grizzly and black bears.

Carrie Hunt's research also took her through the full range of tools available (at that time) for use in conditioning ursids to avoid people—rubber bullets, firecracker shells, noisemakers—and she saw limitations in each.

The first limitation was simply in the "reach" of the mechanical devices then available—how far can firecracker shells reach? Rubber bullets? For that matter, the newly developed pepper spray had its limitations, also. She discovered food-conditioned animals soon learned to associate humans with the noisemakers or the sting of rubber bullets. As a consequence, the animals learned to avoid humans, moving with impunity just beyond reach of their annoying devices.

The second limitation the researcher recognized was our relatively weak senses—we simply didn't always know when a grizzly bear nosed around our garbage can or bird feeder. And despite the dominance of our cunning and creative brains, our coordination and agility is nothing like that of bears and other animals, wild or tame. Therefore, even if we spotted a bear in our territory, often our reaction was too slow to apply aversive conditioning. As a result, if we can't see them, or react with dispatch when we do, the world belongs to other creatures, every one of whom can smell and hear better and react more swiftly than we *Homo sapiens*.

The third limitation is one of effective security surveillance. We simply cannot maintain high-level alertness throughout twenty-four-hour days.

Because of our limitations, Carrie Hunt thought, bears conditioned to finding food around human habitation would continue returning to those places. If nothing bad happened to them when they did—if their prior aversive conditioning wasn't reinforced with another dose—then they received mixed signals: that food gathered by ransacking cabins or garbage cans or horse barns isn't *always* met with a dose of pepper or rubber bullets or firecracker shells.

About the time Ms. Hunt mulled over the problem of inconsistent aversive conditioning, she heard of a special breed of dog from the border region between Finland and Russia. The dogs, so it was said, were bred for the specific purpose of hazing bears. Intrigued, the lady investigated the Karelian Bear dogs in the land where the breed was developed, became infatuated, and returned home to experiment with raising them as tools for aversive conditioning of problem American bears.

"Just as a Border Collie has an instinct for handling sheep," she writes, "Karelians enter the world with an instinct for handling bears safely."

Carrie Hunt established the Wind River Bear Institute at Heber City, Utah and after she'd properly trained her first Karelian bear dogs, opened her doors as a consultant on bear management to wildlife biologists and land managers around the world—not without success.

It was to Carrie Hunt that Glacier Park officials put in a call after Craig Dahl's remains were discovered and the decision was made to take no action against the bears until officials had proof.

The Park Service Summary of Case/Incident #980106, carried this entry for May 30, 1998:

> *... at approximately 1200 hours [noon] received results of the DNA analysis, results were positive. Initial planning session to discuss management action of suspected grizzly family group. First sighting of female with a large dark colored male, they were on the south face of Rising Wolf. Uncertain how long the female and cubs have been split up.*

The disquieting news of the family's breakup was followed the next day with a brief sentence about the Karelian dogs' arrival, placed at the end of a dispatch detailing the placement of snares and culvert traps:

> *Tim Manley and Carrie Hunt arrived in the valley at 2000 hours [8:00 pm].*

Now the players were all in place.

Tim Manley, a grizzly bear specialist with Montana's Department of Fish, Wildlife & Parks, is one of the most respected grizzly trappers and bear management specialist for the state of Montana. He's also vitally interested in aversive conditioning and a convert to Carrie Hunt's enthusiasm for Karelian Bear dogs and their possibilities for future bear management. Since his introduction to the breed, Tim also raises and trains Karelians—which accounts for his arrival on the scene.

At the time Carrie and Tim were invited to the Two Medicine, management concern was primarily directed at keeping Chocolate Legs and her cubs from visitors and investigators. But by the time of their arrival, the focus had shifted to evaluating the practicality of aversive conditioning, especially for the subadult female.

It's important to understand that individuals within the National Park Service are human, too; that differing philosophies are constantly at play, pushing and pulling at competing beliefs.

Views are driven by operational goals and objectives but influenced by on-the-ground exigencies. Perhaps a day-to-day ranger struggling to keep bears and people apart might view a situation differently from an official responsible for directing Park operations within Washington guidelines that are, in turn, set by national politics and national interests.

Those tugs, low-key and invisible to outsiders though they may be, are constant. Biologists are, as is the nature of their profession, more interested in the theoretical than managers, say, who are the ones who must fend off criticism when tactics go awry. The simple thing, from the outset, would have been to eliminate Chocolate Legs and her cubs and be done with it.

But to eliminate the bears without ensuring they were the animals involved would've invited massive criticism through the press, as well as from environmental and animal rights groups. Besides, acting swiftly without thoroughly exploring their options might also be contrary to the Endangered Species Act and its recovery goals, which has clearly identified the retention of breeding females as key to recovery of grizzly bears in the Lower 48.

On the other hand, rangers at Two Medicine were dealing with not one, but three probable killer bears who were still moving freely about within their jurisdiction. And that's not to mention that a concern for human safety was overriding with all involved officials.

Yet might the young female be spared? Might she be rehabilitated through aversive conditioning? If aversive conditioning were to succeed in assuring the young female developed a healthy respect for humans, it was obvious to everyone that she would have to be conditioned in the field, not in a lab. Moreover, she would have to be conditioned to avoid people in the backcountry, not just along roadsides and in auto campgrounds. In short, it would be necessary to "work" the subadult in the backcountry by pursuing her with dogs and perhaps hit her with a dose of cracker shells or rubber bullets or capsaicin pepper spray each time she neared humans.

But taking the Karelian dogs into the backcountry to "work" a bear is an entirely new approach and would require management rethinking, as well as retooling of long-standing policy relative to the use of dogs in Glacier. Could it even be done? Would visitors accept it if the decision was to make the attempt?

Would managers themselves accept it? Would Carrie Hunt try it with her dogs?

In the final analysis, the attempt would be a major experimental effort in attempting grizzly bear behavioral modification. The question was put to Carrie Hunt and Tim Manley. The two Karelian handlers needed more information: What was the Park's goals and objectives? Without clear delineation of objectives, how could an operational plan be designed? Did Carrie wish to risk her and her dogs' reputation on such a high profile case without more information on what was expected?

It was in these crucial days that the first results of DNA lab analysis were returned and the official decision was to eliminate the bears. The May 30 DNA results, which positively identified Chocolate Legs and her cubs as the bears scavenging Craig Dahl's remains, were still incomplete. However, the final report, arriving a week later, were more extensive. According to a June 8 press release:

> *Additional DNA test results received over the weekend confirm that human DNA was isolated and identified in six of 11 bear scat (feces) samples collected at the scene of the incident. Human DNA was also identified in samples that contained the adult female grizzlies' genotype. Hair samples previously taken from the male grizzly in 1997 were matched to hair samples collected where Dahl's body was found. The two-year-old female's DNA was also matched with that of samples collected at the scene.*

Now one begins to comprehend the importance of the hair samples Dan Carney took from both Chocolate Legs and her male cub when he trapped the bears in the Red Eagle Campground in 1997. Had the Blackfeet Tribe's biologist not supplied the investigation with his hair sample data, scientists could not have positively identified which bears were involved without first collecting samples of their own.

And that's not to mention the collar—without pulse beats from the tribe's radio collar around her neck, officials might have lost track of Chocolate Legs altogether.

So they had positive matchups with Chocolate Legs and her male offspring as having been involved in scavenging the body. But Carney hadn't trapped the young female, thus could've taken no hair samples from her. How did scientific analysis get a positive matchup that she had been in on the scavenging, as indicated in the final report? Here's how:

May 31, 1998, at 0300 [3:00 am] telemetry signal showing female moving up valley. Evening, set three culvert trap (two at foot bridge in campground and one in bone yard near the trail spur) and two trail snare sets....

June 1, 1998, telemetry places the female in the Upper Two Medicine drainage. No sign found during a patrol of the Upper Two Medicine Lake and Northshore Trail. Placed a bait snare and two modified trail sets across the foot of Two Medicine Lake

June 2, 1998, telemetry placed the female in the Upper Two Medicine drainage this morning. At approximately 1200 hours [noon] rangers observed the female and large male grizzly in the avalanche chute on Sinopah while patrolling the lake. The male appeared to be pushing (moving fast) the female east on the Southshore Trail.

Located one cub on southeast slope of Rising Wolf, appears to be moving down slope towards the bait. Cub came into bait area, four rangers were sent to attempt a free range dart. Cub sensed people when they were within 40 yards and ran up slope. The cub returned within 15 minutes and tripped the trail sets. Hair was collected from a stab the cub ran into. Approximately one-half hour later, cub returned to bait area, sprung the two snares and fed on the bait. Darting was again attempted, but unsuccessful.

As it turned out, this was indeed the female cub and hair samples collected from the broken stick she'd ran into were forwarded for DNA analysis. Sticking with official insistence on giving the bears every benefit of doubt, a determination was made to wait for the results of analysis before making a final decision as to the young female's fate. With the teenage female hanging around the campground area, capture seemed the only option open at this time.

As we've seen, when one tactic designed to capture her

failed, another was attempted. Still from the June 2, *Chronology*:

> *... Bear dogs were used to attempt treeing or bay-up the cub. Bear ran up the rock cliff band, the trees in the area were not adequate for the bear to climb. Re-baited the snag and reset snares, put in additional snare at the snag. Hung more bait 30 yards away, along with another snare.*
>
> *June 3, 1998, telemetry placed female on south slope of Sinopah. At 0900 hours [9:00 am] spotted one cub on slope of Rising Wolf, it eventually picked up the bait scent in the large avalanche chute and followed it to the snare set. Cub was caught in the snare at approximately 1625 hours [4:25 pm]. At 1630 hour the first Telaxol dart was shot at the cub; the workup was completed at 1900 hours (Handling and Immobilization form completed). The cub was placed in a culvert trap near the foot bridge in the Two Medicine Campground....*

The plan was to use the caged female cub to lure the missing male cub (whose death sentence had already been pronounced) into the area. Meanwhile, officials still awaited the DNA analysis of hair samples from the young female before making any decision on her fate.

And Carrie Hunt yet mulled the question posed to her about whether she and her Karelian Bear dogs could aversively condition the young bear by hounding her in the backcountry. (And Glacier Park officials discussed whether the effort would be advisable, and if so, what Glacier Park's goals and objectives should be?)

Meanwhile, the net was closing. Through careful monitoring of the telemetry signals emanating from her collar, officials kept tabs on Chocolate Legs' location. With the female cub behind bars, only the young male was out of touch and out of reach.

33

Flight from the Net

The end came for Chocolate Legs at 2:02 pm, Thursday, June 4, 1998. It came at the hand of a Glacier National Park ranger equipped with telemetry receiver for location, a helicopter for transportation, and a high-powered rifle to ring down the curtain on her sometimes obscure, sometimes show-stopping, sometimes tragic life.

The *Chronology* Summary of Case/Incident Number 980106 carries this terse announcement under a strange prior paragraph:

> *June 4, 1998 A large black colored black bear was caught in the culvert trap in the bone yard. It was an inadvertent catch and it was released and hazed using the Karelian Bear dogs, rubber bullets, and cracker rounds.*
>
> *Signal of female Upper Two Medicine Drainage. A decision was made to use a helicopter to determine if the male was still with the female. The female was soon located and shot near No Name Lake.*

Glacier National Park's press release for the following day proved equally detail-sparse:

> *West Glacier, Mont - The 13+-year-old female grizzly bear believed to have killed Craig Dahl has been destroyed, Superintendent Butch Farabee announced today. One of the female's two subadult young has also been trapped.*
>
> *Farabee indicated that rangers located the radio-collared female on Thursday in the Upper Two Medicine Valley. Rangers, in cooperation with Blackfeet Tribal biologist Dan Carney, shot and killed the bear at*

approximately 2 p.m. Thursday afternoon, near No Name Lake. The adult bear appeared to be in generally good health, but a routine necropsy (animal autopsy) will be requested.

Ordinarily one can trust the news media to ferret out more depth from a story; especially one occupying so much public interest. But in the case of Chocolate Legs' demise, there was little additional information. Jim Mann's front page story in Kalispell's *Daily Inter Lake* began with these three brief sentences before continuing on with seven additional paragraphs summarizing what had gone before:

Glacier National Park rangers Thursday shot and killed a female grizzly bear suspected of killing a hiker in Two Medicine Valley last month.

The sow was spotted from a helicopter near No Name Lake, at the west end of the valley. After landing near No Name Pass, rangers shot the 13-year-old bear as she crossed a snow field at about 2 p.m.

And in a June 11, *Hungry Horse News* story by Emmett Berg, there was another few crumbs:

... Chocolate Legs was dispatched by rangers after a helicopter search June 4 found her in the Bighorn Basin above No Name Lake. Recently accompanied by an unrelated adult male, rangers found her alone running down a trail.

Dick Mattson, acting District Ranger for Glacier Park's eastern portion and a low-key, can-do guy with extensive experience as a hunter, hiker, horseman, and general outdoors enthusiast, was assigned the job as executioner because he was on-site and qualified. Mattson was accompanied by Ranger Dona Taylor.

Mattson's respect for the competence, courage, and radio telemetry of Dan Carney led him to invite the tribal biologist as the ranger's backup. Had Chocolate Legs known and been capable of human analysis, she might've been proud that she was pursued by the best huntsmen in Glacier Park and the Blackfeet nation.

But bears can't reason in the same manner as humans. Nor could she know of the consequences of helicopters and transmitter location devices. And so she died, running down a trail, crossing a snowfield.

According to the *mortality form* filled out after the action, Chocolate Legs was deemed in "good" condition. Her physical description was listed as "Blonde w/ dark legs, white claws on front feet." Her total length was 55-1/4 inches and her contour length was 68-3/4 inches. The bear's estimated weight was 220 pounds, but her actual weight proved 240.

An examination of her teeth found worn/broken lower incisors. She was lactating.

Chocolate Legs took her last helicopter ride on the way down-valley from Bighorn Basin. Her carcass was photographed in the back of a pickup truck parked at road's end, at Two Medicine.

The blond bombshell with such distinctively colored legs was skinned out and her hide preserved for posterity.

Ranger Dick Mattson also signed off on the June 3rd capture form for Chocolate Legs' female offspring. The subadult bears' weight was estimated at 150 pounds, but actually weighed 130. According to the form, she was darted twice after a left front foot catch in a baited snare one-quarter mile up Northshore Trail from the Pray Lake outlet. The form also advised:

> ... *This appears to be a target sub adult griz involved in Dahl depredation (CI#980106) due to light body and dark legs ... If this is a target bear it will be removed from ecosystem. Used as bait to draw in sibling on 6/4/98.*

Even though it sounded as though the young female's fate was already sealed, there was still enough of a question about it that she was fitted with a tiny, yellow radio transmitter attached to an ear.

While she was still unconscious, her head circumference was measured at twenty-two inches and her neck at twenty-one inches. Rangers also took four vials of blood, assumedly for DNA analysis.

The cub languished in her cage for four days while rangers waited for her sibling's return. The second cub wouldn't play their game, however:

> *June 5, 1998, culvert traps remain empty and we continue to search for the second cub.*
>
> *June 6, 1998, culvert traps remain empty. Completed an aerial search for the second cub.*

And on June 7, the DNA analysis was returned identifying the female cub to the same genesis group as the mother and her male sibling. The Summary of Case Incident Number 980106 for this date tersely states: "A management decision was made to destroy the female cub."

The NPS press release for June 8, 1998 explained the action:

> *West Glacier, Mont - Glacier National Park officials report that the previously captured two-year-old female was being held in an attempt to lure her male sibling into a trap, but after four days in a culvert trap, was humanely killed by park rangers Sunday, June 7.*
>
> *Park managers kept the adolescent female bear alive in captivity strictly for the purpose of attracting the grizzly's sibling into a snare or culvert trap. Typically, after two-year-old grizzlies have been turned out by their mother, they will wander off alone and rejoin their siblings numerous times before ultimately venturing out on their own. Although it was hoped that the juvenile female would bring the other sibling close enough to trap, after four days of holding the bear in a culvert trap, a management decision was made to euthanize her.*

Again, Dick Mattson was tapped for the chore. Then it was two down, one to go. But Chocolate Legs' male cub—the only one of the trio still at large—wasn't cooperating:

> *June 8, 1998 until June 10, 1998, Two Medicine Valley remains closed.*

June 11, 1998, several armed rangers patrolled the trails in the Two Medicine Valley. No significant finding. Second cub has not been seen in the valley since May 31, 1998.

Actually, concern over the whereabouts of the male subadult was more than merely confusing. Patrols moved from one end of the valley to the other, as well as to the passes leading over the mountains. Those patrols didn't just fail to locate the target bear, they found almost no bear sign of any kind—tracks, scat, or tell-tale digs or torn logs or fresh rub trees. Throughout the Two Medicine Valley there appeared to be a dearth of bears of any stripe.

The rangers' absent-ursid reports led to a June 12 press release that had the concessionaires at Two Medicine breathing a sigh of relief, but leaving Park rangers responsible for public safety disquieted:

> *West Glacier, Mont. - Glacier National Park officials today announced plans to reopen portions of the Two Medicine area. This weekend a female grizzly and female subadult involved in the recent fatality of a solo hiker were removed from the area. Park rangers will continue in their efforts to locate and remove the male subadult, also involved in the incident.*
>
> *Bear traps, which are in place to catch the remaining bear, will be removed Thursday, June 11, and the Two Medicine Campground is expected to open for overnight camping on Friday, June 12. Boat tours will begin operations on Thursday, June 11.*
>
> *Bear management rangers will continue patrolling and closely monitoring Two Medicine trails for signs of bear activity. Trails will reopen to the public as conditions permit. Information on current trail status will be available at the Two Medicine Ranger Station....*

When Glacier Park officials made a decision to reopen the Two Medicine Valley to the public, the young male had not been seen for twelve days. Helicopter searches had been conducted. Ground searches by armed rangers had thoroughly covered trails in the Two Medicine environs. In the meantime, his sister had been trapped and euthanized, his mother killed. If the youthful fugitive bruin was still in the valley, he was certainly staying well hidden. If he'd left the area, where did he go?

There was a sense of unease among veteran rangers. Few expected that the final chapter of the Dahl tragedy had already unfolded. Most thought the young male would surface again and there was a general fear that a similar incident would occur, again with tragic consequences.

Amid the void, rumors took root. A report in a June 18 issue of Columbia Falls' *Hungry Horse News* is a case in point:

> *Two Medicine - The final member of the Chocolate Legs grizzly family that mauled and devoured hiker Craig Dahl is still at large.*
>
> *Glacier Park authorities are continuing patrols for the two-year-old male grizzly in the Two Medicine and Upper Two Medicine Lake areas but have seen no sign of the bear.*
>
> *Two Medicine subdistrict ranger Dona Taylor said there was no trace of the animal. She said she was familiar with speculative reports that the boar grizzly seen frequenting the area with Chocolate Legs had killed the fugitive subadult. At the moment, there was no evidence to support that conclusion, she said. The cub's disappearance was also aided by recent weather in the valley.*
>
> *"It's been straight rain here," Taylor said. "Tomorrow they've forecasted thunderstorms, which almost seems like an improvement."*
>
> *Authorities conducted an aerial search for the bear while on an unrelated mission in the past week but found nothing.*
>
> *The entire Two Medicine Valley is open to visitor use. In fact, all Glacier Park trails are open to visitors, spokeswoman Amy Vanderbilt reported.*

The very next day, Kalispell's *Daily Inter Lake* reported:

> *The search for a young grizzly bear believed to have been involved in the mauling death of a Colorado man in Glacier National Park's Two Medicine Valley has been scaled back.*
>
> *"We've had intensive ground surveillance over there,*

but we never saw a thing. That bear just kind of vanished," said Jack Potter, the park's assistant chief ranger.

The two-year-old male hasn't been seen since May 31....

Potter said rangers will continue an "opportunistic" search for the remaining grizzly on routine patrols. If the bear is found, it most likely will be destroyed.

Potter discounted speculation that the bear may have been killed by a large boar grizzly that was seen with the mother grizzly shortly before she was destroyed.

"I don't think we have a good hard theory of what happened to it," he said. "It could have been forced from the area" by the larger bear, or it may have simply moved out of the Two Medicine Valley.

Trails and campgrounds in the Two Medicine Valley were closed for several weeks after [Craig] Dahl's remains were found. Now visitors are being advised to report any sightings of bears that fit the fugitive grizzly's description. Flyers are being posted throughout the valley, Potter said.

The bear is said to weigh 125-150 pounds, has dark legs and a lighter colored body. It has an aluminum tag on its left ear, placed there after the bear was captured with his mother in a campground on the Blackfeet reservation last year.

But every report still begged the question for on-the-ground rangers: Where had the young fugitive *Ursus arctos horribilis* gone? And would he return?

34

Return of the Fugitive

On the 21st of June, Father's Day came and Father's Day went without word of the fugitive grizzly. Glacier Park officials breathed a little easier after each passing day. Perhaps the young male bruin saw what happened to sis and mom and left the Two Medicine country for healthier climes. Or perhaps the big silvertip that split the family really did kill the cub. Or perhaps an internal reformation had taken place deep within the subadult ursid.

An entire raft of questions about the illusive animal were answered at 2:45 in the afternoon of June 24, when the last of what some wags referred to as the "Ma Barker" bear family stalked a party of seventeen hikers on their way down from a visit to Twin Falls, heading for the boat dock at the upper end of Two Medicine Lake. Someone in the close-packed tour group from the Glacier Park Boat Company discovered the oncoming bruin and shouted "Bear!"

The group's interpreter, Tony McDermott, acting with courage and dispatch, stayed between the bear and his party, guiding the group into an open-sided shelter at the end of the lake. With the group protected from three sides, the guide radioed his tour boat, the Sinopah, which was only a short distance off-shore, for a rescue. Meanwhile, Chocolate Legs' son continued to menace the party.

McDermott feared for other hikers who might be in the vicinity. Here's the tale in his own words, as reported in the Investigation Summary, Case/Incident Number 980106:

> *I returned from my Twin Falls walk with a group of 16 people. We arrived at the shelter at 1445 hours as a condensed group. One of the people shouted bear and I*

saw a young subadult grizzly running towards the group. The bear left his direction of travel, approximately 30 yards [away], and started north. I told my group of people to stay together in the shelter until the boat arrived and then to proceed on the boat slowly. I proceeded up the trail to the outhouse to see if anyone was there. As I moved up the trail I noticed the bear following me 30 yards parallel to the trail and myself. I arrived at the outhouse and no one was there. Seconds later the bear appeared in front of me in the trees and charged to a distance of 20-30 feet....

Was this a new type of human to the obviously predatory young bear? He didn't run. He didn't play dead. Instead, he warily faced the young bear at every turn—as we later find out, armed with a half-filled canister of pepper spray.

... The bear aborted its charge, stood on its hind legs and growled and clacked his teeth, and then took off into the trees. I walked down the trail to the shelter and helped the boat leave. I stayed at the shelter to wait for incoming hikers. Approximately 5 minutes after the boat left I noticed the bear once again. He walked around for 10-15 minutes and then charged me again. He started his charge at about 50 yards away from my location. I attempted to climb on top of the shelter and fell. I noticed that the bear stopped his charge when I hit the ground. Two [incoming] hikers witnessed the charge and my fall. The boat arrived back at the dock and we went back to the other side of the lake.

The Sinopah returned with Glacier National Park law enforcement officer, Joe Manley, armed with a shotgun. McDermott told the officer he clearly saw an aluminum ear tag in the blond, chocolate-legged bear. Manley got a glimpse of a bear, but could not positively identify it as the fugitive subadult.

There's one other interesting passage in the Summary:

Ranger Manley was assisted by three Tribal employees in searching the area thoroughly, but the bear was not seen again.

That Dan Carney! He has a penchant for turning up wherever those chocolate-legged bears violate their paroles.

The entire incident at Pray Shelter deserves closer scrutiny: First of all, the bear in question could hardly have been in a more predatory mode. Steve Frye, Glacier's Chief Ranger, characterized the bear's behavior as very aggressive. "Surprisingly so for a bear that age and that size. Especially when you consider the size of the group of people."

Ranger Frye's assessment should be considered a classic understatement. In the annals of recorded western history, accounts of a single bear trying to cut out human prey from a large party of people (my God, seventeen!) is virtually non-existent, demonstrating either a streak of madness in this particular creature, or a clear lack of judgement. In fact, the only similar accounts that can be recalled was when an animal was wounded and suicidally charged its attackers.

This was obviously a demented bear with little or no regard for humans, probably hungry to the extreme—a lethal combination when mixed with an animal, even a young one—capable of turning into a killing machine.

Consider also the heroism and judgment of Tony McDermott. From the time a member of his tour group shouted, "Bear!" until McDermott and the last hikers for which he felt responsible were boarded on the Sinopah, the young man demonstrated decisiveness and valor. It took guts to venture alone to the Pray Shelter toilet to ensure no one was unwittingly left behind, especially while being stalked by a known killer grizzly bear. It took even more guts to stay behind when the boat pulled away with his charges, so that he might warn possible incoming hikers of their danger.

Emmett Berg, writing in the July 2, 1998 issue of *Hungry Horse News* treats the McDermott subject well:

> *... The guide, who was between the grizzly and the hikers, said the bear approached within 30 yards and then aborted the charge, choosing instead to jump across a creek that paralleled the trail....*

The guide then approached nearby pit toilets in an attempt to locate two hikers that reportedly were using the facilities and had not yet been accounted for. During the short journey he was shadowed by the grizzly, who woofed and sidestepped the man in predatory fashion. He arrived at the toilet, finding no one. The grizzly was off to his right and charged him again for a short distance, he said. The animal stood on its hind legs growling and clacking his teeth. The guide was armed with something less than a full canister of bear spray, but he was not forced to use it.

The bear soon went away and the guide returned to the boat dock to help load the hikers on to the Sinopah, which was just off shore when the first incident occurred and turned around immediately. Visitors on board reported seeing the grizzly nearby as the boat pulled away....

Let's put ourselves in McDermott's position at this point. What went through the young man's mind as the boat pulled away, leaving him alone at Pray Shelter while a hungry grizzly bear sizing him up for porterhouse possibilities prowled nearby.

... The guide stayed behind to warn a group of hikers that was reportedly stranded at the head of the Two Medicine Valley.

In the 15 minutes after the boat left, the guide watched the grizzly, who appeared uninterested in his human observer. But hikers approaching the shelter said the bear charged him [McDermott] one final time, charging down from the creek bed, causing the guide to climb on top of the shelter....

(That, too, sounds like an understatement. I'd rather imagine the desperate guide "scrambled" for the roof. Probably in a great deal of haste.) To continue on:

... He slipped on the logs on his way up and fell, breaking the radio and losing his wind....

(The breath was knocked from him on impact.)

... That was when the guide grew afraid for the first time, he said. He was on the ground and wondering if he could withstand a grizzly bite without screaming.

But the grizzly stopped his charge when the guide fell, he said. The bear cocked his head and emitted a low, sorrowful moan. Then the bear disappeared.

Fortunately we can only guess what might have happened had a lone hiker chanced down the trail at the upper end of Two Medicine Lake that day. Or a smaller party—say a family group with young children. It's not unusual for just such families to visit there. Or what might've happened had the maddened bear even managed to carve one frightened person from the party of 17?

Naturally the near-tragic incident at Pray Shelter precipitated an all-out bear hunt. Park officials once again closed all trails in the Two Medicine Valley to public use and a call for armed rangers to head for the Two Medicine went out all over the Park. Enforcement officer Joe Manley was soon followed by others, and before nightfall, the upper end of Two Medicine Lake resembled an armed camp. At the lower end of the lake, "Incident" leaders burned late-night oil planning for the following day.

The following day was a Thursday, June 25; rangers searched the Upper Two Medicine Valley for the bear with little results. Two rangers with orders to shoot to kill patrolled the Northshore Trail to Upper Two Medicine Lake and two more rangers patrolled the South Shore Trail to Cobalt Lake. As the day progressed, one of the pair of armed rangers hiked up the Dawson Pass Trail and the other did sentry duty between Two Medicine and Upper Two Medicine lakes.

Again, the young male had seemingly disappeared.

A culvert trap was dispatched by patrol boat to the upper end of Two Medicine Lake, intended for use in an attempt to trap the fugitive grizzly. However, as the boat neared the lake's west end, there was a radio message that a possible sighting of the errant bear had been made. Here's a report lifted from the

Chronology Summary of Case/Incident Number 980106:

> *... On their return [from Dawson Pass] Ranger Yates observed the bear on the north slope of Sinopah in a large avalanche chute.*
>
> *The bear was pegged to be at about the 6,000-foot level, digging for roots in the avalanche area.*

Incident Commander and can-do Ranger Dick Mattson was again tapped for the job. He was accompanied by Ranger Chuck Cameron. Tag alder and false huckleberry brush was dense as Mattson and Cameron made the 800-foot climb up the steep mountain.

Time was a factor—they began their assent in the early evening, conscious that night would soon be stealing upon the sheltered north slope of Sinopah. Meanwhile, rangers stationed on the Upper Two Medicine Lake Trail watched the bear through a spotting scope throughout the stalk. Mattson and Cameron finally eased within range, sighted the animal, set up their own spotting scope and positively identified the bear via the aluminum ear tag as the one sought.

Rangers watching from below said the golden bruin with dark legs never seemed aware that humans approached. Mattson dropped the bear with four shots from a .300 H&H magnum. All four were hits. The last of the bad news family of chocolate-legged grizzly bears fell at 8:50 pm on June 25, 1998.

The male cub must have been a handsome brute. According to the *reporting form* filled out on the action, he had a "blond" body with very dark legs. Dark around eyes. His estimated weight was 140 pounds. His condition appeared to be "good." Due to the lateness of the hour and terrain difficulty, no measurements were taken. The subadult's age was of course established as two-and-a-half years. An ear was taken for DNA sampling purposes.

Otherwise the male cub was left at his death site because the location was sufficiently remote that even if the carcass attracted other animals—as it was sure to do—it posed no threat to human safety.

It was over. Over for the bears, over for the rangers on the front lines. Emmett Berg, the thoughtful staff writer for Columbia Falls' *Hungry Horse News* interviewed Dick Mattson, the guy called upon to execute the death sentence on each of the Chocolate Legs' family of grizzlies. Excerpts from that interview follow:

> *Glacier Park — Glacier National Park Ranger Dick Mattson has been a sportsman and a hunter for nearly all of his 51 years, but the sporting pursuit of wild game was far from his mind during the destruction of the Chocolate Legs grizzly bear family in recent weeks....*
>
> *... Previous to this season, Mattson has removed just two other bears (both black) in his 27-year tenure at Glacier.*
>
> *For rangers, the destruction of wild animals is not easy. But asked if the killing was the most difficult part of his job as a ranger, Mattson said it was not.*
>
> *"Killing is not something I enjoy," he said. "But in this case, it needed to be done."*

Mattson touched on the relief on-the-ground rangers could now feel knowing the wild ride in the Two Medicine was finally over:

> *He explained that part of the Park's mission was to protect visitors as well as wildlife. And in rare cases such as these, he said, management actions were necessary.*
>
> *The events of last week in Two Medicine brought a sense of relief to the rangers in the area, Mattson said. Prior to last week, there was a general sense of unease among the rangers as to how the final chapter of the tragedy would unfold.*
>
> *"In the back of our minds we were worried about a possible similar incident," he said. "It was unlikely but the potential was still there, maybe now or in the future."*

Dick Mattson's boss said he was chosen because he was "the right person at the right place at the right time."

Chief Park Ranger Steve Frye said, "There are a number of rangers who are qualified to do what Dick did. But he is among the best qualified and the best trained."

Frye added, "Dick has excellent judgment and is never reluctant to step up to the plate when we have a difficult task."

The writer, Berg, waxed eloquent in an earlier opinion column about what he called "Grizzly Heaven"—the high, wild country grizzly bears need in order to live and flourish. He imagined a landscape with shining snowfields and "miles of plump huckleberries, abundant herds of deer, elk and goats, shady caves, and clear streams."

Then his editorial turned to a darker side by describing "Grizzly Hell"—in essence the same as the above, but with humans included.

Certainly the Scenic Point Trail was Grizzly Heaven on May 17, 1998, as Craig Dahl hiked it. Then, as Emmett Berg pointed out, it turned to Grizzly Hell ... for both Craig Dahl and the Chocolate Legs family.

The "What If" Game

The story of Chocolate Legs ended with the echoes of the .300 magnum bouncing from the north slope of Sinopah Mountain to one lofty summit after another until it was so worn it failed even to whisper. Chocolate Legs will no longer turn over talus rocks for cutworm moths on Rising Wolf or either of her two sister peaks, nor lay on her back in a flower-filled meadow in Buttercup Park and gather her cubs to her nipples in ecstasy.

But neither will she stalk boldly through campgrounds, seemingly "friendly" to novices to bear behavior from Schenectady or Shreveport.

The blond bombshell with the chocolate-colored legs and dark mask around the eyes will no longer turn tourist heads from mountain scenes so stunning as to make Swiss Alps blush with envy. Nor will she boost the stock of Kodak and Nikon and One Hour Photos across the land by merely pausing in a meadow in late afternoon and staring disinterestedly at a covey of Californians bunched in a nearby crowd.

But neither will the wheels within her brain grind slowly to a mind fork as she weighs an oncoming hiker *for* food or *as* food.

Chocolate Legs is dead. And dying with her is a dream that we have at last learned something about the habits and habitats of grizzly bears; enough so that we may presume to play God with their lives and loves and day-to-day goals and objectives.

Dead, too, is Craig Dahl, and perhaps Matthew Truszkowski—dead on a battlefield of rising human population and Manifest Destiny, or the Endangered Species Act. The tragedy of their deaths, and those of Chocolate Legs' chocolate-legged son and, most of all, her golden daughter, is that each one may have died in vain: that we've all—bears and humans—learned nothing about how to coexist in a world that's shrinking around us through e-mail and Concordes and bull markets in Singapore and Tokyo and New York City.

The greatest tragedy of Chocolate Legs and her story, of course, is in our knowing it almost worked—rescuing the beautiful blond damsel-bear with such distinctively dark legs from delinquency amid a good neighborhood in a great land to lead an exemplary life in a great neighborhood in a good land.

That much we know for sure, but that's all we know. What we don't know is legion: like when and why and how and exactly where she reverted to earlier form. What is worse, we don't know the circumstances leading to her and her cubs going off the deep end—the actual point of viewing people *as* food.

We can play the "what if" game, supposing a multitude of scenarios leading to the turn listed as Case/Incident Number 980106 at Two Medicine, in Glacier National Park. And we should, for that is all we have left to work with.

Since from the outset, I've admitted that much of this book is pure speculation by the author, I've opened myself to ready criticism by a scientific community trained never to speculate without first having every factual "i" dotted and every biological "t" crossed. In defense, I can only plead ignorance—theirs and mine. I hope my mind is open, receptive to new information as it's accumulated and disseminated. In the interim, though, I still believe in "what ifs" as long as they're based on the best information we have, trusting on analysis of the scanty facts to give direction. And as long as logic is utilized to make some deductive hypotheses.

Meanwhile I'll wait for better information.

But that's information that can only be accumulated by the scientific community. And they're precisely the ones who should first be disseminating it in order that lay people make orderly and factual interpretations. That there's a dearth of information about the habits and habitats of grizzly bears is not my fault, nor is it the fault of millions of folks who travel through Glacier or Yellowstone or Banff or Denali parks, and who have a genuine interest in the fate of bears, as well as a personal interest in their own fate while visiting the bears' home.

The argument, of course, can be made by science that the lack of information isn't a fault of scientists, either. They might say the proper gathering of information is a function that must be supported by proper funding and allocation of sufficient blocks of time to do systematic, quality research. But the ink spilled on this point misses the mark. Science itself is usually governed by the body politic. But it's also governed in part by internal machinations of a diffusion of bureaucracies, each operating under a slightly different management paradigm.

For instance, Glacier Park management very much favors a hands-off policy of wildlife research, believing tourists visiting the Park might consider collared animals a form of visual pollution. (See *Learning to Talk Bear*, pages 96-98). But Blackfeet Tribal Management has no such compunctions, believing it proper to have some sort of handle on what a potential problem bear might be up to. Thus, Dan Carney trapped and collared Chocolate Legs from a tribal campground in the spring of 1997.

One wonders—and it's the wondering where speculation begins—how the Craig Dahl tragedy would've unfolded had not Carney placed that collar? Would Dahl's remains even have been found? If Dahl was never found, how could authorities identify the culprits? Or, assuming they'd somehow identified Chocolate Legs and her family as the killers, how could they have tracked them 'til death did them part?

Yes, the argument could be made that had Park officials suspected Chocolate Legs of being a problem bear, they themselves might well have installed a collar on her for security purposes. But they didn't. And logic says the golden-bear family didn't turn into problem bruins the day they stalked into the Red Eagle Campground on the Blackfeet Reservation. Too, rumblings from the Park leads one to believe a blond sow grizzly with two blond cubs was already well on the way to viewing humans with, if not disdain, then certainly indifference before her Red Eagle foray.

The truth is, there's a stout management aversion to radio collars on wildlife in Glacier National Park. It's a paradigm difference between Park philosophy and Blackfeet philosophy. As one of the biologists responsible for Park research told me: "In my mind, I'd rather monitor bears somewhere else"—which is strange, given that Glacier Park is where grizzly bears are, and where humans are sometimes killed and eaten by the great beasts.

Somebody must research grizzly bears *somewhere* in order that Glacier officials understand how to best manage ursids and ourselves to perpetuate both into future centuries. Chocolate Legs serves as an example of a breakdown in that process. She also serves as a reminder that no matter how much Park biologists would prefer grizzlies be studied elsewhere, "elsewhere research" was conducted on this particular Glacier Park animal as much as it could in the brief window of opportunity allotted to non-Park researchers.

As a matter of fact, the Park has sometimes been criticized by state, federal, and tribal officials managing lands around the perimeter of Glacier because Park personnel sometimes fail to share reliable information on bears ranging in and out of Glacier. And they're not the only ones—Glacier National Park was criticized in 1995 by the General Accounting Office for their lack of adequate wildlife research. That criticism came in testimony before U.S. House and Senate subcommittees that oversee the National Park Service.

Today, there's a three-year DNA study of grizzly bears going on in Glacier. That study uses non-intrusive collection of bear hair and scat samples for study purposes and it has enormous potential for counting the number of grizzlies in the Park, as well as delineating their bloodlines. But cataloging DNA types can in no way provide the information managers needed for analysis of cause and effect on the bear Chocolate Legs during her years without a radio transmitter. DNA hair or scat samples could in no way have disclosed why or when Chocolate Legs turned from passive to aggressive, from ursid-normal to savage killer.

Thus it's still a Park enigma, why those bears suddenly turned to pursuit of human prey.

Chris Servheen, coordinator of the U.S. Fish & Wildlife Service's grizzly bear recovery program and a member of the panel of bear experts that overwhelmingly recommended Chocolate Legs' ultimate fate, suggested that something happened in the summer of 1997 to cause Chocolate Legs to view people as food.

Some bear experts believe otherwise, as was reported in an August 18, 1998 story by Mark Derr in the *New York Times*:

> ... *Other experts suggest that the key to understanding what happened lies buried in the particular events of the bear's life and personality. But common threads are habituation and a regular diet of human and pet foods. "If you look at bears that have killed and eaten people, except those provoked by photographers, you see that they have a history of habituation and food conditioning," said*

> *Stephen Herrero, professor emeritus of environmental science at the University of Calgary and a leading authority on bear attacks.*
>
> *But, he cautioned, "Bears are complex, intelligent and individualistic, and so we can't predict their behavior as if they were stimulus-response machines."*

Quoted in the same article:

> *"The amazing thing," Mr. Servheen added, "is that this doesn't happen more often, given that there are people all over their home range. That it does not is evidence that bears generally prefer to let people go their own way."*

Servheen, quoted in a June 18, 1998 *Hungry Horse News* article gave a more comprehensive run-down on why the advisory panel of bear experts eventually concluded to turn thumbs down on Chocolate Legs and her offspring:

> *"... The evidence we had indicated that he (Dahl) fled downhill, that he tried to deter the bears with his pack and clothing," Servheen said. "All of these items were ignored by the bears. His remains were at the end of the trail where the bears caught him. So we have chasing, killing and consumption. That is not classified as natural aggression. We do not tolerate predatory grizzly bears. Period."*
>
> *Servheen said the above combination of circumstances led him to his decision. He noted that in bear mauling incidents, removal of the bear implicated in the matter was not always warranted. He cited the example of Libby photographer Chuck Gibbs, who was mauled and died on April 25, 1987, in Glacier Park after getting too close to a sow grizzly and her three cubs. In that case, the grizzly killed Gibbs but did not feed on his body. No action was taken on the grizzly.*
>
> *"Usually in any kind of natural encounter (between grizzlies and humans) you don't have this long-distance chase and there isn't consumption," Servheen said. "Together, they indicate predation. That makes it unnatural aggression."*

What of Dr. Servheen's hypothesis that something happened in 1997 to cause Chocolate Legs to view people as food? If so, what might it have been?

There's no way we can know, of course, but the first thing coming to mind is that she was trapped for the first time in the Red Eagle Campground—a traumatic experience to the middle-aged mother. And, as if the trapping wasn't dreadful enough, she was handled by humans for the second time. Might that experience have precipitated a change in attitudes toward humans from indifference to impatience to disdain?

These are the kinds of "what ifs?" one loves to ask scientists. And it's the one that usually elicits abrupt replies.

But one thoughtful management biologist studied me for a full two minutes before counseling me to be cautious while writing this book about Chocolate Legs. "I have a problem with ascribing human terms to animals, Roland—to anthropomorphising their feelings and actions."

I thought about his statement for a long time because the man is a gentle, thinking kind of guy, given to meditation and understatement—precisely the kind of biologist/scientist to whom I want to listen long and evaluate carefully. But I came to the conclusion that it might be just as wrong to ascribe no attributes we humans understand to animals as it might be to try to judge their actions as if they were propelled by human motives. Isn't there an opposite to anthropomorphising animals? Who's to say they don't—or can't—love, hate, feel pain, ecstasy, disdain?

Which begs the question—might her caging at the Red Eagle Campground be the trigger that turned Chocolate Legs into a killer?

Well, yes, maybe—if she was that close to the edge, it might. But there are dozens of grizzly bears every year who are trapped and who never become killers because of it. In fact, it's a subject that has been thoroughly researched and the findings are just the opposite—that the experience of being trapped and handled before being loosed actually reinforces the idea that humans are the biggest, baddest gorillas on the block; someone to avoid.

But since I've agreed to ascribe *some* human attributes to bears, I'll likewise have to agree that she might have harbored some resentment toward the guy who had so ignobly handled her—at least Dan Carney thinks she was hunting him that day when she came sniffing into the meadow where he crouched with his radio monitor. But she'd already encountered other people by the time Matthew Truszkowski disappeared. And she encountered other people after, including some single individuals, without leaving a record of aggressive moves.

All right, Roland, you might say, if it wasn't the trapping that turned Chocolate Legs into a killer in 1997, what then?

Well, maybe it's permissible to disagree with the good Dr. Servheen about her year. Why 1997? Why not before? Why not embrace Dr. Herrero's hypothesis that her drift toward viewing humans *as* food instead of merely associating them *with* food might have taken years to accomplish?

But who's to know what happened to Chocolate Legs during the years she was off-radar, without a collar? In fact, who's to know what happened on a day-to-day, hour-by-hour, minute-by-minute basis even during the years she was wearing a collar? Checked just once each week at best, the blond bruin with the dark legs could've pilfered Park Service cabins, organized campsite raids that went unreported, begged copious candy bars from travelers who had every reason not to squeal about their feeding bears to the next ranger they met.

She could have found discarded fish guts from humans' excursions to the lakes and streams of the Continental Divide country. She could've—and did—raid backpacks, cycle through campgrounds, and amble along paved roads where tourists ogled the blond knock-out and probably sneaked sandwiches out of car windows to ensure close-up pictures.

Yet if those things happened, they occurred over many years, not just in 1997. To conclude anything else defies logic.

However, I have a modicum of trouble with the slow-evolvement line of reasoning, too. For instance, there's the question of just when Chocolate Legs moved into the Two Medicine Valley for good. After all, we have three solid years of information on her range prior to June, 1986. And she was only peripherally into the Two Medicine country during that period.

Leaping ahead to the information provided by her radio collar in 1997 and until she was killed in 1998, she spent virtually every minute in the heart of the Two Medicine Basin. So admittedly the golden bear could've shifted her home range to the Two Medicine as early as 1987, but certainly anytime during the decade 1987-96.

But—and it's a big *but*—Chocolate Legs was often recorded

as a very distinctively colored bear. Her blond body, dark mask, and chocolate-colored legs was thought of as a dead giveaway to anyone who got a good look at her. In addition, the record clearly shows she was, until the last, indifferent toward humans, usually unassuming and always unafraid. It would've been out of character, from the outset, for her to have deliberately avoided humans, as well as impossible to have avoided them if she'd dwelled long in the Two Medicine Valley, where humans were plentiful. Yet it wasn't until 1995 that a report came to rangers that a blond bear with dark legs had frightened a couple of hikers at the head of the valley, and raided their packs.

With that incident as reference, I believe it logical to assume Chocolate Legs never really moved into the Two Medicine Valley until 1995. If so, the question then becomes, why wait until then?

I believe it may have been because the Burlington Northern corn spills were cleaned up in 1993. That possibility is why I've concluded Chocolate Legs actually did visit the spills and why I've taken her there in the book.

We humans tend to be smug about our evaluative processes. But as good as we are at linear thinking, we sometimes miss cause and effect. While it is certainly true that grizzly bears were dying on rail tracks and highways because of those corn spills and it would've been better for the endangered bruins had the derailments never occurred, it seems logical that their precipitate removal must have proved a hardship for those bears who'd come to rely on the fermenting corn for their spring food source at a time when they needed it the most.

The cause and effect of the corn cleanup probably was similar to when Yellowstone and Glacier National parks cleaned up their garbage dumps and cut off bears, who for generations had come to depend upon them for sustenance. At that time, the Craighead brothers—deep into a long-time study of grizzly bears—warned the Park Service that it would've been better to have phased the dumps out slowly, rather than remove them all at once; that grizzly bears bereft of that food source would seek food elsewhere and get into trouble and die. The brothers were right enough on the issue that the Yellowstone grizzly bear population declined alarmingly, taking years to find its way back based on more natural food sources.

Yeah, I'm talking apples and oranges here—grizzlies were dying on the tracks because of the grain anyway. And I'm certainly not implying that the corn shouldn't have been removed for the bears' welfare. But it's Chocolate Legs we're talking about here, and whether the corn cleanup might have contributed to her move to the Two Medicine Valley, where she reverted to the other source of spring food she knew—from people.

The timing was right and I think she did.

Another piece of supporting evidence to that hypothesis lies in the Summary of Activities of Grizzly Bear Family in Two Medicine Drainage, 1997 (Female #235, BIR): That summary, based on sightings and telemetry tracking, shows Chocolate Legs around and often approaching people until mid-July, when cutworm moths and berries were plentiful. Then, though she still utilized the bottom of the valley on occasion, she had no further encounters with humans throughout the remainder of the year (except for one incident on Sept. 19, which may have been another bear).

If she actually avoided people later in the season, when natural foods were abundant, then that fact seems to support the belief that she only considered humans as sources for food in times of stress.

In addition, if you'll allow this last piece of supporting evidence for a late move into the Two Medicine Valley: When she did shift her home base, she apparently moved in aggressively—the telemetry readings delineates her home range as relatively small, the heart of the Two Medicine region. That seems to me to indicate a *dominant* female who knew what she wanted and took it.

Her new home range, incidentally, is also the section of the Two Medicine country that is most used by humans. I see no reason for her to carve out the heart of the Two Medicine as home unless Chocolate Legs had identified humans as a source for food and identified the valley as being her prime food gathering ground.

I also see no evidence to believe she moved there until after the corn spill disappeared.

This hypothesis, of course, begs the question of *why* and *when* she turned the corner from viewing humans as *suppliers* of food to viewing humans *as* food.

But I have a theory about that, too.

36

Who Did It?

History is replete with examples of great rivalries: Achilles had his Hector, Caesar his Cicero, Napoleon his Wellington, Hitler his Churchill. There were Gladstone and Disraeli, Lincoln and Lee, Nixon and Woodward & Bernstein. Great figures, to be elevated, require great adversaries. Chocolate Legs rose to national and international notoriety, in part because she found her perfect foil in Daniel Wade Carney.

It was Carney the management specialist who set two culvert bear traps at Red Eagle Campground on May 28, 1997, trapping two bears.

Because Carney the control specialist set two traps and captured two bears, it allowed Carney the research biologist to take hair samples that provided the basic means for later identification of Chocolate Legs and her male son as participants in a particularly noxious crime.

It was Carney the probation officer, in collaboration with Carney the court judge who decided Chocolate Legs should be installed with a monitoring device, and that she and her cub should have identifying aluminum tags clipped to their ears.

It was Carney the inspector who used both telemetry equipment and deductive powers to play a role in the search where Craig Dahl's remains were found.

It was Carney the techie who provided much—or even most—of the radio expertise to monitor Chocolate Legs' movements through 1997 and '98.

And it was Carney the cop who seemed to have an instinct for being just around the corner whenever Chocolate Legs and her miscreant cubs surfaced.

And last of all, it was Carney the cool, experienced field man who was asked in as reliable backup by rangers charged with carrying out the death sentence to Chocolate Legs.

Dan Carney knew his adversary, studied her, did his sums on the animal. What makes this such a compelling rivalry is that she, too, may have known. Had Frederick Forsyth had such rivalry at his fingertips, he might have foregone writing *Eye of the Jackal* to do one on Chocolate nee Carney.

Rivalries aside, we've still not adequately responded to the question of Chocolate Legs, the killer—when, why, where, and how? Was it a sudden thing? A creeping thing? What role did humans play in the blond beauty ultimately becoming a man-killer? Or was it simply a function of her turning cranky with advancing age?

I'm not sure it was any of the above. It may not have happened suddenly or crept upon her over a dozen years. Humans may never have had anything at all to do with turning her into a killer. And age might have made her more patient instead of shortening her fuse. Why, then, did she kill Craig Dahl?

Perhaps she didn't.

Craig Dahl was killed by a bear, yes. Craig Dahl was also pursued down the mountain, then done in and eaten at the end of his flight path. The Chocolate Legs family consumed him, yes. But in lieu of subsequent events, is it not possible that the male subadult—the equivalent of a mad-dog human teenager—did the deed, and not either the mother or the daughter?

Again, let's return to the record. In the days after the tragedy, there is no report of Chocolate Legs demonstrating any aggressive traits.

I'd just mentioned my theory to Tim Manley that it might not have been Chocolate Legs that initiated the attack on Craig Dahl; that instead, it might have been the male two-year-old that was subsequently proven aggressive. "What do you think, Tim? You were there."

The bear management specialist with Montana's Department of Fish, Wildlife & Parks, one of the most respected field biologists in the business, peered at me as he weighed his words. "I think it's possible," he said. "You know, when we tried to run the bears from the campground, she wanted to leave—it was the cubs who wouldn't. The mother ran across the bridge and up on the mountain, then hung around waiting for her cubs. So we cracker-shelled them and one of the cubs ran across the bridge, but the other one didn't seem to want to leave. Even after firing another round—one of the rangers actually hit him with a cracker shell—he didn't want to go. Finally he trotted across the bridge and the mother gathered them together and went up on Rising Wolf Mountain."

He paused, thinking. His already large eyes, outsized through glasses, seemed to be focused in another dimension. "Then, when I heard later that the male cub had actually charged a big group of people, I thought ..." He trailed off.

"What about the female cub?" I asked.

"She seemed much more shy. After they split up [when Chocolate Legs was again coming into estrus and had forced the young bears from the nest] and we were waiting for the DNA results, we decided to capture the cubs. So we put bait out, then set snares. The female cub came into it, sprung the snares, but wasn't caught. So we decided to dart her and we couldn't even get close enough—every time she spotted us, she took off up the mountain. No, she was shy around people, too."

"But not the male cub?"

"Nope. He was bold!"

Chocolate Legs' male cub certainly was bold. Insane, too. Out on his own for just four short weeks and already he acted as if he'd been on a straight diet of loco weed. Without his mother's restraining hand, the young creature was doomed by his own actions. The question was how many innocent people might he take with him on his way to his mountainside mortuary? Fortunately for visitors to Two Medicine on that fateful June 24 day, the first human the masked *Ursus arctos horribilis* met was Tony McDermott.

If Chocolate Legs' perfect foil was Blackfeet biologist, Dan Carney, then her son's equivalent foil turned out to be the courageous Glacier Park Boat Company guide.

Again, let's examine the record to get a sense of what occurred:

It's obvious the fugitive ursid teenager had already made the leap to regard humans as food and he obviously had predation on his mind when he first rushed, then stalked, the hiking group of seventeen people near Pray Shelter. Most of what bears know about life and their environment, including food gathering techniques, they either learn from their mothers or pick up on their own.

Yes, it's possible that the young bear had learned human predation from his mother's knee, but he certainly never learned to prey on packs of humans—a technique shunned even by giant cave bears during an era when humans were equipped with no more than stones and clubs for defense.

That's why I believe the young male grizzly who'd already developed a taste for humans—and thought that they were easier to acquire than chasing mountain goats around cliff ledges—did not learn the hunting technique from his mother. After all, the young bear had not even learned to differentiate between one human and many humans. Had his mother taught him, it seems reasonable to assume she would've also taught him that numbers of the puny smooth-skinned beasts compound threat by compounding quantity.

In short, I believe it was the subadult male grizzly who followed Craig Dahl down the mountain on that fateful day. I believe it was the masked male juvenile who charged after the young man when he broke and ran. And if Craig Dahl tried to play dead as a defensive measure, I believe it was the young, probably already demented, male grizzly who began to tear into the prostrate figure.

Again, examine the record. The young male was crazed, but without his mother's experience to help him cope with erratic humans. When Glacier Park Boat Company's Tony McDermott wheeled to face the bear with a can of capsaicin pepper spray in his hand, he presented a different image than the one the young bear had previously encountered with Craig Dahl.

And when Tony McDermott stood up to the grizzly's charge in front of the Pray Shelter outhouse and even presented a posture threatening the young bear it must have confounded the animal, simply because he'd had no previous experience with the tactic.

Finally, when the bear had screwed up sufficient courage to once again charge and Tony McDermott fell heavily while trying to scramble to the Pray Shelter roof, the bear was presented with yet another action situation with which he was unfamiliar—despite his best chance to polish off the young guide at a moment of helplessness.

Nope, the entire affair smacks of immaturity on the young bear's part—an immaturity that requires no stretch for me to believe the animal did not use tactics passed down from generations. Neither does it require too much of a stretch for me to believe Chocolate Legs and her daughter may have had no more of a role in the Craig Dahl affair than that they fed on the remains after the fact.

If there's any validity to the above points, then one might also conclude that by eliminating the mother, the Park Service may have eliminated the only restraining influence on her demented offspring. Certainly the events of June 24, at Pray Shelter seemed to indicate a certain element of truth in that idea.

And what of Matthew Truszkowski?

Um, yes. Well, I have a little more trouble with that one—assuming Truszkowski's remains lies somewhere on Sinopah Mountain in Glacier Park, instead of off a remote South Sea island's shore, or in a Paris Potter's Field. And assuming Truszkowski died at the hands of a grizzly bear, instead of falling from a cliff, and assuming Truszkowski was killed by one of these grizzly bears, it would have to have been the mother, because the cubs were only 40- to 50-pound yearlings and less capable of savagery.

But even if Matthew Truszkowski was mauled by a grizzly bear and that that grizzly was Chocolate Legs, we can't know the circumstances of the encounter. Did the man surprise the mom and did she make a preemptive strike in defense of her cubs?

If in fact, the golden bear with brown legs did kill the human in a surprise encounter, it would've been unusual to scavenge from the body so soon after. But what if one member of the family—the young male—was already demented? What if the cub saw the body of the man as no more than that of an elk or a goat or a deer killed in an avalanche? What if the other family members saw what the male cub was doing and thought, `What the hell?'

The *Great Falls Tribune*, one of the newspapers carrying my weekly column, asked me to do an article for their Summer 2000 insert, *Guide to Glacier National Park*. I chose to do a recap of the Chocolate Legs' story. It follows:

> *Ghosts inhabit the Two Medicine Valley in Glacier National Park. One can catch glimpses of them in the mirror magic of stunning mountains reflected on the surface of beaver ponds, and in the fitful breezes that shatter those reflections. There are hints of specters in frost vanishing as a red prairie sun leaps free of the eastern horizon. Eerie moans are in the muted roar of distant waterfalls, in wind soughing through trees overhead, in the hollow cackle of a common loon from one of a dozen lakes.*
>
> *The ghosts are of fine, handsome young men in full strength, vital with superb health and a sense of their own immortality. There are ghosts, too, of a grizzly bear family: a mother, son, and daughter.*
>
> *She was, by all our anthropomorphic accounts, a beautiful bear—a blond bombshell from social lineage so impeccable she could look down her nose at admirers, perhaps even hold them in contempt. Her markings were so distinctive that her name became trademark: Chocolate Legs.*
>
> *Chocolate Legs first attracted show-stopping attention 15 years earlier, before ghosting off into Two Medicine legend. She did so by strolling the roadsides of Many Glacier, accepting treats from open-mouthed admirers. As with any Diana-like celebrity, the paparazzi pursued her.*
>
> *Authorities became concerned that the young siren-like bear with such distinctively attractive legs was becoming too accustomed to her fans and that, sooner or later, a thoughtless individual might intrude on her space and an injury occur.*
>
> *A decision was made to dart Chocolate Legs and move her to one of Glacier's more remote regions. When she regained consciousness, she found herself far from any road, surrounded with unfamiliar mountains, in a far-off land she'd never before visited.*
>
> *The golden bear spent most of the remainder of her life exploring her new home. She learned she could live*

quite well, thank you, without the preferred treats of human admirers. She discovered bistort roots and glacier lily bulbs in the spring, huckleberries in the summer, whitebark pine nuts in the fall. And when finally she wandered over another mountain ridge and found herself once again among humans, their trails and roads, the gorgeous blond bruin felt no need to revert to youthful food gathering means—for a while.

During her life, Chocolate Legs could've had as many as five litters of cubs. There were, for the next decade, tantalizing off-and-on reports of a blond grizzly with cubs at her side inhabiting the highland between Two Medicine and the Park's southern boundary. But little can be documented until she and her last offspring began attracting attention.

Bear mothers have an especially hard time making ends meet. Cubs are born while their dam is asleep for the winter. Upon emerging into a not-yet-productive land, the mother, who hasn't eaten for six months, must not only provide nourishment for her young, but also replenish her own energy reserves. That may explain why Chocolate Legs, cubs in tow, reverted to roadside and campground beggary. After at least a dozen years of exemplary bear behavior, the blond bombshell, a little older and a little wiser, returned from exile.

Now, however, as befitting her middle-age demeanor and motherly demands, it became more and more difficult for her to take no for an answer. She and her cubs started raiding hikers' camps and frightening them on trails, then ransacking their abandoned packs.

In 1997, 25-year-old Matthew Truszkowski disappeared while hiking alone in the Two Medicine Valley. His remains have never been found, and many folks pray he is still alive in some distant part of the world. But the following year, when 26-year-old Craig Dahl disappeared in the same valley, Truszkowski's specter began haunting the region in earnest.

Dahl's mutilated remains were discovered. Human DNA samples were isolated from nearby grizzly scat. Conclusive evidence was garnered that Chocolate Legs and her offspring were the culprits. They were condemned to death and executed, the daughter by lethal injection, mother and son by rangers carrying high-powered rifles. Chocolate Legs' and her cubs' ghosts joined that of Matthew Truszkowski, along with that of Craig Dahl's.

Many questions remain: Did the bears actually kill Dahl or did they merely scavenge his remains? What actually happened to Matthew Truszkowski?

But to me, the most haunting question is this: Was Chocolate Legs the marauding killer we humans believe? Or was she, at least from a bear's viewpoint, an especially good mother?

Or both.

37

Logic Bounces Where Theories Abound

To be sure, there are other theories than the ones I've put for-ward about what turned the bad news bears into man-killers. Chocolate Legs could've went off the deep end and both cubs joined her in a savage frenzy. Maybe Craig Dahl blundered into the family and without any of the principals in the affair intending to do so, the brouhaha turned into a flight/attack mania.

Whatever happened on that fateful day—whatever Craig Dahl did when he was on the way down from Scenic Point and whatever course the bears took—it was the wrong thing with the guy and the wrong thing with the wrong bears on the wrong mountain at the wrong time.

There are many who criticize the Park Service for the actions they ultimately took in destroying Chocolate Legs and her family, but I'm not one. Instead, I believe they practiced commendable restraint in the affair, choosing to await DNA results before assigning blame and passing judgment. Had I been the person with whom the buck ultimately stopped, I, too, would've had to make the same decisions, no matter how much I care for grizzly bears or how much I wrung my hands in agony. In the final analysis, they had no other choice.

Not all that many years ago—well within the memory of many middle-aged Montanans—every grizzly bear that chanced to be in the Scenic Point/Appistoki vicinity would've died to avenge Dahl's death. But today, with grizzlies in critically short supply, the emphasis has changed to saving the great beasts instead of dispensing with them.

It took guts for the Park Service to wait for proof before acting—especially when we understand that officials knew it probable the bears might split up before the DNA results could be known. Because the agency stood firm, they've been accused of going overboard in being fair to the bears instead of ensuring safety for the visiting public.

Not only should Glacier officials be commended for their restraint, they also should be congratulated for the quality of personnel they assigned to the incident. We've come to expect coolness and courage from Park rangers when under pressure. But in the past, we've not always seen the monogamous National Park Service invite individuals from outside the Service to fill on-the-ground holes where their rangers might be weak.

I'm satisfied with the way the Case/Incident Number 980106 was handled. And that includes the way this family of clearly killer bears finally played out.

But that doesn't mean I'm satisfied we're even as much as one iota smarter about handling a second—or third—Chocolate Legs of the future. It doesn't mean I'm satisfied that policy would even allow development of response techniques before the indifference of future Chocolate Legs turns to disdain. Have we learned nothing from this incident? Indeed, have we learned anything at all about the science of handling potentially problem grizzlies from the entire Chocolate Legs' story?

"What techniques will you use for another young Chocolate Legs who's panhandling at Many Glacier?" I asked a biologist who cares about these kinds of things. "What can you do? After all, Chocolate Legs was relocated into some of the most prime and remote habitat in all of Glacier National Park."

"If I was the one making the decision, Roland," he replied, "I wouldn't move her at all. Instead, I would apply on-site aversive conditioning and try to break her of her bad habits while she stays to grow in a land with which she is familiar."

I'll admit his reply stunned me—I wasn't ready for what sounded like a new innovation in the management of problem grizzlies and so I fell silent. But on reflection, I wonder if Glacier Park is ready for on-site aversive conditioning of problem grizzlies.

What kind of conditioning are we talking about? Surely he knows, better than I, that aversive conditioning applied only when a bear is trapped and confined might not stick to a free ranging grizzly bear roaming over miles of wild country. Surely he knows, better than I, that aversive conditioning applied only along a roadside might break a bear of the roadside human habit, but might not affect the animal's trailside manners or backcountry camp-raiding habit.

It seems to me that aversive conditioning, in order to work, must be applied wherever a bear routinely associates too closely with people and whenever that bear appears to treat people with indifference. It mustn't make the bear hate people, but make the animal's time around people unpleasant enough so that he'll want to go elsewhere. And above all, the aversive conditioning must be consistent enough in application that the bear will prefer to seek out natural foods in natural settings, surrounded by a natural environment.

To effectively apply that sort of aversive conditioning on a problem bear would, of course, require some sort of monitoring system for that bear. And it would require a commitment of people and means for applying the aversive conditioning. That requires gearing up for backcountry applications. And it means developing guidelines for working on specific problems with specific bears.

Is Glacier Park ready to trap problem bears so that adequate monitoring devices—and that presently means radio collars—can be installed, then reinstalled when necessary? Are they ready to monitor these bears throughout?

Or will they simply be trained to stay away from roadsides and auto campgrounds?

Or will they once again be moved to remote mountains in the middle of the Park?

Or will another "Chocolate Legs" visit the Two Medicine Valley someday in the future? Will another grizzly sow and her offspring stalk through campgrounds in the Two Medicine country, staring indifferently through humans as though they don't exist?

The answer is yes.

She already has.

Even as I toiled on this book in the first summer of the new millennium, news reports flashed a story about a grizzly bear and her cub who entered a campground at a remote Two Medicine area lake.

Talk about déja `vu!

Here's the story by Jim Mann as it appeared July 17, 2000 in Kalispell's *Daily Inter Lake*:

> *A stubborn grizzly bear with little concern for humans forced the evacuation of a campsite near Old*

Man Lake on Glacier National Park's east side Saturday evening.

The female bear, with a cub-of-the-year, approached within 30 feet of the campsite as a group of campers tried to haze it away, said Amy Vanderbilt, Glacier's public information officer.

"They were yelling and shouting in an attempt to haze her from the campsite area," Vanderbilt said. "And she did not respond to that hazing. She apparently demonstrated no awareness of the humans."

Instead, the bear appeared to be entirely preoccupied with grazing on grasses and digging for glacier lily bulbs. The cub fled the area twice, but both times it returned when its mother didn't follow.

The grizzly gradually wandered over to a tent and caused some minor damage to it, in what rangers say was more of an effort to continue digging around the tent than an aggressive action.

Eventually, it wandered toward a tent that was occupied by two people.

A backcountry ranger who happened to be camping at the lake retrieved his handgun, concerned for the safety of the people inside the tent.

He fired a shot over the bear's head into a hillside, but the bear did not retreat.

"After a second shot was fired, she ran a short distance, stopped, pawed at the ground and walked off in the direction that her cub had fled," Vanderbilt said.

The incident started at about 9:00 pm and when it concluded, the ranger instructed all seven campers to break camp and pack up their belongings to return to Two Medicine.

Two other rangers met the group and helped escort them. The group arrived at the Two Medicine Ranger Station at about 1:00 am.

The Old Man lake area, as well as the trail from Dry Fork Junction to Pitamakin Pass have been closed. Rangers are patrolling the area for further sign of the bears.

The female bear's behavior is of concern to rangers.

"She didn't receive any food reward," Vanderbilt

said. "But her tolerance to humans in close proximity, in addition to the shouting and hazing, is of particular concern."

I'll repeat the question: Have we learned nothing? Is there anyone alive who thinks we won't hear from this animal again?

If ever a bear needs a monitoring device of some sort, this Old Man Lake sow does. Yet all that happened was the indifferent female grizzly bear was hazed from the area. Where's the radio collar when it's needed?

Where's the DNA samples? Isn't anyone curious to know whether this sow's DNA is a genotype-match with that of Chocolate Legs? Don't we want to know if this is Chocolate Legs' daughter? And her granddaughter or grandson?

Or lacking that, where was the ballyhooed aversive conditioning? I read nothing about the use of pepper spray in the entire account. If not, why not? Surely by now, the majority of backcountry travelers in Glacier National Park know that capsaicin pepper spray is the best line of defense to deter aggressive grizzlies. From the news report, it's difficult to imagine a more perfect opportunity to apply a proven method to drive home a point to a problem grizzly sow.

Grizzly Country

Somewhere in Glacier or Yellowstone, or in Wyoming's Wind River Range, or Montana's Yaak country, or Idaho's Selkirk Mountains, or Washington's North Cascades, there's a sparklingly delightful stream. Its water is clear and nicely cool in late June; the kind from which it's a pleasure for a body to belly up and drink. The stream might be a hundred yards from bank to bank, or it might be merely step-across wide. But lots of rocks break its flow and cause it to gurgle or roar, depending on its size or the measure of peace lurking between the listener's ears.

The rocks embraced by this stream are smooth, the bottom mostly gravel. Along its banks are many fine lounging places, each purposely designed by God to provide proper solitude and atmosphere for contemplation and restoration.

The young of many species play in the stream's coolness during summer's heat, gamboling along its banks and from rock to rock as chance and mood and sport and play arises. They splash the others and roll and dive and choke and cough and gasp and grin. They call. They swim. They flee. They chase. Most of all, they make merry.

Surrounding mountains are like so many jumbles of monstrous broken glass, shards thrusting skyward to catch the first rays of a fascinated morning sun who first fondles, then pets, and at last glorifies them. Sometimes a break-of-day fog drifts from the stream up to those distant peaks, first hiding, then exposing them like a celestial game played by court jesters in training.

Gradually autumn's equinoctial tilt transform the stream's banks by painting surrounding vegetation with vivid pastels of every imaginable color. It begins with different shades of greens and blacks. One looks away to the first brushing of snow on touch-the-clouds peaks and when he or she glances back, suddenly there are golds and reds and yellows and oranges everywhere. The pastels begin zig-zagging groundward—off the shoulder, onto the head, past the elbow, carpeting the feet. The first thought is to stand in awe. Then one wishes to applaud. But to whom should you direct your applause? At last a leaf is caught and turned over and over, and its veins examined in a way one never thinks to do when the leaf is green and full of chlorophyll and sturdy with new growth.

Soon, bankside trees are but stark trunks and starker limbs waving disconsolately skyward. The snowline creeps down those broken mountain shards. Then there's nothing but the floating blankness of winter and the monotonous white and unfriendly pools of blue-black shadows lurking amid the stark forest. Through it all burbles the last of a rushing mountain freshet reined in to pace itself for the coming busy season.

That season comes with yet another tilt of the earth's axis. It begins in February with the embarrassed blush of a young virgin stumbling over an indecent proposal, then turns in March to the muted sobs of the same maiden suffering irreplaceable loss. A tear here, a tear there and the land's seasonal makeup smears and the soil's dampening qualities turns as sodden as a sleeve-cuff hanky. And with the April jilting by her cad-lover and the maiden's lamentation-flood, the soil will no longer sop up all the moisture.

Spring run-off begins first on the sunstruck slopes as the ice-out releases the stream. Snowbanks and snowfields retreat into recesses and behind bulwarks, then take panicked flight down mountainsides and into gullies and finally to swell the stream. It bloats and finally bursts as the land warms and north-side snow-banks-in-hiding begin seeping, then weeping, and finally flooding in cascades to the lowest valleys.

Spring, of course, is the forgiveness of nature. And amid the maiden's deepest snow-melting lamentations, she's handed a taste of redemption via her first floral adornment—buttercups and spring beauties and glacier lilies. As a suitor, nature is lavish, if nothing else. And throughout spring and much of summer, bouquets follow bouquets—colors so extravagant to beggar a rainbow: bluebell and penstammon, larkspur and dandelion and aster and cinquefoil and mariposa. Even bushes flower: mock orange and serviceberry and hawthorn and dogwood.

With the land bursting with life, our maiden (or any

maiden, for that matter) finds succor and new love. Ducks and geese wing honking overhead, heading God knows where to procreate and populate. Songbirds twitter from meadow grass at morning and evening, and flutter to the tag game all day between.

"And God blessed them, and God said unto them, Be fruitful and multiply and replenish the earth...."

And they did: beaver and bobcat, titmouse and toad. While our stream bursts from its banks in spring flood, elk cows nuzzle spotted calves amid geranium blossoms in isolated hillside glades. Even as flood-tide tears at tree roots and glacial tills, blind coyote pups snuggle to their bitch's teats amid the inky blackness of their den.

By late June, the sun completes its swing to the north and is, at last, prepared to baste spring's promise with summer's delivery. Most high country snowbanks have dissipated, aquifers charged, springs bubbling, streams tamed. Days are warm and sunny, nights pleasantly cool. Seedpods head, berries ripen, cones mature.

Owls hoot from nearby forests, water ouzels bob atop our stream's boulders. Trout rise to dimple the surface and lunkers swirl in the turbulence of side-stream seamlines or in the pools behind sweepers or log jams or outsized stones.

Harlequin ducks and mergansers ply the fast water and buffleheads and wood ducks and mallards paddle the pools. Near our stream—perhaps across our stream—stretches beaver dams where the industrious rodents have toiled for many strokes of eternity's hour hand to created regimes that both God and wildlife love. There are marshes and swamps and fens and bogs. Moose come here often and stay long.

Bears amble our stream's shores and blink down into its depths, wade its swamps, and swim its marshes. They nip nearby berries and graze the grass of nearby glades. They sleep along its bank and watch their cubs splash and play.

In a few favored places in the continental United States the bears might be more than merely *Ursus americanus*, the black bears—norm for most other places. In Glacier or Yellowstone National parks, or Wyoming's Wind River Range, or Montana's Yaak River country, or Idaho's Selkirk Mountains, or Washington's North Cascades, it's still possible that the cubs splashing in wild abandon amid our stream might be of the genus *Ursus arctos horribilis*—the grizzly bear.

It's still possible in these few places for a silvertipped mother to lie in contentment and fondly observe her offspring at play. And may God help us all if these mightiest of all bears disappear from these last few wild places.

I've hiked or horsebacked or driven through each of these wild mountain places and hiked or horsebacked or driven through most of the rest of the West's best. And it's my considered opinion that mountain ranges or valley bottoms where the grizzly bear roams are grander and prettier and more compelling than any of the weaker, wimpier, wussier places where they don't.

Somehow, at the turn of this new millennium, we must come to grips as a nation with the sheer dynamism of purpose and poise the grizzly bear brings to our land. Somehow we must learn to accommodate his presence and share space with him. We must bring a mandate with that accommodation that to successfully share, we must first understand. In order to first understand, is it not appropriate for us to ask why the National Park Service spends less than three (.03) percent of its budget on research of any type?

I want to know what turned Chocolate Legs from a poster girl for enlightened management to Ma Barker in a fur coat. I want to know how we, as a species so brilliant that we can clone a sheep and alter human genetics with a few applicational imperatives, can so clumsily drop the ball when it comes to learning how to help one of the most charismatic of God's creatures survive.

I want to at least hope that when the clock ticks into the next millennium that the children's children of my children can still find an occasional grizzly bear in Glacier and Yellowstone and Wyoming's Wind Rivers or Montana's Yaak country or Idaho's Selkirks or Washington's North Cascades. Anything less—if grizzlies disappear from even one of these places—I'll know Chocolate Legs lived and died in vain.

And I will have done the same.

—the end—

RESOURCES

Blond bear sightings at Many Glacier, 1983, as compiled from BIMS (Bear Information Management System) reports.

Case Incident Record, Grizzly Bear Transplant / relocation, July 28, 1983. Bear #251.

GNP Telemetry Locations for Grizzly Bear #251 (1983)

GNP Telemetry Locations for Grizzly Bear #251 (1984)

GNP Telemetry Locations for Grizzly Bear #251 (1985)

GNP Telemetry Locations for Grizzly Bear #251 (1986)

"Grizzly Bear Use Of Army Cutworm Moths In The Yellowstone Ecosystem;" Stephen P. French, Marilynn G. French, and Richard R. Knight / A compilation of selected papers from the Ninth International Conference on Bear Research and Management.

"Grizzly Bear Use of Alpine Insect Aggregation Sites, Absaroka Mountains, Wyoming" / Sean L. O'Brien and Dr. Frederick Lindzey, Wyoming Cooperative Fish and Widlife Research Unit, University of Wyoming (1992).

Project Summary Report, Corn Spill Clean-up Activities South of Glacier National Park Near Essex, Montana / Prepared For Burlington Northern Railroad by KRW Consulting, Inc., July 1993.

Site Assessment and Remediation Report, The Burlington Northern and Santa Fe Railway Company / Grain Train Derailment, Blacktail, Montana, Line Segment 0036, Mile Post 1157.1 / August 29, 1998 / Report Date: November 23, 1998.

Blackfeet Fish & Wildlife grizzly bear capture list, 1987 - 1999.

Selected newspaper reports and Glacier National Park press releases relative to the disappearance of Matthew Truszkowski, July 5, 1997.

"Partners In Life" Program, Wind River Karelian Bear Dogs / Wind River Bear Institute.

Summary of Activities of Grizzly Bear Family in Two Medicine Drainage, 1997 (Female #235, BIR)

National Park Service Case Incident Record, Number 980106, Dahl Search / Summary.

National Park Service Supplementary Case/Incident Record, Number 980106, Dahl Search / Results of Investigation.

Selected National Park Service press releases relative to Craig Dahl Incident.

Selected news accounts relative to Craig Dahl incident.

Glacier National Park Bear Handling & Immobilization Form (Mortality, female cub).

Glacier National Park Bear Handling & Immobilization Form (Mortality, #235).

Glacier National Park Bear Handling & Immobilization Form (Mortality, #238 [male cub]).

National Park Service press releases and selected news reports relative to unknown grizzly bear family at Old Man Lake, July 15, 2000.

Index

About *Learning to Talk Bear*

God's music is wind soughing through treetops, dove wings whispering at waterholes, the mournful cry of a lost-in-the-fog honker. It's a harmony that became addictive, and carries even into my dotage. Elk music took me to the dance. Bears-particularly grizzly bears—keep me dancing.

Grizzlies, you see, are the Marine Band of the animal world. They swagger with the calm indifference of an animal who knows he has nothing left to prove. So why does this John Phihp Sousa of wildlife resonance—an animal who not only fears not, but cares not—receive such a bum rap from the planet's most fearsome other creatures—us?

Good question; not all grizzly bears are Jeffrey Dahmers in fur coats. Perhaps that's the "why" for this book.

from readers:

"It [Learning to Talk Bear] *reminded me of two other books: John McPhee's* Coming Into the Country, *about Alaska, and Sebastian Junger's* The Perfect Storm.*"* Franklin Marchman in an amazon.com review

"The book was informational, intriguing, humorous, and above all—genuine. " J.W., Lori, Megan, and Dakota Westman
El Dorado, KS

from reviewers:

"Cheek is at his best when he's describing bears in action, and at his best, he's excellent." Bob Mottram / Tacoma's News Tribune

"New book paints perfect portrait of grizzlies."
Mark Henckel / Billings Gazette

"Roland Cheek is an extraordinary teller of outdoor tales."
Explore! Magazine

About *The Phantom Ghost of Harriet Lou*

In the beginning there was heaven and earth; and the earth was without form and void and little towheaded boys wandered around barefoot with hands in pockets because there was nothing upon the land to catch their imagination. And God looked upon His work and saw it was not yet good that no thing existed to challenge those boys. And so an autumn came to pass when eerie whistlings drifted into the valleys from distant mountainsides and the by-then lanky teenage boys threw away their toys and accepted the wapiti challenge that would make them men!

And God and girls saw that it was good.

If you've heard a different version of this story, that's your problem. I heard it but once—this way. And so I became an elk hunter. Then I became infatuated with all creatures, and eventually a believer that God's handiwork is composed of such intricacy that a quest to understand will take the rest of my life. The Phantom Ghost of Harriet Lou is about that quest.

reviews! reviews! reviews!

"Roland Cheek probably has forgotten more about elk hunting than many of us will know. But what the veteran outfitter/guide and outdoor writer remembers and packs into his book makes it worthwhile for anybody who pursues the elk." Michael Babcock / Great Falls Tribune

"If you are, were, or ever hope to be an elk hunter, The Phantom Ghost of Harriet Lou *is a must-read book. It should be mandatory reading for every hunter education student as well as instructor."*

Jack McNeel / Coeur d'Alene Press

and readers say:

"I am enjoying The Phantom Ghost of Harriet Lou. *It is so good I want to order one for my hunting partner and life-long friend. "*

Robert Anderson / Helena, MT

"My wife tells me it is the first book she has seen me read and not put down until I'm exhausted. "

Asa Asaturian / Carbondale, IL

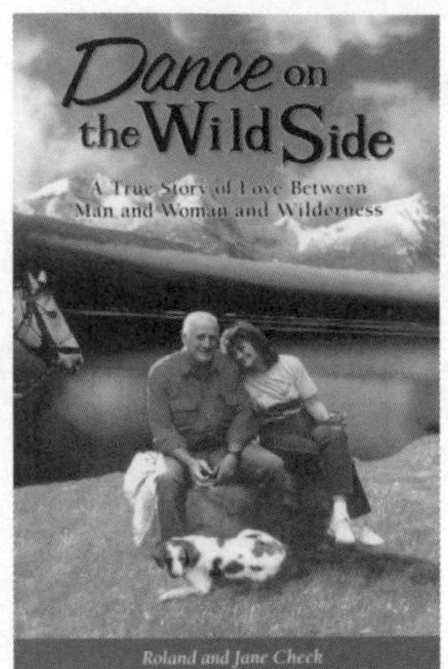

About *Dance on the Wild Side*

It was her idea to compete in a man's world. "Competing in a man's world" is the way my wife Jane refers to her growing involvement and enchantment in outdoors adventure. That concept infuriates me. I understand that people must struggle with everyday problems and relationships. I realize love must be learned and earned, and that it can be lost through mistakes or choices made throughout life. Some might applaud the thought of a lady determined to become her "own woman" in a man's world. Not me. What bothers me is not that my petite wife of more than four decades wants to compete in outdoors proficiency, but where in the hell does she—or anyone else—get the idea that all in nature belongs to men?

This book, then, is about two people in love sharing a life of exciting adventure—and growing in the process. In reality it's about everyone over forty who has lived and loved and struggled together toward a common dream. What makes this particular book's storyline remarkable is how many times these people fell on their butts while doing it.

Within a month of the book's May 1, 1999 release, readers weighed in:

"I haven't put it down since I opened the package.... This was a story that begged to be told. The two of you have lived quite a life together. "
letter from Scott Taylor/Wolf Point, MT (former guide)

"Dance on the Wild Side *rates a 4-Star (****) gold in my literary experience, with a must-read recommendation for family and friends."*
letter from the Honorable Judge Larry Cole/Baker City, OR

"Devoured the book yesterday in a single—very long!—sitting. Jane, you are a lucky woman, having a 300 odd page love letter written for you. "
e-mail from Jean Rafferty, feature writer
Glasgow, Scotland

"Enjoyed your Dance on the Wild Side *very much. How about a sequel after the dance? "*
ham radiogram relay from Lewis Shearer / Wasau, WI

About *My Best Work is Done at the Office*

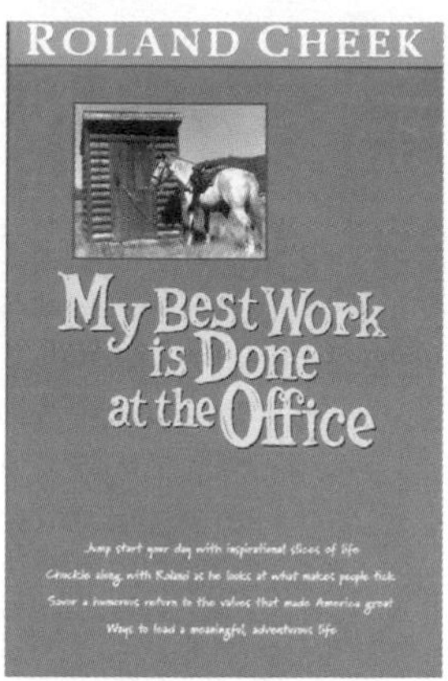

Roland Cheek's popular stories of low chuckles and high adventures got their start around wilderness campfires, far from bierstube and beltway. The best of those riveting tales of wild people, wild places, and wild things eventually made their way into newspaper columns and radio scripts. As a result, Roland's audience exploded from a handful of campfire gatherers to a coast-to-coast mushroom cloud numbering in the hundreds of thousands.

Now there's a book composed of the choicest of those stories. *My Best Work is Done at the Office* is the one for which readers and listeners all over America have repeatedly asked. Now you can see for yourself why Roland Cheek is widely known as America's Rocky Mountain Sage; why his tongue-in-cheek wit is so irreverent, but so relevant; why fans re-read old newspapers for his columns and pause in their work or sleep to listen to him on the radio.

from readers:

"I enjoy your radio program very much. I set my alarm so I can listen to it just before I get up each morning. I've always loved the outdoors and your program makes me feel like I'm right there on your outdoor adventures."
Cassandra Syme/Raymond, MT

"Not often do I re-read old newspapers—but I sometimes do for your column."
Bill Johnson/Cameron, WI

"I like your program very much. So much in fact that I have trouble getting going in the morning because I hang around the radio waiting for it to come on."
Don Kilgrow/Monticello, UT

"I really enjoy listening to you. They air your program at 10:55 a.m., so I try to save that time to answer letters or do something that will keep me in the house then."
Mary Ellen Schnur/Townsend, MT

"My dad has sent me the Thursday Great Falls Tribune *no matter where I am in the world for the last 13 years. I have always enjoyed your writing...."*
Joel Stewart/USS Fife DD 991